"Here I Am, Lord"

"Here I Am, Lord"

The Letters and Writings of Ita Ford

Selected with Commentary by
Jeanne Evans

ORBIS BOOKS
Maryknoll, New York

Founded in 1970, Orbis Books endeavors to publish works that enlighten the mind, nourish the spirit, and challenge the conscience. The publishing arm of the Maryknoll Fathers and Brothers, Orbis seeks to explore the global dimensions of the Christian faith and mission, to invite dialogue with diverse cultures and religious traditions, and to serve the cause of reconciliation and peace. The books published reflect the views of their authors and do not represent the official position of the Maryknoll Society. To learn more about Maryknoll and Orbis Books, please visit our website at www.maryknoll.org.

Published by Orbis Books, Maryknoll, NY 10545-0308.

Designed by Roberta Savage

Manufactured in the United States of America

Library of Congress Cataloging-in-Publications Data

Ford, Ita, d. 1980
    Here I am, Lord : the letters and writings of Ita Ford / selected with commentary by Jeanne Evans.
        p. cm.
    ISBN-13: 978-1-57075-605-4 (pbk.)
    1. Ford, Ita, d. 1980. 2. Maryknoll Sisters—Latin America—Biography. 3. Missionaries—Latin America—Biography. 4. Christian martyrs—El Salvador—Biography. I. Evans, Jeanne, 1949- II. Title.
    BV2300.M4F67 2005
    266'.2'092—dc22
                            2005021059

CONTENTS

ACKNOWLEDGMENTS

I have many people to thank for their help and support in developing this project of bringing together the letters and writings of Sr. Ita Ford, MM. The idea for this collection was inspired by her brother Bill Ford's visit to Marymount Manhattan College and a talk he gave to our students about his sister and her death in El Salvador in 1980 alongside three other North American churchwomen. He recommended *The Same Fate as the Poor*, Maryknoll Sister Judith Noone's account of the death of Ita Ford, Maura Clarke, and a third Maryknoller, Sister Carla Piette. After reading Judith Noone's book, I wondered if it was possible to read more of Ita's letters. Her brother Bill confirmed that there were many and that they were very powerful to read. I am grateful to Bill Ford and the Ford family for their help.

I felt many people could benefit from the opportunity to hear Ita's voice. I knew my students wanted to know more and read more of her own words, their interest heightened by the discovery that Ita Ford was herself a 1961 graduate of Marymount Manhattan College.

In 2003-2004 I received a junior fellowship from the College as support for this project. I particularly want to thank my Chair, Dr. David Linton of the Humanities Division, for encouraging and fostering this project, along with Dean Dawn Weber, Dr. Eileen Tynan, Dr. Maureen Grant, and Professor John Costello. The help of the librarian archivist, Dr. Mary Brown, has been extraordinary.

But most importantly I am grateful to the Maryknoll Sisters who granted me permission to use their archives and to research the letters of Sr. Ita Ford. Sr. Judith Noone's book, her organization of Ita's letters and papers in the archives, as well as the testimony of many people who knew Ita Ford, have been enormously helpful. The Maryknoll archivists were extremely generous and patient, particularly Sr. Martha Bourne, MM and Eileen Pierce. In addition I would like to thank the Maryknoll Sisters who read the manuscript and served as my advisors: Sr. Patricia Desaulniers, Sr. Joanna Chan, and Sr. Julie Miller. The Maryknoll Fathers also offered wonderful hospitality. Dr. Curt Cadorette, MM in particular contributed important insights about liberation theology and the importance of bringing forward Ita Ford's articulation of what it means to live in accompaniment of the poor.

Friends and family have been enormously supportive, among them Joan Loncich on Cape Cod, and most especially my husband, Lou McNeil. I am deeply grateful to my editor, Robert Ellsberg, for his guidance and support of this project at Orbis Books.

This book appears on the twenty-fifth anniversary of the murders of Maryknoll Sisters Ita Ford and Maura Clarke, Ursuline Sister Dorothy Kazel, and lay missioner Jean Donovan. It is with heartfelt hope and care that I dedicate this book to them and to the more than 75,000 civilians who died during the war in El Salvador.

INTRODUCTION

Twenty-five years ago, on December 2, 1980, four North American churchwomen were murdered in El Salvador by Salvadoran security forces. Their names were Maryknoll Sisters Maura Clarke and Ita Ford, Ursuline Sister Dorothy Kazel, and lay missioner, Jean Donovan. It was an event that shocked the world, clearly exposing the savagery of the Salvadoran regime. In their deaths these women joined thousands of previous victims — mostly poor and unrecognized by the wider world — including many priests, lay catechists, and even the archbishop of San Salvador, Oscar Romero, assassinated earlier in the same year. But for North Americans the deaths of the four women brought a new level of awareness about the brutal reality of El Salvador, while also raising new questions. Who were these women? Why had they died? What kind of faith or commitment had brought them to this fate?

The four women shared much in common — a commitment to the poor, faith in Christ. Each had followed a separate path that converged in a shallow grave in a cow field in El Salvador. This book of the letters and writings of Maryknoll Sister Ita Ford follows and illuminates the journey of one of these women — telling her story in her own words, mostly through letters to friends and family. Her letters through the years return us to the vitality of her youth and the intensity of the search that led her to embrace the values and ideals that brought her first to Chile and then to El Salvador.

Ita Ford loved words and she wrote often to seek clarity and to communicate her effort to discern the direction of her life. Her friendships were broad and active and her letters sustained and con-

nected her to longstanding friends of her youth. Though some of her
friends saw her as an extraordinary person, she did not. Her writings
articulate her effort to seek her own inner counsel as well her desire
to create for her community a record of the missionary experience.
Her reflections seek to connect a wider audience to that experience
and awaken their imagination to the insights and plight of the poor
and the responsibility of all people to seek justice for one another.
Her life was anchored by a foundation in a loving family. She felt a
strong desire to give back because she felt she had received so much.

Who was Ita Ford? She grew up in Brooklyn in a happy Irish-
American family. She was educated in Catholic schools, graduating
in 1961 from Marymount Manhattan College in New York City. Ita's
youth was circumscribed by Brooklyn and Manhattan, a tidy, secure,
homogenous world. But at an early age she felt drawn to the Maryknoll Sisters.

Her cousin was Bishop Francis Xavier Ford, who died a martyr
in communist China when Ita was twelve. He was one of the founding members of the Maryknoll Fathers and Brothers and Ita's tem-
perament, like his, was adventurous and compassionate. After a college trip to Russia in her senior year of college, she became more
conscious of the desire to dedicate her life to a wider horizon of service. Her letters during these years capture her youthful spirit and
voice as she tried to articulate her dreams and the interior shift she
was experiencing. She wished to break beyond the safe and tidy
world of her childhood and young adulthood to connect with people
of other traditions and countries, to learn from them, as well as to
give something back. This was the era of John F. Kennedy and the
Peace Corps, when many young people were drawn to the spirit of
idealism and new frontiers. For Ita, the strongest attraction was to
religious life — but not the secure life of the convent. She was
attracted to the adventurous life of a Maryknoll missioner.

The Maryknollers were known for their outreach to the poor in
places like China, Japan, Latin America, and Africa. In a *Time* magazine article of the fifties they were characterized as the "women on
horseback," who creatively solved problems and served in extraordinary circumstances. Heeding her parents' plea that she wait at least

until she had graduated from college, Ita joined the Maryknoll Sisters in 1961. Initially she was unsettled by the institutional aura and the hierarchical discipline of this pre-Vatican II period. But she valued the spiritual training of the novitiate, which demanded a stripping away of the self in order to follow an interior journey. Ita came to embrace profoundly this spirituality, and its lessons for her evolved through many years.

Her early letters convey youthful chafing at the rules and regulations of the order, and at the same time a determination to build a spiritual foundation for her future life. But in 1964, just as she readied to take her vows, she ran aground of physical problems — a nervous stomach that made eating difficult. Because of these physical problems the leadership of the Maryknoll Sisters decided that she was not a good candidate for the hardships of living in distant countries in rudimentary conditions and they advised that for health reasons she seek a different religious community or vocation. This decision took Ita by surprise and she found it deeply unsettling and painful. She returned to her family in Brooklyn in 1964 to rethink her future. Her letters show her effort to struggle with this reversal in her life and consider new possibilities that could incorporate her ideals of service and activism.

From 1964 until 1971 Ita Ford worked with great success and skill as an editor for Sadlier Publishing Company, a Catholic publisher of religious textbooks. She moved to an apartment near Greenwich Village and reconnected to friends from college. These were important years of growth. She led a busy, active life in New York encompassing a burgeoning career as well as myriad volunteer activities. She was part of a group of young, progressive, Catholic laypeople coming to grips with the currents of the Second Vatican Council, civil rights, the Vietnam War, the sexual revolution, and the feminist awakening. The extraordinary optimism of the early sixties was tempered over time with a growing awareness of the complexity and difficulty of achieving authentic transformation and social justice.

After much prayer and soul searching, she rejoined the Maryknoll Sisters in 1971. Her friends and family were not surprised. She easily overcame any resistance the Maryknoll Sisters offered. Both

Ita and the Sisters had evolved in these years and this time it was a fitting match. In the post-Vatican II era many women's religious communities were embracing a new model of religious life, focused not on separation from the world but living alongside the poor, sharing their life experience, and bearing witness to the gospel in the midst of these struggles. For the Maryknoll Sisters this was not a big stretch. It brought them, in some ways, closer to the ideals of their founder, Mollie Rogers. To her new formation in Maryknoll Ita brought much greater life experience, confidence in her gifts and abilities, and greater maturity. After a year of study in St. Louis at the Jesuit School of Theology and taking vows, she left for language immersion school in Cochabamba, Bolivia, and from there traveled to Chile to begin her first mission assignment.

Ita Ford arrived in Bolivia and Chile at a remarkable time of social and political unrest, and a time of transition in the Latin American Church, as it took on, increasingly, a prophetic role in solidarity with the poor and marginalized. Soon after Ita arrived in Chile she settled into life in a shantytown outside of Santiago called La Bandera. But almost immediately came news of her father's death. As she prepared to return home for his funeral, the country erupted in chaos. On September 11, 1973, the socialist government of Salvador Allende fell to a military coup led by General Augusto Pinochet. Ita had witnessed briefly the hope fostered among the poor by Allende's government, and she would witness firsthand the crushing brutality and oppression that followed. Friends and neighbors were among those swept up by the military, some to be tortured and imprisoned, and some never to be seen again. This was the journey she walked in faith. In 1977 she wrote: "The challenge that we live daily is to enter into the paschal mystery with faith. Am I willing to suffer with the people here, the suffering of the powerless? Can I say to my neighbors, 'I have no solution to this situation, I don't know the answers, but I will walk with you, search with you, be with you.'"

In 1978 she returned for a year of renewal at Maryknoll, New York, in preparation for final vows. She did not want to leave Chile. The shantytown of La Bandera had become her home, a place of living intensely and knowing more fully the meaning of life. As she

returned to the United States she was shocked by the lack of awareness of the poverty and injustice she had witnessed and the ignorance of so many about the role of the United States in supporting
and bolstering the military junta's oppression of the Chilean people.

The year of renewal at Maryknoll is charted through her letters
to friends, interviews, and her spiritual journals. They show her
growing on an interior level, wrestling with her anger, even as she
lovingly dialogued with friends and family. The letters tell of her
life's journey, a journey she came to see, increasingly, as a process, a
set of detours, not a straight path. She was captivated by T. S. Eliot's
"Ash Wednesday" and his image of the spiral staircase on which we
meet ourselves again and again. Her retreat journals convey the
sense that, after much struggle, she had broken through to a deeper
level of self-acceptance and awareness of Christ's love with a freedom and joy that she had rarely experienced before.

The last year of her life brought her to El Salvador, responding
to Archbishop Romero's request for help from the Maryknoll Sisters
in the way of experienced missioners. While en route to this new
assignment she heard the shocking news of Romero's assassination.
In El Salvador she joined her fellow Maryknoll Sister Carla Piette, a
particularly close friend, with whom she had worked and lived in
community in La Bandera. They learned quickly that El Salvador was
far more violent and brutal than Chile. In their ministry to the
refugees of Chalatenango in northern El Salvador they repeatedly
accompanied the poor as they retrieved the murdered and disfigured
bodies of their loved ones.

In August, Sr. Carla Piette drowned when the Jeep in which they
were traveling was caught in a flash flood. Ita barely survived, along
with two seminarians accompanying them. In the following months
she struggled to overcome the physical and emotional effects of this
trauma. Some urged her to leave El Salvador, especially as the situation
became increasingly dangerous. But she chose to stay. With her new
companion, Sister Maura Clarke, she carried on with her work, determined to live fully the virtues of faith, hope, and love, walking this road
of accompaniment with the poor on the path to God's kingdom.

Ita Ford rises in these letters to speak of a life lived with passion and courage. From her youth to her death we are engaged by her energy and zest for life as she pushed herself to make a difference in the world, while at the same time pursuing an inward journey to realize her fullest spiritual potential. All her life she was propelled by a deep desire to give her life over to others. Her path broadened as she listened to the poor and discerned the signs of her mission to walk alongside them.

Her letters tell her story in her own voice, a story that is so much broader and more meaningful than simply the circumstances of her death. They vividly bring us into contact with the significant detours and complexities of the road she traveled to El Salvador with three other women of faith who shared her commitment and courage. From a distance of twenty-five years, her letters bear a message of hope, and a challenge to live daily and enter more deeply into the paschal mystery that leads to resurrection.

1.

The Early Years in Brooklyn: 1940–1957

Ita Ford was born in Brooklyn on April 23, 1940. The Second World War was underway in Europe, but the United States had not yet entered the conflict. The population of Brooklyn in this period was largely immigrant, with multitudes of Catholics, each ethnic group with its own enclave and church, all of them seeking to support the next generation's hope for greater stability and prosperity. Many families still struggled to overcome the legacy of the Great Depression.

The Ford family was vitally connected to the dreams and aspirations of other Irish immigrant Americans. Yet in one respect — their highly educated background — they stood apart. Ita's father, William Patrick Ford, was related to Austin Ford, a prominent Catholic journalist, whose branch of the family had immigrated to America before the Civil War. Austin Ford edited several Catholic newspapers, the *Irish World*, the *Freeman's Journal,* and the *Catholic Register.* The latter two were newspapers specially developed for the Irish Catholic immigrant community in New York. Previously in Ireland he had edited the *Irish World,* whose fiery editorials defending Irish freedom had resulted in its being banned by the occupying British authorities. On American soil, Ford continued to convey a strong message of social justice rooted in the tradition of Catholic social teaching. His papers supported the labor movement, showing that papal encyclicals supported the rights of workers to a just living wage, an eight-hour working day, safety in the work place, and the right to unionize.

Austin Ford's advocacy of social justice, his love of language and literature, and the intellectual exchange he fostered around the family dinner table were traits that shaped the destiny of his son Francis

1

Xavier Ford, the youngest of six children in the family. Francis, in turn, became one of the original members of the Maryknoll Fathers and Brothers, the first Catholic foreign missionary society in America. Maryknoll was founded in 1911 with a vision of serving the poor and bringing the message of the gospel to distant shores. Up to that point foreign missionary work was essentially a Protestant enterprise, with the Catholic Church struggling simply to meet the needs of its immigrant flock. The founding of Maryknoll — first the Society of Fathers and Brothers, and a year later the Congregation of Maryknoll Sisters — represented a new, expansive vision for the American Catholic Church.

After joining Maryknoll, Francis Ford went to China, where he became a bishop and eventually died as a martyr in a Communist prison camp in 1952. His story was prominently covered in the newspapers of the day, and his book, *Come, Holy Spirit,* was published posthumously in 1953. Certainly all this loomed large in the consciousness of the Ford family — Ita was twelve at the time of her cousin's death — and undoubtedly affected her own ideals and sense of vocation.

Ita's father, William Patrick Ford, passed on to his children the Ford tradition of Catholicism, with its concern for justice and equality. To Ita, with whom he was particularly close, he also passed along his love of language, literature, and music. And yet for much of her early life her father's health was shadowed by bouts of tuberculosis. Her mother recalls:

> *My husband was a recovered tuberculosis patient before our marriage. When the girls were in high school he had a relapse and spent about a year and a half in a mountain sanitarium. After that he had a disability retirement. His business was insurance. He was extremely well read. He kept up with the current bestsellers but his greatest love was Russian writers. He took adult courses at the New School — several in creative writing. Words fascinated him. He did the* Times *crossword puzzle everyday. He wrote some amusing short stories — which I always intended sending away for a small private printing for the family and friends. He wrote some poems for special occasions. His letters to Ita were carefully planned.*

His closeness to Ita wasn't a matter of his being available. It was a chemistry between them. It was their joy in singing — their love of literature — their radical beliefs in social justice and equal opportunity.

Ita was the second of three children. She had an older brother Bill and a younger sister Irene. Her mother, Mildred Teresa O'Beirne, taught public school for ten years prior to her marriage in the early thirties. She continued her career as a teacher while married for a total of over forty years. Thus, Ita saw in her mother a strong professional woman, who nurtured the family and managed a teaching career. At the same time, Ita benefited from her father's presence and mentoring role in the household.

Ita's childhood was a secure and happy one supported by a loving family and an extended network of Irish relatives. The family lived in a detached frame house, number 1023 57th Street, Brooklyn. She attended Catholic girls' schools in Bay Ridge, starting at age five in 1945 at Visitation Academy, a school founded by the Visitation Sisters. The Sisters were semi-cloistered and known for their high educational standards. Classes were small and Ita developed lasting friendships that served her all her life. She had a gift for sustaining friendships over a lifetime. Her classmates were like herself, for the most part, middle-class and Irish Catholic.

She was an excellent student. She won the General Excellence Award both at Visitation Academy and later in high school at Fontbonne Hall. Fontbonne Hall was an all girls' high school founded by the Sisters of St. Joseph. It was situated in a nineteenth-century mansion of Bay Ridge that had once belonged to the actress Lillian Russell, mistress of Diamond Jim Brady. At Fontbonne Hall she edited the student newspaper and worked on the yearbook. As a gadfly, she vigorously supported freedom of the press and found herself on one occasion standing up for her principles when challenged about an article in the school newspaper. This incident raised some eyebrows in her first application to the Maryknoll Sisters as a result of the contradictory letters of reference from a teacher and the school principal who each recalled the incident. She was admonished by the Maryknoll Sister reviewing her application to control her "flip tongue" and "her critical attitude at the base of which is pride." She was also urged to begin right away to practice greater humility — in that period, the cardinal virtue for Religious life.

Ita's friend Grace Monahan remembers her as something of a chatterbox, secure in her world, comfortable with herself and the quest to discover more. She and Grace shared many hours together in adolescence talking about the future. Grace recalls that by age fifteen Ita entertained a desire to enter Maryknoll one day and to be a missionary reaching out to people in other cultures. They often rode their bikes along Shore Road and climbed over the fence to sit on the rocks and look out at the water.

> *Ita and I sat and talked for long periods during our high school years. Ita felt that she wanted to not just be a nun — but be a part of Maryknoll at that time. She wasn't insistent that it be right "then," unlike some of us who wanted what we wanted "now," but thought a great deal as well as talked about it seriously. She wasn't outgoing about this particular idea. It wasn't an ever-present topic of discussion, but it was there, and periodically we'd hash it out.*
>
> *We'd get on our bikes, ride down to Shore Road, which is a particularly lovely and peaceful area along the water (the Narrows), park our bikes, climb over the railing, and sit on the rocks. We'd stay there for a couple of hours, sometimes talking, sometimes not saying a word.*

At five-feet-two, Ita was slight in build, but graceful, a good dancer, endowed with youthful wit and humor, a gentle and vivacious personality. She was enamored with the cartoons of the *New Yorker* magazine, especially enjoying the droll humor of James Thurber, Charles Addams, and S.J. Perelmen. Ita engaged in life with intensity, and carefully considered the different sides of questions. As she matured, her words and sentences became more measured and carefully wrought. She was curious, analytical, and, like her father, a voracious reader — especially fiction and poetry, and later in life, works on politics and theology.

A wealthy relative fostered Ita's love of music and the arts by bringing her to concerts, the opera, plays, and museums. According to her mother, she often visited a cousin her age in the suburbs and was exposed to the country club aspirations of this world. But she was not drawn to such a life. As she sifted through these experiences she continued in her desire to serve and seek a wider horizon of experience. In high school and college, marriage was not the vocation she envisioned for herself. While her mother encouraged Ita to explore, supporting her sense of adventure, she advised her daughter against entering religious life right out of high school. Instead she counseled Ita to finish her college education before making any decisions.

Nevertheless, it was always Maryknoll that captured Ita's imagination, rather than the more traditional orders of teaching nuns represented by the Visitation Sisters of her grammar school, the Sisters of St. Joseph at Fonbonne Hall, or later the Sisters of the Sacred Heart of Mary, the founders of Marymount Manhattan College, the all-women's college that Ita would attend. These religious communities, which originated in Europe, were known for their service as educators and administrators of schools. Ita, instead, was drawn to the more adventurous vocation of being a foreign missioner. The Maryknoll Sisters, serving in Africa, Asia, and Latin America, represented a more pioneering and active life beyond the boundaries of the convent, or even the more traditional roles available to secular women of that time. The Maryknoll Sisters ventured to new frontiers of need, creatively meeting extraordinary challenges in far-off places and cultures, such as Hong Kong, Kenya, and Bolivia. Perhaps she was inspired by the example of her cousin, Bishop Francis X. Ford, whose service in China and whose heroic death helped spark a passionate interest in the poor and posed the ideal of giving one's life for the love of others.

But Ita's journey to Maryknoll and her search for meaning and commitment took many detours. These detours nurtured and enlarged her vision and deepened her experience of life. And yet invariably they brought her back to her first love, the Maryknoll Sisters, in whose company she saw the way to express her faith in God and her love for others.

2.

Marymount Manhattan to Maryknoll: 1958–1961

Introduction

From 1957-1961 Ita Ford attended the all-women's Marymount College on the East Side of New York City. The college had opened prior to the Second World War as a satellite campus of Marymount College, located in Tarrytown in Westchester County. In 1961, during Ita's senior year, Marymount Manhattan College became separately incorporated as an independent college from its Tarrytown counterpart. At that time, the Sisters of the Sacred Heart of Mary, the college founders, commissioned a new coat of arms with the motto: "Direct us by thy light."

In Ita's day the faculty consisted of a mix of laywomen and Religious. The Sisters of the Sacred Heart of Mary, originally a French order, were noted internationally for their founding of six colleges. As educated women committed to high standards of scholarship and international awareness, the Sisters presented themselves as models to their students. The mission of the college was to offer young women an educational experience comparable in standard to Ivy League colleges like Barnard and Radcliffe, but shaped by a Catholic vision and religious values. The college was founded to serve an economically diverse population and to "instill an awareness of the political, cultural, and ethical participation in and improvement of society." Classes were small. For the most part, the students commuted from the boroughs of New York and represented the descendants of Catholic immigrants. Ita's class consisted primarily of the granddaughters of Irish immigrants.

For the most part, women's education at the time was still directed toward forming competent marriage partners who could support the careers of their upwardly mobile spouses. But the times were changing and a feminist critique of these assumptions and the questioning of the status quo were beginning to emerge, represented in 1963 with the publication of Betty Friedan's *The Feminine Mystique.*

The time was marked by a great upsurge of pride for American Catholics and the seeking of new post-war opportunities. In 1956 Senator John F. Kennedy, the grandson of Irish immigrant Catholics, whose family epitomized the successful realization of power, riches, and status, was nominated to be Adlai Stevenson's vice presidential running mate. While he did not win the nomination, his supporters were galvanized, and four years later, in the fall of Ita's senior year, he was elected the first Catholic president of the United States.

For all these new hopes, it was also a time of fear. The Cold War contest between the West and the Soviet Bloc was at its height. The Berlin Wall was built in 1961, followed the next year by the Cuban Missile Crisis. The Soviets meanwhile were making startling advances in science and exploration of space. In 1957, Ita's freshman year, they beat the United States by successfully launching Sputnik, the world's first unmanned satellite. In 1961, the year she graduated, they followed with the first manned spaceship.

The Church itself was in a time of change and transition, beginning in 1958 with the election of a new pope, John XXIII. Through his leadership for renewal and change, a new horizon for the Roman Catholic Church was emerging. Under his leadership the Second Vatican Council began in 1962, a year after Ita graduated college and entered the Maryknoll Sisters. A new idealism fueled the dreams of this generation. Many joined the Peace Corps, taking to heart President Kennedy's dictum: "Ask not what your country can do for you; ask what can you do for your country." The principles of service and giving back to create a more just world, to alleviate hunger, and to develop global peace were important ingredients of this era's vision. For Catholics this idealism found its roots in a new appreciation for the social message of the gospel, as enunciated in Catholic social teaching, coupled with the American belief in equality and opportunity for all.

Like many others of her generation, Ita was restless, eager to learn and commit to a life of service. In the letters she writes to her high school friend Jean Reardon (Bauman), we catch glimpses of her sense of fun and of the emerging sense of her vocation. Her teasing relationship with her younger sister, Irene (fondly Rene to her friends), emerges as she writes a poem that her father publishes as "My Sister Sophia." She toys with the idea of transferring to Barnard College, perhaps seeking a more challenging academic environment. At the same time she is pursuing inquiries about Maryknoll, perhaps chafing at the parental requirement that she finish college first.

Ita Ford worked various part-time jobs through college. She waitressed in the summer at Spring Lake, New Jersey. She managed to do volunteer work even as she participated in school plays. Swimming and sports were required at Marymount Manhattan College and Ita enjoyed the pool on the eighth floor. She kept up with friends from Fontbonne Hall, particularly Jean Reardon Bauman, and her letters serve as a sounding board and space for self-exploration and dialogue.

Her major at Marymount Manhattan College was English, with minors in comparative literature and philosophy. Every student at the college had to fulfill annual requirements in philosophy and theology. These were not her favorite courses and she appeared bored by them. Ita expected to be challenged and worried that she was not realizing her full potential. She loved poetry, however, and the English classes of Dr. Clancy, a published poet and playwright. She saw in Dr. Drennan, her philosophy professor, a model of authenticity and the quest, as she put it, "to give oneself over" and transcend the limits of self-absorption.

She was active in the college, serving as business editor of the school newspaper, the *Corivae,* for which she occasionally wrote, and, in her senior year, as editor of the yearbook, *Avelan.* The highlight of her senior year was a trip to Russia, which opened up a whole new world of experience and deepened her commitment to enter Maryknoll. Ita's father loved Russian writers like Tolstoy and Dostoevsky.

She shared his passion and embraced in this trip the opportunity to venture to the land of America's Cold War enemy in a spirit of friendship and cultural exchange. As she traveled she especially admired the Russian people she saw in churches, their fervent piety, and their thirst for religious freedom.

Prior to this trip her brother Bill married and the next year her sister Irene followed suit. Ita's own entrance to the Maryknoll Sisters in the fall of 1961 was the realization of a long-sought goal, one that she discussed and shared with friends and family. Her letters to Jean at Easter convey the seismic shift she felt. She desired to reach out to others beyond the homogeneity of her Marymount Manhattan College world and to experience the culture and religious longings of people different than herself. She sought to know herself through this kinship with the other. It was a pivotal turning point.

Through these letters during the Marymount Manhattan years, we catch glimpses of Ita's struggle to gain entrance to Maryknoll, overcoming all obstacles in a complicated and forbidding entrance process. Through it all she was eager, full of energy, and sure that this was the place where she was meant to be.

Letters and Writings

1. To Jean Reardon, November 24, 1958

Dear Jean,

I'm writing again. This time in Bloomingdale's, what a rat race, 5 nights a week, 5–9 PM. No Saturdays, which is not that bad, except that I'm slightly tired when I crawl home (like now).

I've been waiting for Barnard's catalog, but it hasn't come yet so, in order to appear dutiful — I'm writing ahead of it. I hope to have Eloise arrive before you depart on your Christmas trip to wherever you're going. Pat Murdorf was asking for you.

I've acquired a preliminary questionnaire for Maryknoll, and I expect to go up there Christmas week to look the place over (I've a contract with the Mafia to case the joint). So I'm doing my level best to make this thing work for next September. Maybe, it'll and, maybe it won't. I even have mother partly convinced. Aren't you proud of me? You see I haven't been sitting around here doing nothing.

There's a new Charles Addams book out, *Adam and Evil,* and S.J. Perelman has a book out too. The *New Yorker* has been lively. I had to write a poem for Dr. Clancy's class, so I wrote about Rene. Well, I sent it up to my father, who's in a sanitarium Upstate (for T.B.) and he put it in the local press. They made a few mistakes, but I got a kick out of seeing it. He put down the title as "My Sister Sophie" so Rene, after she murdered her 5th husband, wouldn't say it all stemmed from a neurosis that her sister nurtured by writing a derogatory poem about her.

Went out to Brentwood yesterday and saw Pat. From Mary's car she just flashed the famous P.C. smile and that's it, after all, no fraternizing with the guests allowed.

Well sweets, how are you coming along? Does the Alpine air suit you or do you miss the roaring, filthy, corrupt metropolis (hovel) N.Y.C. It misses you, so do Bonwit's, Lord & Taylor, Saks 5th Avenue who have published papers of bankruptcy since the Reardon Sisters have gone on their Grand Tour! They had to lay off 20 clerks who used to compute your bill alone, you rat, the least you should do is send them a $5000 donation of good will.

School is brutal this year. Marks are going to be lousy, at least, all C's. I'm going to miss those crazy B's and the coveted A's. *C'est dommage* — as you Swiss say. I'd write in French, but the only affiliation I've had with the language is Mary's homework. I must brush up so I can say hello when you get home.

I promise to write very soon, but please you do so too. I know I'm alive but I'm beginning to think you're underneath an avalanche.

Ita

2. *The poem by Ita, referred to above, as printed in a local newspaper, after her proud father submitted it for publication.*

"My Sister Sophia"   November 24, 1958
    William P. Ford of Ray Brook brought the following poem to the *Enterprise*. It was written by his daughter, Ita, "My Sister Sophia." She is sixteen.

> And the world is hers to do
>   with what she will.
> But her ambition is nil.
>   She's young
> And the horizon stretches
>   Before her far and wide
> But she only turns aside.
>   She lacks responsibility
> Doesn't want troubles and cares.
>   They only bring gray hairs.
> She wants to have fun
>   Be crazy and carefree
> Who wants maturity?
>   She's careless and sloppy
> Her clothes are strewn around
>   the room
> Yet she expects to nail
>   a groom.
> She's boy crazy
>   Runs after anything in pants
> called a mister
>   And she's my sister!

Ita Ford, Sophomore.
Marymount College

3. *November 15, 1960*

Dear Jean

This was an extraordinary day! It began normally enough. I went to Comparative Literature, that's Dr. Clancy's seminar, and we usually bring in coffee and on the whole it's pretty relaxed. Today we had coffee and caviar, Black and Red. It was left over from a cocktail party, so one of the nuts brought it in with crackers. It doesn't go very well with coffee, particularly after farina!

Then I spent a half hour convincing Sr. M. Dymphina that my dissertation [on "Graham Greene and Death"] didn't have to have the revisions she thought necessary. I brought her down quite a ways until I was happy.

But tonight, on the subway I lost my dissertation between 68th and 59th Streets. I don't think it really has hit me yet. In fact, it won't bother me until I start to rewrite it. I have a rough draft around someplace, and my notes, so it's not a complete loss, but rewriting it is going to be the biggest pain in the neck. In fact, I still can't believe I lost it. I don't go for tragedies major or minor, and in school this will be considered overpowering. I'll have to say something, though, because I was to have a revision by next week.

So, how are you, now that I've wept on your shoulder? If Ann was confused by the gibberish on her birthday card, so was I. I am now having confused days. I have so much on my feeble mind that I continually think about it, instead of doing anything constructive. Like I've been meaning to write to you for two weeks, and it took a lost paper to make me sit down. So maybe it's worth it!

This is the sickening season of showers. Friday night, there's one for a former classmate of mine, and Saturday, Mary, Grace and I are giving one for Regina. This was more of a surprise to me than it ever will be for Regina. But that's the game. I hate showers and here I am spending $50.00 this weekend on something against my very nature. Then in two weeks we have another twin bill. On Saturday one of my cousins is giving Mary Anne a party (that's the King's name for the tradition) only this will be a little different, just our family, meeting the prospective addition. The following day, her bridal party is host to another round! I'm all in favor of elopement.

So I'll see you next week, come back looking healthy, Ann too. I'll teach you the words of Brendan Behan's song "I'm Lady Chatterley's' Lover," which goes to "Pomp and Circumstance." He was on "Open End Sunday," along with Tennessee Williams, Anthony Quinn, Jack Lemmon and an English director, and as he sang another song, it was interrupted by a commercial. The N.Y. public doesn't have natural taste, except when they pay $10 for an orchestra seat!

I'm beginning to ramble, so good night.

Love,
Ita

4. *February 7, 1961*

Dear Jean,

Bill [Ita's older brother] got married in 17 inches of snow! What a day. No limousine for Mary Anne, no extra guests in the church except the immediate families (it was an intimate wedding). The reception was a little sparse, considering that it was to be small any-way, no music, except from a woman piano player who I'm sure came from the Bowery Follies. But on the whole it was a day we won't forget. The bride looked beautiful, but she came all wrapped up in sheets and plastic, and one bridesmaid rode the subway with paper bags around her legs.

School has started with a bang. The reading lists are immense, but today I received consolation. My marks came and for the first time in my four years I made the dean's list. But I'm convinced that it wasn't all my ability, but a good deal of luck, especially in theology.

I still haven't written that letter. I don't know what to say! It's slightly ridiculous my being lost for words.

This is short, I know, just a hello because I'm going to get the jump on those 15 novels for prose fiction. My eyes are going to fall out because that's only the first list.

Love,
Ita

5. *February 25, 1961*

Dear Jean,

I was going to write the "right" way. I put the paper in the hand way and this is how it would look! [She illustrates this.]

You sure were right when you said your letter had arrived a little too late for inspiration. I had already gotten an answer. That woman is crazy and as surly as I remembered.* I'm to stop, as of 10 days ago, smoking and social drinking. It's now all medicinal. She wants a little schedule of my dating habits (they're clean) and I can only go out once or twice a month and not with the same boy. But to remedy that I'll have to start a special Maryknoll escort service for girls who can't get attached to men. She should know that you can't overcome temptation if it's not put in your way.

Oh by the way, I'm going on an Easter trip — sit down! — to Poland and Russia, just a little 18 day tour. Fordham's Russian Institute chartered a plane, but they didn't fill it up, so they called Marymount and offered us the spare seats at $1/2$ price, $500. Such a bargain couldn't be passed up. So far eight of us from school are going and my sister is coming to chaperone me! It's odd my father can't picture Rene in Moscow.

We leave March 28th for Warsaw (three days there) then we go to Czestochowa, which is a national shrine, then to Krakow. There's an eight-hour 'scenic' R.R. trip to the Soviet border, then to Lvan, then two days in Kiev, then three in Leningrad and three to four in Moscow.

It winds up either the 14th or 15th of April. We miss a week of school, and oral exams. The dean is so excited that I think she'd excuse us from the rest of the semester.

Monday we have to get passports. Then Fordham arranges for the visas to Poland and Russia. My mother's still in shock. Yesterday she said I could go. Then Rene decided to go and it's all rush because Fordham is getting all the visas (except Marymount's) on March 1st.

---

* Ita refers to the Maryknoll nun by whom she has been interviewed and who is advising her regarding her interest in joining the Maryknoll Sisters.

We have to have 7 passport pictures. I guess the Russians really want to know who's visiting.

I would tell you more about the trip, except I don't know anymore. All I have is an itinerary. Next Saturday we have to go up to the Campus and get briefed.

Love,
Ita (Catbravanya)

6. *March 17, 1961*

Dear Jean,

This is the first year that I haven't marched and it would have been with a new school too. We are now separately chartered under the name Marymount Manhattan College. Marymount, NYC is now a defunct institution.

Yesterday I gave the yearbook, minus 13 pages, to the printer. It took 2 whole nights in school to wrap it up, and stiff bones from sleeping on the student council office floor, but I had to get it done before the jaunt.

Today was the first day I was free to do anything — so I got the smallpox shot. I still can't get organized enough to really believe I'm going [to Poland and Russia]. It seems like a magic carpet affair.

Jean, you have a twin at Marymount, not physically, but spirit wise. She's a young nun, in the Art Department, who's moderator of the yearbook. I couldn't pin it down until last night, what it was that struck me about her. Somehow, I don't know the reason, she doesn't quite fit in at school with the rest of the nuns. She has an independent streak, which she suppresses in the weirdest ways and gets upset about things that seem so trivial. It isn't this exactly that's like you, but many little things and a kind of loneliness, which she tries to hide. Yet I'm not really comfortable with her, as I recall I wasn't with you when I first knew you. I can't quite fathom her, I'm not sure I want to, but at least I feel better now that I've pinned it down.

I've been so involved in the show and yearbook this semester that schoolwork has gone out the window. I'm up to last month's work and Russia throws the rest out the window. Our orals are 2 days after we get back, so that should be fine. I don't want to bring the books with me, since it's four years' work, but I can't see how one weekend is going to solve the problem either.

I wrote to Maryknoll for re-application after a warm up letter, and today I was answered with, "wait until you get back from your trip." Maybe I can take my medical on graduation morning, at the rate I'm going.

Well, it's a short life and a merry one. When do you come home for Easter vacation? Hello to Ann.

Love,
Ita

7. *Easter Sunday 1961*

Dear Jean,

I hope the bunny was very good to you. This trip gets better as it progresses. I think I told you that in Warsaw we spent a day with students. Well our first night in Krakow (Friday) we met French engineering students on their holidays. We spent the craziest 6 hours with them (that is 4 from school, Rene and myself) communicating in French, English and, at one point, one junior was spouting Spanish. They were all boys around 22 or so. The Poles [with whom they were traveling] in Warsaw were mixed [ages] and about 25. Yesterday Joe, a student at Krakow University, who is trying for a scholarship at Columbia, took us around in the afternoon. I wanted to get to the student center, but everything in Krakow closes tight at 4:00 o'clock Holy Saturday to Monday, except churches. There's not even a restaurant open.

The money situation is crazy. We changed $10 Wednesday night (I guess actually it was Thursday morning around 3) and we haven't spent much. I bought a bottle of wine and some postage. I think Rene still must have all of hers and we can't change it back and we can't take it out of the country. We leave at midnight tonight for Russia and nothing is open today. What I am going to do with my 70 *zlotys* and 90 *grozys,* I don't know yet, since I actually only have $3, and some kids still have their original 240 *zlotys.* There was nothing to buy, nothing even in the line of souvenirs. Everything was junk. In Krakow we couldn't even find a place to buy postcards.

This is a beautiful city compared to Warsaw, which is almost entirely rebuilt (93% of it was destroyed by the Germans). The rebuilding is really lousy. They don't seem to care if bricks are in a line or not. The cement is all over the bricks and buildings up 2 years are already cracked and have large chunks of facing out of the walls. But Krakow wasn't touched by the war and it still has the 14th century university in the heart of the city. Nothing is much newer than the market square, which was a medieval trade route stop from Western Europe to Asia. It really had charm. But the drivers are mad. They purposely aim cars at you in the narrow streets.

Mass this morning (at 6 a.m.) took 2 1/2 hours. There was a one-hour procession. Women carried every statue in the church around on poles. And they sang loud and strong. We were nearly trampled to death, since everyone has the right of way and the church is like a free for all. Only here are the people downright impolite. On the street they're lambs — in church they're monsters. But I'm getting adept at stepping over the mobs who kneel in the middle aisle and who won't move no matter how much traffic.

We have been warned that although we have found the people friendly so far, the Russians won't be as open, particularly in Moscow where we won't be such a novelty as we have been so far. Tonight will tell. I guess our luck couldn't keep up too long. It's been almost too easy in Poland. Everyone wants to talk to you and through sign language. We do get through.

I'm going to try and sleep for an hour. I've had about 16 hours since last Monday night. We've been promised that it will be impossible to sleep on the train tonight. But I'm so overtired, I can't sleep — but I'll try.

Love,
Ita

8. To a Sister who advises young women interested in membership in the Maryknoll Sisters, April 19, 1961.

Dear Sister,

Now that I am home, and regretfully so because I feel eighteen days isn't enough to really get to know any country, particularly one as complex as Russia, I would like to request the papers for application.

After the whirlwind of the last month of school has died down, I would very much like to come and tell you what I saw and heard on the trip. I guess it was worth about ten years of college.

I can comply with the requests on dating, drinking and smoking.

Sincerely yours,
Ita Ford

9. April 19, 1961

Dear Jean,

I really missed you while I was away. I did a lot of thinking. The wise apple is on the way out. I think I have recently just begun to know myself and have evaluated a lot of things, which used to seem so important to me. I understand that when you used to say that I was your best friend, you meant it. I was always non-committal. But now I know, I think, what you meant for the first time. And this would be much easier if you were here to tell you, but I feel I can't wait another month and a half to do so. Thanks. I hope I can be as good to you as you've been to me.

If you think I've gone mad, I haven't. But I have gotten a new set of values. This isn't completely from the trip. It started about a month or two ago, but being in Russia did help. I can't explain it, but at times I want to hug the whole entire world — no matter the cost — or anything. I can't even seem to say what I feel. May be I have snapped, but it's great.

Maybe I'm beginning to break through my shell. For the first time in my life I really feel at ease. I'm not trying to hide everything with a wisecrack. And for the first time I'm positively sure what I want to do. You can't imagine what it was like being in Russia and feeling so impotent when people needed your help. A man next to me during a Russian Orthodox service cried during the whole Credo, which the congregation chants. Religious barriers made no difference then. It no longer matters to whom one pledges allegiance, the pope or patriarch. It was the idea that these people, the only ones I saw, really believed in God — not a lip service offering as my own is — but a soul wrenching belief. The ones who really deserved freedom of religion, they were the ones denied it. It was pathetic and nauseating at the same time. I wanted so much to do something and couldn't. It was this, more than anything else in my life, which has made me aware now that I really have to go to Maryknoll. I couldn't ever stay away after being in Russia. Even if it doesn't happen in our lifetime that overtures can be made to the Russian people, I can realize that this must exist through the world. Before I had a feeling of wanting to do something without really knowing what. Now I hope I understand a little.

In rereading what I've written so far, I realize you've probably never seen me so intense. But I can't help it. In fact it's pretty funny, because I get so fired with zeal and then I fall asleep because I'm so overtired. Today we had orals and I'm still in a traumatic shock. I'm falling asleep, but after this week, I'll have to tell you, calmly, about the trip. It was really great. Historically, I guess we couldn't have been in Moscow at a better time than from last Wednesday to Friday. I could never really describe what I saw happen. It's too unbelievable. The whole trip actually was unbelievable. But I guess most details will have to wait until June.

Love,
Ita

3.

The Maryknoll Sisters and Back: 1961–1964

Introduction

Ita Ford entered the Maryknoll Sisters in the Fall of 1961. The day she entered, Mrs. Ford recalls, the family drove up with Ita and stopped for a festive lunch in Westchester, where there were swan boats on a small lake, to mark the occasion and come to terms with her departure and new venture. Once they arrived at the Maryknoll Sisters in Ossining, Ita changed into the uniform of the Maryknoll postulant, a black dress, black veil, and white collar and cuffs. She said good-bye to her family and began the journey toward her new life. She joined a class of 64 entering that year, ranging in age from eighteen to thirty-two. Some were coming just after high school, others like Ita with a college degree, and some with further experience beyond that. It was still a period of extraordinary growth and expansion for religious communities, a time when few Catholic women thought of pursuing a professional career. The choices for most were either marriage and motherhood or religious life.

The Maryknoll Sisters had grown and expanded tremendously from their founding in 1912. The American spirit of the early pioneers under the leadership of their founder, Mollie Rogers (later known as Mother Mary Joseph), was still there with its liveliness and sense of adventure. Through the fifties the Maryknoll Sisters received extraordinary coverage in *Time, Look,* and *Cosmopolitan,* due in no small part to the journalistic training and public relations savvy of Maryknoll Sister Maria Del Rey. Mother Mary Columba, the congregation's leader at the time, even graced the cover of *Time* magazine in 1955. According to *Time*, "The sisters know how to drive Jeeps (and repair them), how to administer hypodermics and do major surgery, how to teach Christian doctrine . . . When they return from the missions to the Motherhouse on the Hudson, they are received with laughter and merry chatter."

When Ita first applied to Maryknoll, during her sophomore year of college, she felt that she was storming the walls. There were many applicants in those days, and they were carefully and selectively screened, particularly with a view to the rigors of mission life. Novitiate required a three-year process of spiritual formation in preparation for going out to the missions. This was still the pre-Vatican II era, and Ita quickly encountered the rules and institutional strictures that Maryknoll shared with other religious communities of this period. The convent was like a women's college in its atmosphere, but with a multitude of rules and directives that regimented the postulants' and novices' lives from 5:30 a.m. until 9:30 p.m. Rules covered every facet of their daily routine. "No chewing gum, no loud laughter, no food left on the plate." They were not allowed to have newspapers or magazines. Outgoing mail was to be unsealed and incoming mail was opened before they received it. Particular friendships and even talking in twos was forbidden, as well as mingling with novices or professed Sisters during the postulancy period.

A weekly "Chapter of Faults" required public confession of one's infractions and penance. At meals they heard readings from the diaries of missioners. At first, Ita appeared to feel alienated and impatient with the system. This was very different from the freedom she had known throughout all of her schooling. As her mother put it, "I think now the reason Ita had such problems when she entered Maryknoll was that up to that time she never had to do the goose step." Dialogue, conversation, and analysis were no longer encouraged in quite the same way as she had experienced them previously through her many close friendships from high school and college. She felt these strictures, the loneliness, and the loss of access to the *New York Times* and her beloved *New Yorker*. Yet Maryknoll for its time offered more freedom than many religious communities.

There were picnics and sports and the spirit of fun that had been essential to its founders. They were not cut off fully from their family and friends, who were allowed monthly visits at the Motherhouse.

Those who survived the first nine months, as Ita did, graduated from postulant to the status of novice. They received the community's religious habit and new Religious names. The training focused on spirituality and the formation of an interior prayer life. At first Ita, like many others, found the process numbing. She welcomed kitchen duty and the chance to be by herself among the pots and pans.

Gradually, however, she turned a corner and embraced the opportunity to struggle with her spiritual life. She was much taken by Francis Thompson's poem, "The Hound of Heaven," which she rediscovered and understood more deeply than before. She found that it articulated the struggle she was experiencing to give herself over, against the constant temptation to run from the spiritual encounter with God. At one point in Lent she highlights an insight regarding the tenth station of the cross — where Christ is stripped — and ponders what that means. She connects to it as a portrayal of the struggle to submit her will, the need to strip away the mask and smart self of her youth, and to face someone within.

She rediscovers the symbolic power of the Annunciation, and sees in Mary's commitment a model of giving oneself over. In her letters she begins to use the phrase *Ecce Ancilla Domini* (Behold the handmaid of the Lord). She seeks to identify and parallel her life commitment to Mary's witness. At the same time, a new theological scope also begins to develop through her reading and study of Teilhard de Chardin's *Hymn of the Universe* and the lectures on tape of Barry Ulanov, a professor at Barnard College, who developed a similar theology to Teilhard "for the realm of the arts." It was the ability to see transcendence in immanence and to discover God in the sacramentality of the world and the expression of its beauty. God was in the world, drawing it towards transcendence. She notes in her letters to Jean that this new perspective was worth the three years of formation.

The novitiate in Topsfield, Massachusetts, connected her even more to the beauty of nature, and represented a significant stage in her journey. Yet the letters reveal an interior struggle. She developed problems with her health and could not keep food down. This was just weeks prior to her scheduled profession of vows on June 24, 1964. Many of the novices felt similar pressure during this period. By the last weeks of the novitiate, half of those who had entered had been sent home. There was never any explanation given. At dinner there would simply be an empty seat at the table.

Ita was sent to see a doctor, who advised that the pressure be lifted. To calm her nerves she was assigned to pulling weeds at Topsfield and did an eight-day retreat. But although she had the support of her novice mistress, others thought it wiser to send her home. The rigors of mission life were great and health problems in missioners were to be avoided, if possible. For Ita, who so feared falling short of the ideal, it was a terribly difficult process. Years later she would still wonder out loud and seem puzzled by it all: "Who else had ever been sent home for a nervous stomach?" But she would also refer to this detour as a positive and enriching life experience, and trust that it had all been part of God's mysterious plan.

Letters and Writings

10. To Jean Reardon, November 8, 1961, from Maryknoll

Dear Wall Washer turned Shop Girl,

It sounds like a rags to riches story. If I were home I would have counseled otherwise. You'll either lose your sanity or all your finer feelings in the toy department (it matters not the store) at Christmas time.

You want an honest report. I'll try, but it might not be coherent. As for the kitchen, I'm convinced it's one of the best jobs to be had, once you build up your biceps. No one bothers me, and if I'm in a mood, I take it out on the pots, which is a very healthy vent for my emotions.

School wise, the only thing new is Gregorian Chant. I get very bored because most of the classes seem repetitious and ridiculous. I try to pay attention, but I sleep through many of them. I feel very stagnant. I've unfortunately been given a few really dull spiritual reading books, so I've had nothing in my mind. That's been a very hard transition to make, and I admit I'm doing it grudgingly. I don't want to become, what I very rashly perhaps see as — a dullard.

We've been having a series of lectures by Barry Ulanov from Barnard (a friend of Dr. Clancy's). Monday he spoke on the Modern Theatre. This is a tease. It's a drop of water to a great thirst.

For the group around me, 59 very different people, I know them all, and not at all. For the next three years it's not allowed to recreate in twos. And about one's knees, mine no longer talk to me, in other words they're stiffer than hell. You also in the beginning anyway have to reconcile yourself to be a 'number' for a while. This is sheer institution, because of the large group, and I hate this phase of it to the point that, when I thought I'd climb a wall, I expected to see everyone else there too. I could always take much more of the crowd than you, but when you eat, sleep, and even go to the 'john' at the same time, it's a little nerve wracking.

Now you'll think but there's some good side, 'the hundredfold return,' but it's impossible to communicate mob style. The ages range from 18–32 and no one is very offensive and there are many affable ones.

It's lonely, not in the sense of being alone in a crowd, but in an emotional way. No one knows you well enough to be able to say the right thing when you need it. And as yet, no one cares enough.

Naturally being separated from the things that crowded my life, I can now look at them, not in a disinterested way, but like a little removed from them. I miss many people, some much more than others, you, a lot. There's so much I seem to want to tell you. I'm not going to preach. If you're ever going to do this Jean, forget 'there.' Well, I'm patiently waiting, no that's a lie. In fact my whole problem, the one that's plagued me my whole life is impatience. I expect to conquer everything in one try and with one look. You don't do that with a new life. The outrageously petty things continuously trip me up to the point of exasperation.

Many people find prayer a great consolation. Me, I'm just learning how to pray. It makes it very hard when you've nothing to fall back on. That's my only advice.

As for next Sunday, it's a long trip for a mob scene. If you do come, come a little later, like around 3 p.m. That way I can see my family, talk to them, and then to you. Last month was very bad. I talked at everyone and spoke to no one.

That letter you wrote after last visiting, saying you wouldn't complain to me because I've a lot on my mind, Jean, 3/4's of each day there's nothing on my mind. I wish you'd spill some of your complexities onto paper. I'd be more than happy to listen, just as I've made you do now.

As I understand more, I'll report further.

Love,
Ita

11. To Jean, December 28, 1961

I just opened the envelope and read what I wrote yesterday. It sounds a little psychotic 24 hours later. But it's a true picture of me in one of my crazy moods.

It took snow flurries to stop us from having our Thursday night supper outside. Last week it was insane, especially now that it's dark here by 5. All the food had to be carried down by flashlight, down stone steps (the kind piled one on top of the others) then there were candles on the tables and a roaring bon fire. And we all freeze to death in just sweaters. Rumor has it we're being trained for a new mission in Labrador.

Today Julie Miller from Savannah, Georgia saw snow for the first time. There are a few others, one from Hawaii and California, who've only seen it a few times. It was strange to watch them look at it. Just like kids,

Thursday night is confession night and every week I resist the impulse to go and say bless me father, I'm a saint. But tonight, as I was gabbing away, the priest said I could have the *New Yorker* after I've digested all of St. Paul's Epistles to the point of application.

Speaking of the *New Yorker*, it was a surprise to learn about Thurber's death, especially since I didn't know he was sick. Another good man gone to 'God's Little Acre.'

My hands are a mass of scratches. Yesterday afternoon we dug up rose bushes. The novitiate garden has been relegated for a parking lot. The nun in charge of horticulture nearly collapsed when she saw one of the postulants go at a persistent root with a long handled axe. Never hack a rose bush root! I don't know how many rosaries the kid got as a penance. Ignorance here is neither bliss nor an excuse.

Such is spiritual formation. My love to your mother and father . . . Some for you too.

Ita

12. *January 7, 1962*

Dear Jean,

Your letter started me off on a thinking bout. But when I think I have an answer it's inadequate when on paper. I need lots of time, like on the front porch with a pillow, because words don't even mean the same when used by 2 people. And letter writing can confuse the issue. But here goes.

Contentment is not a descriptive word for here, particularly because it always seemed to me to imply a satisfaction with the status quo. I can't say that I am, because I'm in a hurry to get involved. This gives me a lot of unrest. I get annoyed at myself for having so many hampering things that hold me back. It's like a vicious circle. It's not that we're so different. It's more that you and I seem to be aware of the situation, but still lack the ability to remedy it. I always said, the one thing I didn't want to be was mediocre. Then I turn and I look the word "All" in the eye. That to be mediocre implies a full jump — a giving of all — think about it. It's like a kick in the stomach.

Then come the platitudes about detachment. When you get

there, and I say this only from my limited 4 months of trial and error, known as experience, that regarding possessions—it doesn't hurt at all. No, that's too general. The first weeks I thought my brain might deteriorate if I couldn't have access to the 800s of the Dewey Decimal System. I thought a few books wouldn't break me, that the *New Yorker* would be nice, and that I was starved for news. So it was barbaric that we were deprived of the *Times*. Now you could answer that they've succeeded in making you happy living in a vacuum. No, not at all. There's a substitution, not a tit-for-tat, not the *Tablet* for the *Times,* rather it's on the inside of yourself that you deal. You spend more time trying to understand. Anyway I was saying that now I really don't mind having few belongings, it simplifies things — in fact I never thought a 3rd pair of shoes could be superfluous — now, yes! Detachment becomes a problem with you and me when people are involved. You don't want to let go and, in a sense, you have to. As bad a poem as the *Hound of Heaven* is, it can bring across the point. Everyone wants to run, me most of all. Stop and think of the irony of my being here. I still have a strong distaste for a large group of nuns. When we can talk to them, I've nothing to say and usually walk away and wind up being furious at me that I can't conquer the abhorrence. Maybe a part of it is shyness. I hope so or else it's going to be quite an adjustment problem. That's why I liked the sink job so much. I was by myself. I've gone off the track again (this is why it's hard in a letter) but anyway it's basically what you do with your will. I'm still rebelling in a few ways. It's hard to swallow everything you've paraded as your smart self and accept the fact that, to go all the way, you don't want to be so glib anymore. This was hard for me, not how much room I have, etc. To really be involved means a purification of the sadistic vein of mine which I want to keep and get rid of at the same time, because I sometimes get the feeling that giving all could compromise you into the 'John Raymond' state and, then after a moment of lucidity, I realize that involvement doesn't mean . . . being in a fog. But when you come around to this, being honest with yourself hurts deeply. The more I want to go, the more I realize that I tried so hard to hide all this for so long. That I got into the habit of living one way. That now it's hard to switch to what I want to do.

This is a foggy incomplete attempt, very inadequate but you started it by your letter. So you get the end product. You'll work it out. My one wish for you is a place to sink roots — in peace.

Love,
Ita

13. To Jean, January 25, 1962

I had a letter from Pat this week, which I was going to answer today, but instead I'll talk to you. If you want, you can write to her.

I can and can't see you in front of a class. The idea is ludicrous in part, because you can tell me 'til you're blue in the face and part of me refuses to acknowledge that Jean has a job. I don't care what kind. Somehow it just has been in my blood that you shouldn't be in the eternal rat race.

I know if you're in a 'constructive' mood that you must do and make something with your 22 years of experience and knowledge. You'll feel that I'm a drag against your good intentions, I know. A certain part of me remains in a cloud of nostalgia, when you didn't have to work. If it takes a subway ride and fallen arches to prove to yourself that you're a useful member of society, all right. You've got more will power than I'd have in the same situation. I know I'd be in school, which I think has always stood for me as some kind of security symbol, no? Or else chalk it up to my lazy blood. By the way, my pet, your closing thought, your last letter sounded like a post-mortem tribute to a 'late, great,' neither of which I am. Ask anybody who knows me. My vocabulary should be minus some of my former descriptive words, but they all are still quite applicable to me. The only comfort I give most people is by shutting my eternally going mouth.

Now back to you. I can never organize what I want to say. There's so much I feel now that I never let myself before. Being away from my own 'image' and those who met it every day, things gradually begin to eke out, parts of me that never surfaced before, probably because I wouldn't let them. (I thought I was going back to you.) Well for the first time, and its bizarre that it should be here, I'm allowing myself to love and be loved. You know I was always such an independent [*pauvre,* beggar]. I never accepted anything or ever admitted that I needed affection. Of course, I was wrong. Both ways. It's a constant give and take. Only now, there's no possession except in a very abstract manner, so then you have to love more people. It becomes a matter of being involved in everyone to a certain point, because you can't give yourself to one person. I never thought I could look at a whole roomful of people and honestly say I love them all. I can't explain it. I do. Not all the same, of course not, but it's more than the casual getting along with people that I was fairly adept at before. I managed that because I could keep on a superficial plane and not get involved.

I don't even know now what I was going to say. But if any of my rantings are in the least bit useful as insights, I'm glad. This is sort of like a melting process. A continual stripping of all that could clutter up your wig. And I admit, the first few layers come off very easily. It's only as you get inside that it bursts. I'm not kidding. I told you last time that detachment from material things wasn't that hard. But the only thing that seems to get in the way between divinity and me is me. I think I'm developing a case of 'not yet, Lord,' give me a few more minutes to relish my ill-conceived notions of freedom. Try it sometime. It's not that the spirit is willing and the flesh is weak, so much as the will is strong and as yet won't bend. And ironically even though you want it to, it doesn't happen right away.

Now I must go to you. You think Dick is giving up on you. You can't run your life on a timetable. I'm sure I could find priests who might have predicted that I'd never last through four years of college and still go. Everyone is different. And all the guidance in the world is no use unless you have your own convictions to agree or disagree with it. You know I don't care if you wear a hair shirt or a nightshirt. I care that you're happy and sincere with yourself. Don't let him push you if it is not the time, but don't run away to Europe from a decision either.

I give out advice, as if I could almost dispense it. I don't mean to sound so authoritarian, but rather more like a verbal back rub.

Ita

14. July 15, 1962

Dear Jean,

Answering what you said two weeks ago is of little help. I guess that's the most frustrating thing about the beginnings of this crazy life, holding your tongue and pen until the right time. And then the remarks have little import. You sort of learn to straddle time being now in one month, now in another, skipping back and forth until the people who listen to you are dizzy. I'm sure my family thinks I'm slightly demented at times or, at least, getting very simple.

I know that on every letter that I write, I say the same thing. I'd like just to sit and talk to you. There's no satisfaction at all, except for seeing your faces, on mob days. All those wasted nights on dribble, no not really wasted. They laid a foundation that's there so we can just pick up where we laid off.

I know what you mean of the journey to Topsfield. It does make a big difference. More than I seriously thought about. If finding out about yourself through the unravelings of the past year told me anything, it was mostly that I thought more of myself than was really called for. This is not imposed humility, but more of seeing clearly.

I'm not a sage. And yet I always seem to be writing ponderous advice to you, if not pompous! I haven't come to the point of no return, but it's much easier to live if you assume that you have, otherwise it's one foot in and one foot out and that's a very dangerous game to play. I did it for a while and all you get is malcontented and that's a very contagious disease. It's also a dirty trick to play on others who have it just as hard.

But this doesn't cut us off. I'm here I hope for good, providing I don't louse it up, an ability I seem to be developing. It's very hard to explain, but I still feel close to you and want to say very much for all to go well. You know whatever you do is fine by me, but please don't bide your time too long. Your nature at times underrates yourself, so you shrug your rheumatic little shoulders and sink into the slough of despondence. Remember it was as soft and mushy as a pig-sty, better than quick sand.

You're playing like I was. The temptation to the better thing . . .

or illusions of grandeur or don't bother me now, there's still a good supply of scotch. You say what you 'should do' — or 'sort of want to,' just do something. In my bones I can hear the same thing next July. You make it sound like a sword over your head and the only thing it's giving you is a guilty conscience. That's no way to live. (I'm getting a little violent — no?) I don't mean to be so outspoken and shout pious platitudes at you. But you need a fuse to get you going. I think most of your own atmosphere at home tends towards *status quo* or run away. Don't.

I'm not putting you behind a grill, but I want you to look at it squarely soon instead of always shelving it.

Please write an outraged reply and tell me to stop walking not only all over your toes, but your life too.

Love,
Ita

15. *August 27, 1962*

Dear Jean,

I was just thinking that you should number my replies and then go back and see that after so many months I started pontificating, and now that it's almost a year I can sermonize with the best of them.

I was thinking about you in bed last night. We're on vacation and a group of us have our supper under a few pine trees every night and we're gluttonous about the tea and so it was keeping me awake. I thought of the things that I wanted to tell you that are related to your letter and have hit me during the past year.

The first one's about the tenth station. I'm not much of a station maker* but one day during Lent I was thinking about it. I was particularly struck by the tenth. What could be harder than being stripped, not just of your clothes, but of all that goes to make you up. Yet, what was more necessary than that very thing? Somehow you

---

*Station maker, that is, praying the Stations of the Cross.

have to peel off all the layers you've acquired. All those things that go to hinder you when you really want to make the break. It fascinated me. I could see so many things that had to go, and still have to, if I was to get anywhere.

The second [thing I thought of] is maybe more akin to you. So many times, I wander around feeling very empty, almost numb. Routine takes over, and you can settle into a vacant state. I guess I said something to one of the others and she turned to me and said, "Don't worry about feeling empty because it's only when you're empty, that you can be filled."

It's something that you hear over and over again, from the *Hound of Heaven* high school days, but it never means anything 'til it hurts. You've got to let go of the little you have, to get it back in a downpour of other things too.

It's so sensible, so rational, and yet I know so often, I just can't believe it. What you have now, you can see and enjoy it, no matter how miserable it is. We just don't have enough trust that if we let go of it, we'll get so much more.

It's outrageous here, because everyone has come this far, letting go of the big things (supposedly), only to be tripped up by all the mites. The same with you, it's never going to be obvious what will hold you down. No matter how much we kid, it will never be money or weight. If anything could ruin your life, it's the petty daily stupidities that detract you from the 'all important.'

I might seem way ahead just because I haven't been in the whirl for a while, but you could far out distance me where you are by cutting a few strings. My fear for you is that you'll get bogged down over some stupid trifle, when your beautiful spirit wants to and is capable of soaring. If you get a taste, and find it sweet, don't let anything stop you. I know you can go all the way and that's all I expect from you.

Oh, and don't let personalities, Fr. Dick's, mine, anyone's make or break you, because you know in the end, what do we matter.

Love,
Ita

16. August 18, 1963

*Ecce Ancilla Domine**

Dear Jean,

I'm sure this is going to pass a letter from you on the way, but I thought I'd do one today, and then one on vacation that starts next week. Of course, I really have nothing to say, but you know.

The visit was good, but about a week too short. First I thought it was too bad that we used to waste so much time before, but after rethinking about it, I don't think so. You can live ahead of yourself, and our friendship has come along as we have.

About your 'invite,' I tried to remember back to front porch and pillow sessions. It seems that there's a certain insistence in it, as all along, you know that sometime there's going to be a capitulation. But there's no duress, or unbearable discomfort in it. If you can relax in it (a ridiculous thought when time is so short, I know!). There's a real sense of joy and elation that's light headed.

I'm not much of a fan of the symbolism attached to religious life. But there is a definite relationship to be established with God. And maybe with less sentiment, it could be clearer. But in or out of the cloister, it's the same thing. Why even now I hold back saying such things to others because they'd seem 'nunny,' when we have no prerogative, is silly. Everyone has to do this and, sometimes, when Dr. Drennan used to give his 'asides' in philosophy, you could really see the effect of a person who had given themselves over.

It's joy, it's peace, I can't see it in many people around here. This morning I was doing my spiritual reading, and it struck me, how easy it should be (at least in theory). The only thing that gets in the way, most of the time is ourselves. We say 'yes' with a dozen strings and conditions attached.

But I'm getting off the point. Yes, you have to go, but not under a two edged sword. It's wonderful to be called. It's dizzying to know that you're loved so. I know I don't do very well and I'm very ungracious, and any self-respecting male would have left me

---

* Mary's words to the angel Gabriel: "Behold the handmaiden of the Lord."

long ago, but I'm still here. I don't understand it, but I'm grateful.

Also I have to admit to you, I'm a sneak. I wanted to give something and, of course, I had nothing 'til I thought of the medal.* That pleased me very much, because it's a little way of saying that She's quite a lady. We were never formally introduced and, like some Josephites,† I never paid her much heed. It's a gradual thing, there's so little about her actually to say. It's all in the Annunciation, as you feel more the need to be that way. She stands out more and more. Quite a lady.

Enjoy the cocktails and canapés and check the menu for the first course. I'm with you all the way.

Love,
S. Ita ‡

17. *November 17, 1963*

Ecce Ancilla Domine

Dear Jean,

I think this is the first time I'm answering one of your letters within two hours. It's usually that many months.

Did you like Dr. Ulanov? He lectured at [Marymount Manhattan College] once and gave a series at the [Maryknoll] Motherhouse when we were postulants. When you mentioned him in the last letter, it was just after we had heard one of those tapes. We've had two since then, one on art, yesterday's on drama. They're supplements to classes and also just underline what should be most obvious to us, though of course since some like me are a little dense, the light comes slowly. His theme was always the transcendence and immanence of God, and he illustrated this in all the art forms and scripture, but he also showed how we meet the transcendent in the immanent. Teilhard de Chardin says the same thing, as many others do too. It's a slow process of real-

---

* The medal here is a small medal of the Blessed Virgin Mary that Ita gave to Jean.

† A reference to the Sisters of St. Joseph who taught her in Catholic high school.

‡ The "S." is the abbreviation for "Sister" Ita. This is the first time she signs herself in this manner in the letters we have. It will not be characteristic of her later on.

ization, but as it gradually comes it makes everything capable of being a sacramental. I think it is also developing in me a sense of wonder or awe. I can delight in the beauty of sunsets, in the local flora, in a fish and bird that we discerned. The psalm verses come to mind about all things praising God, how we are so wonderfully made, etc. in all nature, we're the only 'clods,' that being our glory and our downfall.

Sometimes I think all this (3 years) would be worth it just for this new scope. Why were we so pigeonholed before? You said we were never as narrow as your scholars at St. Brendan's, but at least, I was in this way. We might have gone to the Met rather than the Red Apple, but it never got related.

I think of you there at St. Francis. It may be dry and dream-like, but even so, that too has infinite potential. I'm not exaggerating with my adjectives. I have to tell you one thing. I just remembered, a real *non sequitur.*

Remember one night when Ann and we were talking about being women and if it applied? Well, I've been thinking about it. I don't want to be Peter Pan for the rest of my life. Though I may not look the part, I'd like to be womanly, with what that implies, the giving, the selflessness, the strength. Back to you, now that like a clamshell you've been opened up, and hurt, this whole process could be a softening and strengthening. I think the mellowing comes not with the gray hair, but with the suffering used positively. You're always beating me to the punch and it pleases me. I hope we both give all.

Love,
Ita

18. *December 30, 1963*

Dear Jean,

Of course, I dislike what you said in your letter, more than smirking. Please don't put me on any pedestal or distort what I have. It can't be teacher-pupil or what ever else name relationship. It's only friend showing friend. Please just take it that way.

Now that you've taken the plunge again (you and I should publish our memoirs of applications), I realize you've been told very little of what goes on. And sadistic as it sounds I'm not going to enlighten you anymore. It's not that very important. But there are things I want to share with you very much, which I'm going to ruin by words but try and see through the scrawl for what it is.

The beginning of this month, I'm not sure how or why, probably more evolution than anything else, I admitted to myself that I'd wasted 15 months. I'd done nothing to consent to live like this, but had just rolled along in that comfortable little air of complacency that has been around my cubic frame since it replaced the after birth. You don't have the exact thing, but you have similar traits that can choke you as well.

I played with this for a while, it has to take some kind of root, I guess, until last week. Now I've got to start all over again. I was 'hyper,' as we say here, and calming down has left about the biggest void. But I don't mind (that's not exactly true or what I meant), I expected it. I have to go back to the prosaic day-by-day, not as before because I can't live it that way anymore, these small insights into responsibility, mine for you, me, all who I eventually meet — into the overworked 'awareness' themes, all of it. If I wrote this letter Wednesday or Thursday, it would have been an oratorical delight. Now I can't even say it. I guess I finally committed myself. I sort of realize I can only be myself by doing it. Even if it means being a mediocre clod, I've got to be one now, here. It's a little like *The Hound of Heaven,* you run smack right into Him. And in the beginning it's elation. Then you realize what it means. It's good I don't know it all now, but only a little because it would be crushing, especially since I can no longer chuck it.

I don't know if this is clear, I hope it is, to you. Part of the inner clamshell has been pried up some. It hurts, but has to be. I want it that way, masochist that I am! So you know what I mean. I'm happy in the way it's worked out. I hope you don't hold out as long. Everyone tells you how silly it is, but no one can make you budge 'til you want to. It's sort of been a pitting of myself against God and I even had the gall to think the odds were kind of even.

Whether your next mattress is straw or not, please take some of this. I give it with all my love.

Ita

19. June 12, 1964

Ecce Ancilla Domine

Dear Jean,

I don't know if you've been speaking with my family or not, so I don't know how much this will surprise you. My stomach has been on the 'skity,' and last Monday the doctor asked that I not be under the pressure of taking vows on the 24th. The Mother General said all right, so it looks like I'll be summering in Massachusetts.

Rene and Mary Anne are flying up tomorrow, mostly to put everyone's mind at ease that I'm all right, but just need a little time to ease off the pressure.

I think I caught my parents off guard, and of course they were worried and upset, but now I feel they're taking it in stride. Maybe if you talk with them next week, they can report anything they think worthwhile. I'm to make the eight-day retreat, starting Monday night.

After things quiet down, near the end of the month, I'll write again.

Love,
Ita

20. August 18, 1964

Dear Jean,

I'm home. Wednesday afternoon it was official that I couldn't take vows. I didn't want to shock you by calling up or ringing the bell.

Rene's baby will be due within the week. I'll call Tuesday or Wednesday, after I know you've gotten this. It's a shock and disappointment and I don't think I'm operating on all engines, but I'll bounce soon.

Love,
Ita

4.

New York: 1964–1971

Introduction

Ita Ford returned in August 1964 to her family's home in Brooklyn. Ita's sister Rene had called Grace Monahan Neimeyer, an old friend from childhood and high school, to pick her up at LaGuardia Airport. Grace was puzzled but happy to help. As she recalled,

> *After saying "sure" I asked why and Rene told me that Ita was coming home. When I arrived at LaGuardia's Eastern Shuttle, I watched the plane unload and concluded that Ita had missed it. I didn't recognize her!! She came off the plane looking unlike I had ever seen her look.*
>
> *How she suffered during the next few months. She was miserably sick, both in body and spirit. She spent hours listening to Julie's piano recordings [Julie Miller] and crying. She talked about how painful it was and we talked about all of it for hours at a time. I have never seen Ita so totally devastated.*

Ita was fragile when she returned, but resilient. It was as though events had taken over that she could not control or understand. Her family and friends lent their support and suggestions as she considered alternative choices to religious life. With a New York doctor she dutifully kept up with the therapy sessions she had begun in Boston, before concluding that they weren't all that helpful. She kept up friendships with a variety of Maryknoll Sisters, former classmates who were professed, some serving in the States before leaving for mission. As her mother observed, during these years Ita never fully relinquished the connection to the Maryknoll Sisters.

What at first had seemed like a final decision began to appear, over time, as more of a detour. Many testify this was an important time of growth and exploration for Ita. The letters collected in this section convey shifting ideas and plans during her first year home as she continued to communicate with her novice mistress, Sister Mary Galligan. For the first year Ita lived at home, but after getting a job as an editor she moved to an apartment. She wanted greater independence and a place of her own to share with friends, particularly the various Maryknollers who came and went through the city on their way to different destinations.

For Mrs. Ford this period marked an important transition and realization for Ita of her gifts and independence.

Why do I think this was her greatest period of growth? She was now for the first time an independent person — with all its responsibilities. She became an editor of a high school religion series. This was in the 1960s. She became involved in civil rights and other causes. She kept close ties with Maryknoll.

These were years of extraordinary social and political change. The civil rights movement and Vietnam as well as feminism and the sexual revolution filled the popular press. For Catholics, the Second Vatican Council was initiating a new era of reform and renewal. Ita found herself in the midst of these currents, dialoguing with friends and family as she attempted to chart her own course.

She considered teaching and took education courses at Hunter College. But ultimately she chose a different path. One of her college professors at Marymount Manhattan College recommended that she take a job at Sadlier, a Catholic publishing house that specialized in religious education. It was a very apt opportunity for Ita Ford, drawing upon her high school and college experience as an editor of newspapers and yearbooks. It enabled her to plug into the exciting new currents in the post-Vatican II church, providing textbooks that reflected the expanding horizons in theology and biblical scholarship.

She quickly sought out volunteer opportunities, working with young Puerto Rican women at St. Teresa's parish in Chinatown. She observed how little they understood about Catholic doctrine, but how real their practice of Christianity was, and how well they grasped each other's struggles in the city and the problems of drugs and prostitution. She was acutely aware of the superficiality of the religious education she had received in Catholic grammar school, high school, and even college, and she was eager to share the fruit of her experience. Maryknoll, she realized, despite her early complaints, had rewarded her in her three years with a richer understanding of her Catholic faith.

She considered joining a volunteer lay apostolic program (Extension Volunteers) run out of Chicago that would offer her an opportunity to do service in the inner city. She wrote to Sr. Mary Galligan about these plans and requested a letter of recommendation that could clarify her departure from Maryknoll. The problem was not so much the lack of a vocation to religious life as the physical stamina needed for mission life.

These were years marked by protest over the Vietnam war and radical cultural upheaval. Ita, like many with religious faith, invested this period with great hope that through the effort to achieve peace and justice the world could be brought into closer alignment with the Kingdom of God.

Sadlier Publishers opened up a new avenue that fit very naturally with these ambitions. Sadlier was founded by two Irish brothers who arrived in America in 1832 to meet the educational and spiritual needs of the Irish Catholic immigrant population. Through several generations of the family, the Sadlier publishing house had survived and evolved from catechesis to the post-Vatican II era of Ita's time and a range of non-religious as well as religious textbooks entered its lists.

At Sadlier, Ita was fortunate to find a close-knit group of young Catholic liberal professionals seeking to develop the vision of the Catholic lay person in the world and in the Church. They were well read and invested in the culture and dynamism of the city and its life. The *New Yorker* and the *New York Times* were staples for this set, along with *America, Commonweal,* the *National Catholic Reporter,* and the documents of Vatican II. William Reedy was one of the editors with whom Ita worked. She saw in him a mentor and an example of Christian living in the world, grappling with the problems of the times. As Joe Petulla, an author who worked with Ita, recalled about this period:

> She did the editing on all my books. And she was far more than the editor; co-author is more like it. I sent her a dictated draft; she would move material around, add some and send it back; I would do the same and return it. Some of the happiest days of my life were trips to New York to discuss content, revise outlines for new books, and do a lot of writing.
>
> Most of the New York meetings were made up of people from the office and all the advisors and writers, crammed into a room at the City Squire [a café] or at the office itself. We got a lot of work done at those meetings. Ita and I usually spent some time on our books at the office too, and also managed to get to a few plays together or the Museum of Modern Art or whatever hot thing was going on. We carried the discussions of the books over to our wanderings around New York; I think Ita and I represented the left wing at the discussions but I never felt any tension with the others. Ita had a critical mind, non-ideological; even in the mid-sixties we met a fellow taking signatures to stop the building of a nuclear power plant, and Ita challenged the guy to tell us where New York would get power if they didn't build the plant. She said she would think it over before she signed.
>
> Reedy was very funny at our meetings, liked to kid all of us, especially Ita, of whom he was especially fond. I tended to be critical of American institutions. Bill chided me for being too downbeat; Ita pulled us together.
>
> Those days do seem to be so long ago. In a way it seems amazing to me that Ita and I could have been so close and not even consider any kind of covert liaison, and in a way it isn't strange. I wasn't considering leaving the priesthood then, and Ita

had a lot of things on her mind. For one thing she was engaged to a Japanese American fellow, Ray I think. She was considering the best way to live the rest of her life too. She wanted a deep experience of community (as I did), and told me later that she found it at Maryknoll. I lived in several different group arrangements (the overtly political one was the most uncommunity-like, not to say disgusting) out here at Berkeley and San Francisco, and now tend to think that religious communities have the best chance to pull off a community relationship in the sense Ita and I spoke of it.

I was very naïve in those days, but I don't think Ita was. She was very sensitive, compassionate, but at the same time a wonderfully critical thinker. And she got excited about issues, problems, like I do. But unlike me, didn't lose her head.

Cathy Lavin, a colleague from Sadlier during Ita's years there, recalled meeting her in 1969 and being very struck by Ita's openness and extraordinarily sharp mind and capacity for friendship and intellectual engagement:

At that time the Sadlier religion department was a closely knit group who frequently lunched together and stopped after work for a few drinks. Ita was part of that group. Over a period of months we became very good and dear friends. As a friend I was attracted to her by her good nature, her honesty, her openness to friendship — and her sense of humor.

She loved life and loved New York . . . theater, music, the Village, NYU Newman chapel, reading to the blind . . . Since I was single and my apartment was in New Jersey, I would frequently wind up at Ita's and Kate's apartment for the evening. There was much time for talking.

Ita was very well read and had one of the sharpest minds I have ever been in touch with. At the time she was deeply upset about the war in Vietnam. I'm sure she must have marched in Washington too, though I don't remember her being with me. She and Kate and I (and others) went to the play about the Berrigan

*brothers — "The Trail of the Catonsville Nine." One morning I
got a call from Ita asking if I wanted to go to a news conference
with her. One of the Berrigan brothers (Daniel) had been in hiding but was arrested in Rhode Island at the lawyer [William]
Stringfellow's home. Stringfellow was holding a NY press conference to explain his actions. Ita warned me that it was entirely
possible the FBI would be present taking pictures . . . I thought it
over and joined her.*

*I think this incident exemplifies an important aspect of Ita's
personality: although she herself may have held strong convictions
on an issue she never tried to impose her views on others. In the
press conference incident, she had made up her mind but merely
presented the facts to me — along with an invitation.*

Another editor, Roger Marchand of Sadlier reinforces this portrayal of Ita.

*In her apartment on Sheridan Square, during her pre-Mary-
knoll years, Ita had a poster on the wall. The poster said: "What
if they gave a war and nobody came?"*

*What was Ita like during her years as an editor in New
York?*

*In those days — the late '60s early '70s — she seemed just
like the rest of us. Most of us editors were unmarried then. We
were a bunch of "liberal Catholics" who worked together, partied
together, and protested the war in Vietnam. Ita was very much in
the center of all that.*

*As an editor she was superior — a real professional. As a
friend she was generous, fun loving, and (now that I think of it)
totally accepting of everyone. One by one most of us married and
started to raise families. But not Ita.*

From 1968-1970, the years before she reentered the Maryknoll
Sisters, Ita shared an apartment in Sheridan Square, Greenwich Village, with Katherine Monahan Gregg. It was Ita's second apartment
and roommate. She and Katherine were both graduates of Mary-

mount Manhattan College; they had traveled together to Russia in their senior year and had kept up a friendship through a large circle of friends. Katherine at the time was working at IBM and making very good money. Ita, as an editor, was not as prosperous.

Katherine remembers those years as peaceful and a time of youthful exploration in which her post-college renewed friendship with Ita deepened. Ita, though shyer than Katherine, was the one to lead in exploration of the rich possibilities of taking in an art show in the Village, exploring the bookstores and museums, and attending many plays. Ita introduced Katherine to opera. They bought cheap standing-room only tickets, way at the back of the theater. Often after the second act they took the better seats abandoned by the suburbanites who left early.

Ita loved to go to the museums and spend hours absorbing the sights. She taught Katherine the value of participation in community and dialogue, to be active in relation to people rather than spend hours passively being entertained by T.V. Though Katherine insisted that they have a T.V. in the apartment, Ita seldom watched it and Katherine came to appreciate Ita's style and her value of conversation and silent wanderings in the city. Ita introduced her to new ways of being and drew her and others to join protests and to write letters against the Vietnam War. Katherine remembers that Ita initiated and led in these areas while she kept to the background in large crowds.

During these years Ita dated several men. Her mother and others recall that Ita had her most serious relationship with Ray, a Japanese American lawyer. His family had been interned in camps in California during World War II. To many friends they made a great couple. Ita talked of having many children and moving to a rural area, perhaps inspired by Catholic Worker ideals of the period. But the relationship petered out. They remained good friends and he was there at her farewell party before Ita reentered the Maryknoll Sisters.

According to her friend Kate Monahan Gregg, Ita reached thirty and wanted to do something larger with her life. She had grown at Sadlier, having gained more experience and professional competence. She and her friends traveled to Cape Cod, Florida, Washington D.C., California, and Mexico exploring and staying in inexpensive hotels and sharing adventures. She retained her values and simple life style. Her friends described her in this period as pretty and classic. She did not strive to dress as a chic New Yorker. Instead she maintained the same wardrobe she had had since college. Possessions were not important to her. Time spent with friends and intensely experiencing the riches of life and its questions were at the forefront. She wanted to live in community with others and she strove to discover how to realize that in the midst of a culture that emphasized the power of things rather than personal relationships. Urban poverty, racism, despair, riots, and death shadowed hope at the end of this decade of the sixties.

Through this time, the Maryknoll Sisters experienced great change as they grappled with the directives of the Second Vatican Council. The General Chapter of 1964 foreshadowed the change that came more dramatically with their 1968 General Chapter. In 1964 Mother Mary Coleman sent out copies of Cardinal Joseph Suenens' *A Nun in the World* along with the writings of Mother Mary Joseph (Mollie Rogers), their founder. They were seeking to recollect their early vision and open the community to the new challenges. In 1968 they asked themselves, which actually had priority, mission or consecrated religious life? Increasingly the Sisters believed that mission should shape community life. They moved from the hierarchical structure of governance by the Mother General and General Council to a more representative style of government with a President and Central Governing Board. Sr. Barbara Hendricks became their first President. She had served in Peru and knew the Peruvian liberation theologian Gustavo Gutiérrez. The Maryknoll Sisters' new constitution reflected the new focus of "identifying with the poor in the Gospel sense." They felt called to a new mutuality as they approached mission in foreign cultures "to develop community through mutual sharing and deeper understanding of the ultimate meaning of life: building the community of God." Vatican II led them to a renewed commitment to respect other peoples' culture and religion.

Through Ita's ongoing contacts with the Maryknoll Sisters during these years as they visited her in Sheridan Square, she kept up with this conversation of renewal and change. In 1970 she decided to take a trip to Japan with a teachers' tour group that her mother had learned about. She visited Tokyo and her friend Sr. Julie Miller, and they visited numerous Buddhist shrines as they explored Kyoto. As Sr. Julie recalled:

> In the summer of 1970 Ita found a tour of teachers or some odd thing, which was going to Tokyo for two weeks. She got on the tour and arrived. I think her mother found out about the tour and told Ita about it . . . We had a swell visit. We even flew to Hokkaido for a few days. I have pictures of Ita in various temples in Kyoto.
>
> The day before she left Ita asked me what I thought of the idea of her entering Maryknoll again. It was all very casual. I can't remember anything either of us said. She flew off with her tour that she was never with and called me from New York in Tokyo in 1971 saying she was off to St. Louis. She never told me of the hassles she had getting back in, but she had them.

Ita sent a brief postcard to Jean Reardon (now Bauman), in which she also celebrated the beauty of Japan and her love of Buddhist sites. This, like her earlier trip to Russia, prefaced her re-entrance to Maryknoll months later. In each case she reached out to explore another culture, very different from the West. Ray was no longer her future, but he had piqued her curiosity and desire to see Japan as had her friend, Sr. Julie Miller. To go to Japan offered an opportunity to reflect upon the bombing of Hiroshima and Nagasaki and the power of war to destroy. Ita wanted to bridge cultures and learn a way to lend her life to peace and inter-religious dialogue. Vatican II opened this horizon of possibility and a new way of approaching mission. She returned to Maryknoll, ten years older, with greater life experience and awareness of her ability to live in the world and develop her talents. Others remember her intensity and will to experience life at this juncture. Cathy Lavin of Sadlier recalls:

I found out about Ita's decision to return to Maryknoll after she had made up her mind but had not yet been accepted. The community seemed to question whether Ita had the psychological strength for Maryknoll and their doubt stemmed from whatever reasons caused them to ask her to leave in the first place. I would have expected Ita to be nervous about her interviews with the doctor since her future depended so much on what he said. But Ita was her good-natured self. She was very comfortable about who she was and where she was in life. She was sure Maryknoll would learn that for themselves and if they didn't . . . I clearly recall her smiling her impish grin and saying she would leave it in God's hands . . . Her call to be a Religious did not make her better than the rest of the world. That was her job in the world. But the world needs good people in every aspect of life. Her message seemed to be — Do your own thing, but do it well and with a good conscience.

She often engaged in lengthy dialogue about issues as she attempted to come to better understand them. Significantly, she did not turn to friends and query them about this decision of hers to return. Instead, it appears she kept her own counsel and lived with her conviction that the time was right for her to reconnect to the Sisters.

According to Mrs. Ford:

When I questioned Ita about her return to Maryknoll she said the whole atmosphere was very different now than when she first entered and that these were the people she wanted to spend the rest of her life with.

Maryknoll was in the right place for Ita. It was as if the Congregation and she had both been journeying to this crossroad together. In 1962, one hundred and thirty-two postulants had joined the Maryknoll Sisters; many of them had left in the intervening years, in part because of the changing currents of the times. By 1970, only three were to enter. But Ita returned in 1971 very aware of her quest and ready to explore her commitment. This time she found herself entering not in Ossining, New York, but in St. Louis, Missouri.

Letters and Writings

21. *To Sister Mary Galligan, MM, Maryknoll novice mistress, September 10, 1964*

Dear Sister,

It's four weeks since I arrived home, and though it's still very unreal, I am getting settled. Through Marymount, I got a position at Sadlier Text Books, doing editorial work on a new series of high school English books. This is not completely new, for I had been on the staff of the newspaper and yearbook. For right now it seems the best thing to do.

I thought perhaps I might like to teach. Since I regarded education courses in college as a waste of time, I have to start now to get the minimum, which should be finished in the spring. (I am eating all my collegiate bravado, but a slice of humble pie isn't too big a price, if I could be an influence in a classroom).

I also contacted a priest in the New York CCD [Confraternity of Christian Doctrine] office, and I may be teaching catechism on a night when I won't have classes.

This should keep me busy, as I'll be going to Arlington on Saturdays, beginning the middle of next month. I saw the doctor in Newark, before she flew to London.

I haven't contacted too many people yet, as I don't exactly feel at ease, but I have seen S. Maureen Faith, and on Labor Day I visited Rosemarie. (I got the dinner that you missed.) Saturday, I am meeting Adele Noble. Other than that, there doesn't seem to be any desire to see the others just yet, or get involved in their organization.

I used to think I was very flexible and a quick adjuster, but it takes time getting back into things, which are different, if not diametrically opposed to the way I've been thinking for the past three years. But the graces keep coming, so I'm confident it will all work out.

This has been a very ego-centered report. At least it ends with a wish for a very happy year for you and S. de Chantal at St. Mary's. I would be very pleased to hear about it, if you get a chance, and I will write when I begin to see the doctor.

Lovingly,
Ita

22. *December 2, 1964*

Dear Sister [Mary Galligan, MM],

I like your latest stationary better than letterhead. If you don't mind my saying so, it tickled me because it had your touch of the unexpected.

There is no getting around it, I've been a rather poor correspondent and I don't want to be. But I've gotten on a very tight schedule (too tight to my mother's and the doctor's thinking), though I never enjoyed twiddling my thumbs.

You asked about Arlington. I saw the doctor for five Saturdays in a row, but two weeks ago I asked for a month's trial of no visits. It seemed that most of the problems now are just in getting settled. Actually, I think I'm somewhere around the point of last July and August, not "all better," but sort of accepting the *status quo*. A good deal of me wishes I was still the over-ripe novice at Topsfield, but I can accept the wisdom that decided otherwise.

The joy of my existence is a group of sophomore high school girls at St. Teresa's parish in Manhattan. Maybe you have heard of it as some of the Junior Professed [Sisters] teach catechism there. It's not far from Chinatown. They are mostly Puerto Ricans living in the City projects and the kindest euphemism would be to say they're underprivileged. Actually they have nothing in their homes, social set-up, etc.

Theoretically, I teach CCD, but I never teach any topic at all. They were supposed to be studying the Commandments but they hardly know the basic prayers. Though Sunday Mass isn't too high on their priority list, they do have a wonderful Christian attitude toward each other. I guess that's why I love them. Somehow they sense that no matter how badly off they are, they know many in even worse circumstances. They try and help those on dope or the girls who are being used for prostitution. (It startled me when they said this starts in grammar school!!)

Right now I can only get over there once a week, but I hope soon to make it oftener. There's a full-time center (a joint CYO [Catholic Youth Organization] and City Youth Board affair) and they try to schedule something for everyday so that there will be a place that the girls and boys can come to rather than staying on street corners. There's one counselor, who will take all the help she can get, so I'm going to try and give more.

I think you'd enjoy Hunter, not so much for the classes as the students. I go two nights a week and they never stop intriguing me. Having gone to Catholic schools all my life, I get a kick out of the way the Jewish people talk. Education courses seem to be more gab than content, and they have an example or incident for every point. So if the courses are colorless, the people in them aren't.

Did I tell you where I work? I'm doing editorial work at W. H. Sadlier, a Catholic textbook publisher. If you had to pick a more relaxed place, I think you'd have a hard time. So in that respect, it's good. Right now I'm doing an English book for fourth year high school. It's the last of a new series, which are in paperback. It's an impressive anthology, but my work is mostly technical. I also had to put the new liturgical changes into the *Baltimore Catechism*. (Yes, it's still around, used as a jumping off point for all the *kerygmatic** approach.) But I guess I'm neutral as to my feelings about it. I really didn't care what I did, but I guess I'm fortunate to be in such a pleasant place.

Now that I've said so much about myself, how are you? What area in theology are you studying? After poor courses in high school

---

* *Kerygmatic* approach — an approach to catechesis with more emphasis on the message of Jesus rather than on demonstrating the logical content of Catholic doctrine.

and college, I was intrigued and delighted with what we were offered in the novitiate. It was wonderful to realize there was a lot of meat to theology, rather than it just being something you sat through. (I don't doubt that a lot of that was bad attitude, but we never were offered anything comparable.) I wish they gave a good scripture course along the line. But probably a lot of that might change now anyway.

Sister, it's after midnight so I should go to bed. I did want to write before too long a time had passed, and I hope I won't be slow on the next one. Do you think that next semester there might be a chance for an art course? I hope so.

Lovingly,
Ita

23. February 14, 1965

Dear Sister [Mary Galligan, MM]

It's a very long time in between letters, and this one I admit has an ulterior motive. My good intentions to write always get waylaid, but when I have a favor to ask, you see I'm managing the time.

How is school coming this semester? I hope you were able to manage an art course. I'm taking eight hours at Hunter, and this should give me the minimum credits necessary for education. The people in the course are far more interesting than the content. It gives me a good idea of our pluralistic society.

I'm applying to Extension* for volunteer work starting this summer. The application has questions about previous novitiate training and reasons for leaving, along with inquiries about psychiatric treatment and why.

If it is possible, I would very much like to enclose a letter from you with the application. You said last August that you felt my leaving Maryknoll wouldn't be a hindrance in entering another order.

---

* Extension is a Church program that provides support for Home Mission work in the United States.

Right now, I don't feel in a position to make that decision, but I would very much like to be involved in some form of apostolic work. With your help, I thought I could give a clearer reason for not continuing to take vows. I don't want to evade the issue, but I also don't want to answer it and give the impression that I'm a complete misfit. May I ask this of you?

The Director is Rev. John J. Sullivan, Extension Lay Volunteers, 1307 South Wabash Avenue, Chicago. I thought a letter from you would be a better explanation than I could give. And if it arrived with the application it would settle the matter right away.

You must be very busy but I'm asking this because I feel it's important to me, and something which I should try. Thank you very much, Sister.

Love,
Ita

24. May 17, 1965

Dear Sister [Mary Galligan, MM]

Before you change addresses, I thought I would write to tell you what's happening.

While the application was being processed for Extension, I was asked by the pastor at St. Teresa's, where I teach CCD, if I would help as a full-time catechist. He thought it might be possible to get funds from the Archdiocese so I could study in Puerto Rico this summer. As it turned out there are no provisions for lay helpers, only for religious and priests.

Then I was transferred to the Catechetical Department of Sadlier's. I am working under Mr. William Reedy, who is writing a new series of books for high school. As I thought and prayed about it, it seemed as though I should continue where I am right now, so I can learn all that Mr. Reedy is so willing to share, not only in catechetics, but also as a marvelous example of a good Christian man.

Last week, Extension said I had been accepted, so I wrote to ask if they would keep my application on file. Now it's working out so I can 'pick' Mr. Reedy's brains during the week, and then try and share it at St. Teresa's. I'm not a very good middleman, but it's more effective than if I were trying without any source of information.

Several weeks ago, there was a 'reunion' of many of the former novices. I didn't go, but I did get to see Terri Sullivan and Madge Holt before they went home. It was very good seeing them again, but I had no wish, and probably just wasn't able to play *auld lang syne* with a large group.

I'm just beginning to feel as though I'm getting on my feet. I hope I put as much into being a good Christian here, as I wanted to put into Maryknoll. I know I have an advantage by having been there.

This has been a very 'I' letter. I hope you reciprocate in kind.

Lovingly,

Ita

25. To Jean Reardon and John Bauman, undated postcard

Daibutsu at Kamakura, Japan

Dear Jean and John,

There's a great deal to be learned from the Buddhists. In the middle of all the frenzy there are quiet, peaceful pockets that seem a thousand miles away. I keep getting the feeling that I'd just like to sit down and stay a couple of days. May be I will.

See you soon.

Love,

Ita

5.

Maryknoll to Chile: 1971–1978

Introduction

The letters that follow cover the period of Ita Ford's life from 1971 to 1978. During these years the trajectory of her life moves from her return to the Maryknoll Sisters in 1971, through her novitiate and profession, to her mission work in Chile during a remarkable period of turmoil and struggle.

Poetry and scripture spoke to Ita and she often prayed during the Chilean period over the passage in Jeremiah, 18:3ff., which describes God as a potter recasting broken clay vessels. In these years she likened herself to a misshapen clay vessel, returning to the potter's wheel to be recast again and again in God's hands. Like Jeremiah, she struggled to give voice to the meaning and prophetic message of God as it touched her life. What was God's plan for her and her community? She felt trust and faith, and yet it was a process, with much uncertainty about the answers she was seeking.

These were years of extraordinary social and ecclesial change. This time, instead of joining a large class of sixty-four Maryknoll novices, she joined a class of three that expanded to four. They were women like herself who had had the experience of developing careers and traveling to places off the beaten path. They were seeking to commit themselves to work with the poor through community and to deepen their relationship with God as Maryknoll Sisters.

In the fall of 1971 she found herself studying in St. Louis, Missouri, at the Jesuit theologate. She lived with the other Maryknoll

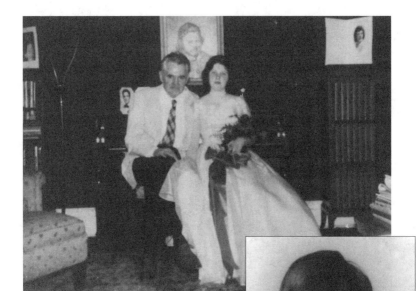

Ita with her father, William Patrick Ford.

Ita's high school graduation photo from Fontbanne Hall.

Editor of the yearbook at Marymount Manhattan College.
(Courtesy Marymount Manhattan College Archives, Thomas J. Shanahan Library.)

Ita in 1961, a postulant at Maryknoll, with her brother Bill.

Ita seated with other Maryknoll novices in 1962.

In the summer of 1971, just before her return to Maryknoll.

Ita in La Bandera, 1978.

*La Bandera,
the shantytown outside
Santiago Chile, where
Ita lived.*

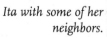

*Ita with some of her
neighbors.*

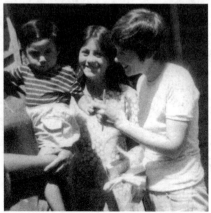

Ita with Maryknoll Sister Carol (Carla) Piette.

Ita and Carla with neighbors in La Bandera.

novices in a large house. This time her experience of community was smaller and more participatory. This was not a mob but a scale that allowed for dialogue and close friendship. The rules had evolved to foster greater participation and the members were now making decisions together about prayer, study, work, and recreation. The classes were challenging and in light of the post-Vatican II changes there was a new emphasis on biblical studies and theology. Her fellow students were drawn from different religious communities that included men and women, as well as some lay people and non-Catholics.

It was altogether a different atmosphere from her first experience of religious life. Ita felt she was on a new path. And yet as she visited the Sisters' "country house" in Valley Park, she was reminded of her earlier experience at Topsfield, Massachusetts, in 1961. So much had intervened. The years of work and experience in New York had shaped her and given her confidence, yet the large institutional grounds reminded her of the earlier training. She realized as she walked and hiked that she was able to reconnect to the depths of the inner search that she had begun seven years before and feel a return to that interior spiritual journey. "In a way I'm back home. Of course it's different and I am too, and I expected that, but sometimes when praying or free-associating, I have the feeling that my heart is moving or being moved as it may have been eight years ago. Either I'm very consistent or I'm still in the same place I was then. This doesn't mean anything to me or bother me, because it's good just to be in an atmosphere that prompts and encourages me to look inside."

Ita enjoyed drawing from the rich menu of courses available at St. Louis in biblical studies, philosophy, theology, and spirituality. Intellectually and spiritually she was always curious and reflective. A course on "Discernment" was particularly helpful. On April 29, 1972, Ita was professed in a ceremony at St. Louis. Sr. Mary Galligan, her former novice mistress, attended, as well as many friends and family members.

Ita considered different options for mission work. Because of her training in religious education through her years at Sadlier,

Chile, or the Philippines, with their large pastoral institutes, seemed to offer the best opportunities for utilizing those skills. In the end she chose Chile, though her work would be quite different than anything she had prepared for.

The Latin American bishops in 1968 in their historic meeting at Medellín, Colombia, had responded to the Second Vatican Council's call for a new model of Church by looking at the problems of injustice and poverty. Traditionally, the Church in Latin America had identified most closely with the rich and powerful. Medellín marked a new horizon of understanding of the Kingdom of God, stressing the social and this-worldly dimension of salvation. The documents addressed the situation of social injustice as a case of "institutionalized violence" and "structural sin," calling for conversion and solidarity.

Ita traveled through several countries on her way to the Maryknoll language school in Cochabamba, Bolivia, a colorful and quaint city of two hundred and fifty thousand. Along the way she spent several days in Lima, Peru, where she experienced firsthand the incongruities of extreme wealth and extreme poverty.

The Maryknoll language school in Cochabamba brought together many Religious from a variety of backgrounds, experiences, and levels of language skills. The classes were very demanding and intense, but there was the pleasure of good company and the excitement of meeting other missioners who were equally committed to the goals she embraced. Humor and camaraderie buoyed the days of intense struggle to grasp another way of speaking and to see the world through another culture and language.

In one letter to her friend Jean Reardon Bauman, Ita asked Jean to see her more clearly as an ordinary human being, seeking to recognize and accept her fallibility as she accepted herself and the love of others. Religious life was not something that should set her apart, she advised, but simply her own way of living out her commitment to God.

Bolivia was experiencing its own economic and political struggle. During the period of her study, a state of siege and martial law was declared. In La Paz, the capital, tanks were rolled out to close down protests and strikes in reaction to the spiraling inflation. But, as Ita noted, the response in Cochabamba was almost casual, as people went about their business. Military dictatorship was nothing new. Repression was part of the fabric of Bolivian life, as much as the contrasting extremes of poverty and wealth.

She was excited by the opportunity to travel and she was eager to see and investigate ancient archeological sites like Machu Picchu, the ancient Inca city in Peru. At Christmas time she ventured to the town of Juli and Lake Titicaca. The sight of Aymara Indians in a remote village affected her on Christmas Day.

In March she faced the end of her weeks of study at Cochabamba and took her leap into the unknown. For weeks after her arrival in Chile she wandered through the country, trying to adapt and find her niche within the region of her assignment. She was happy and felt a sense of harmony with herself and God. This life was not about ecstatic experiences but a calm sense of finding her center.

The Maryknoll Sisters had originally been invited to Chile to found schools which tended to serve the middle and upper classes. The changes in recent years had inspired a new emphasis to move out of the classroom and into the world of the poor.

Ita's travels through the country enabled her to see and understand the country and to discern her own place in the mission work. Feeling most at home in an urban environment, she eventually settled on the area of Santiago.

The capital city of Santiago is in the center of Chile, a long narrow strip of a country that includes the Andean mountains on the east and stretches nearly to Antarctica at the far south. Its climate is milder than the country's other geographical extremes. Santiago is a beautiful city, designed in the typical Spanish style with a *plaza de armas* at the center, from which an octopus of streets extend in every direction. Stately colonial buildings mix with the mansions of the wealthy and the shacks of the very poor. The population of more than five million includes the growing numbers of the rural poor, who fill the shantytowns that encircle the city. At the time of Ita's arrival, Chile prided itself for its long tradition of democracy and political stability. Yet grinding poverty defined the lives of one third of its population, while 50 percent of the wealth was controlled by 10 percent of the population.

Politically the country was in the midst of a building crisis. President Eduardo Frei of the Christian Democratic Party had been elected in 1964 and brought about many social reforms. But in 1970 the Christian Democrats lost in a fragmented election to the leftist Popular Unity Party and its socialist candidate, Salvador Allende. Quickly, Allende tried to introduce reforms to socialize the economy and weaken the influence of multinational corporations. From the beginning he was opposed by the Right and by most business leaders. Joining these forces, under the direction of Richard Nixon and Henry Kissinger, was the U.S. government, which attempted, through subversive channels, to undermine and eventually overthrow the Allende government.

Despite these efforts, Allende's party gained congressional seats in midterm elections in March 1973. The Christian Democrats, disillusioned and shaken by Allende's radical reform measures, aligned themselves increasingly with the Right. President Nixon's efforts to "make the [Chilean] economy scream" were bearing fruit. Strikes and food shortages led to long lines for kerosene, bread, and other staples. Inflation reached 360 percent. The country was rapidly moving toward an explosion.

Many people told Ita that she had come at the best and the worst of times. She noted that, despite the long lines and shortages, people seemed to adapt with humor to the hardship and struggle. Through their involvement in unions, the working poor of Chile had developed a greater degree of solidarity, class-consciousness, and pride. They had helped to elect Allende, and they remained hopeful that his government would defend their interests.

Much of Maryknoll's work in Santiago was in the shantytowns or *poblaciones* that circled the city. Eventually Ita settled into one of these, La Bandera, with three other sisters, Mary Tracy, Carol (Carla) Piette, and Connie Pospisil. La Bandera was one of the toughest and poorest of the shantytowns with a population of between 70,000 and 80,000. The Chilean Church had advocated the importance of building community among the poor, outside the usual institutional structures, to engender small base Christian communities. It was there that Ita would root her ministry.

After returning from a workshop in Talca with Sr. Carla Piette, Ita learned that her father had died on September 10, 1973. Her brother Bill was finally able to get a message through to her at the Maryknoll House in Santiago. Her family wanted her to return for her father's funeral. She was torn. Ita had always been particularly close to her father, and she treasured the beautifully wrought letters that he sent her. But she had only just settled into La Bandera. She talked with the others, who listened carefully to Ita's debate with herself. Finally, Sr. Carla convinced her to go. And yet leaving Chile at that stage turned out to be very difficult.

On September 11, 1973, just as Carla and Fr. Tom Maney were driving into Santiago to arrange for Ita's plane ticket, a military coup was being staged at the Presidential Palace, close to the airline ticket office. They had to run, under gunfire, to get back to their truck and rush back to La Bandera. Before the day was over, Allende was dead and martial law had been declared. General Augusto Pinochet, the architect of the coup, was named as the leader of a military junta. The following weeks were marked by brutal repression, as thousands of dissidents and Allende allies were rounded up. The poor of the shantytowns and their leaders were particularly targeted. Soon the soccer fields, stadiums, and schools were filled with political prisoners, held without charge. Many were tortured, killed, or "disappeared," during this brutal reign of terror.

A few days after the coup, when the curfew was lifted, stores which had been vacant of goods were suddenly full of staples — though available now at exorbitant prices. Ita was on one of the first planes to leave Chile on September 21, 1973. She had missed her father's funeral. But apart from visiting her family, part of her purpose in coming was to tell others outside the country what was taking place. The Watergate scandal was absorbing the country. Nevertheless, as she spoke of the conditions she had witnessed in Chile, many of her friends found it hard to grasp what she described and the possibility of U.S. involvement in Allende's downfall and murder. Her friends and family observed that she was strained and tense.

After two weeks in New York, Ita returned to La Bandera, which she now considered home. She wrote a number of short papers that describe her work and the conditions under the new repression. In "Try to Imagine," she details the fear that gripped the neighborhood as soldiers arrived at dawn to take away men and boys. Three times their own house was searched.

The Chilean bishops responded to the repression with several important documents. In April 1974, they issued "Reconciliation in Chile," which called for a reestablishment of the human rights of the Constitution and its legal guarantees. But the document had no effect. Ita relates the example of a priest who was arrested after arms were found in the tabernacle of his church. Church authorities maintained that the arms were planted. Increasingly the church became a place of refuge and the voice for the persecuted and disappeared. In October 1975, the bishops released the document "Gospel and Peace," that contrasted the military junta's ideology with the spirit of the gospel.

Ita's mother and sister Rene came to visit her in La Bandera in 1974. Rene stayed for a week and her mother for two. Mrs. Ford found it an extraordinary place, both because of the simplicity of the people's lives and the power of the Sisters' commitment. The hospitality and warmth of people who had so little, but who were always generous, impressed her greatly.

Ita described their work as fostering base Christian communities where a number of people could come together, read scripture, and reflect about its significance in the framework of their lives. La Bandera was an open society. Everyone was aware of each other's business. The Sisters were not living apart, coming in from the outside with a warehouse of goods and solutions. Instead they were there to nurture hope and to act in solidarity with the poor, to accompany them, and with them to work out the meaning of the Kingdom of God in their midst.

On Easter 1975, Ita and Sr. Carla met a young British doctor, Sheila Cassidy, at the Maryknoll Center in Santiago. She came for prayer and was impressed by the commitment of the Maryknoll Sisters. Although she had been raised as a Catholic, this was a very different experience of church and of religious life for her. Sheila Cassidy recalled that Ita often referred to the passage from Jeremiah 18:3ff about God as the potter, recasting the imperfect creations from his potter's wheel. Again and again the good clay was taken up and reworked by God. Ita saw herself as the imperfect vessel, and she wished to give herself over to the refashioning. Together they sought the courage to work with the poor in this time of even greater fear and desperation. This entailed real risk. To live the Kingdom of God in these circumstances meant running the risk of being mistaken for a subversive.

In October 1975, Sheila Cassidy was arrested for treating the wounds of an "enemy of the state." She was stripped and tortured. No one knew where she was for days. Eventually they found her at *Tres Alamos* Detention Camp on the outskirts of Santiago, among six hundred prisoners, held without charge, under the provisions of the state of siege. Ita and Carla visited her and smuggled in for her, among the folds of napkins, consecrated hosts. (Cassidy was eventually released after the British government, in stark contrast with U.S. policy, threatened to cut off diplomatic relations.)

Ita worked with refugees and wrote letters to Senator Edward Kennedy and other members of Congress seeking help for those trying to leave and start a new life. The work was carried out on a variety of levels. Occasionally, however, she would go to Santiago for relief and diversion — a trip to the movies, or to McDonald's with friends, to escape the oppressive conditions. She was always aware that, unlike the poor of La Bandera, she lived with a safety net. It pushed her to greater humility and to an analysis of her own values and poverty of spirit. The clash of cultures could be wearing as well. She and the other Sisters were shaped by the values of efficiency and order. At times it was difficult to let go of the urge to take charge and instead to listen and learn and be evangelized by the poor and the culture of La Bandera. She said it was not a comfortable place, but it was the right place to be.

Ita and Carla formed a particularly close bond in those years as they witnessed and struggled to understand the meaning of mission in this context. Carla Piette had already served in Maryknoll for ten years. She was radical in her desire to live side by side with the poor, allowing herself few luxuries. She and Ita shared a great love of literature and poetry. Carla was a creative and exuberant woman who occasionally became deeply depressed by the conditions she felt she could not transform. Ita offered Carla a sense of balance and a patient ear. In turn, Carla shared with Ita her humor and her sense of perspective when Ita would tunnel deep into questions, seeking the answers with her vibrant intellect. Together they helped each other to stay grounded.

Ita was due for her Reflection Year and final vows in 1977. She postponed it a year because she felt it was too great a luxury and too difficult to leave the people in their time of need. Though she saw that she did not have all the answers or solutions, she felt they were living the paschal mystery in Chile. The cup of suffering was great and hope, at times, was hard to contemplate. Yet she attempted to remain faithful to the journey of accompaniment.

Finally, in 1978 Carla convinced her to go, reassuring her that she would keep her peace and balance, even in her absence. And so the journey led back to Maryknoll.

Letters and Writings

26. To Jean Reardon Bauman, October 6, 1971

> Maryknoll Sisters,
> 4484 Westminster Place,
> St. Louis, Missouri 63108

Dear Jean,

Sorry it's taken me so long to answer your notes. My 'sabbatical' year is a little more busy than I anticipated. Between Scripture courses at the Divinity School (one of the five Jesuit theologates in the country) and theology here at the house, the work has been piling up.

I can't remember if you've ever been in St. Louis or not. I haven't seen that much of it: the business downtown area, the university area and the environs of Forest Park, not too far from where we live, but there's a gracious element about it. People passing you on the street often greet you with a nod, a little human touch that is a nice change.

In the area in which we live, which is, [according to] my not yet too clear sense of direction, kind of in the middle of the city, I get a strong feeling of one-time opulence. The houses are large, stone, three-story affairs, fit for comfortable burghers at the beginning of the century. Some have turrets and other interesting architectural features. Now I'm sure they are subdivided into apartments, but from the street, you still get a sense of stability, roots, large families, etc. There are only a few high apartment buildings, but I noticed a few more are on their way.

For the most part our neighbors seem to be students, groups of religious, and black families. I haven't noticed that many white families around, but the area is overrun with different orders of priests and sisters because of the Divinity School. Of course, you can't tell anyone's identity from looking at them. The seminarians look like my neighbors in the village. The priests are about the same, while the sisters still retain some element of being "neat."

A couple of days each week I sit in on religion classes in a nearby high school. At first I thought I might be able to take one, just to see what it's like, but the school is on a modular program, and the classes keep rotating in time and days, so I couldn't match it to my schedule. So I think I might look into the high school CCD program or an adult education situation.

Last Friday afternoon, the three of us who are the brood took off for a twenty-four hour break to our "country house," the 110 acre former novitiate at Valley Park, Missouri, which is up for sale and now staffed by a dozen retired sisters who literally rattle around in the buildings that held over two hundred novices and postulants at one time. It was a good stretch for my legs. I must have walked eight hours altogether. It is larger than Topsfield was, but there's much that reminded me of the past. It didn't bother me though, probably because so much has intervened. After a month, I can say I'm glad I'm here. It's strange to realize that I'm back again going toward what I want, and I may have a case of arrested development, but sometimes I feel I've been through it before, although that just may be the case of getting back into the situation. (Does this paragraph make sense? In a way I feel like "I'm back home." Of course, it's different and I am too. I expected that, but sometimes when 'praying' or free-associating I have the feeling that my heart is moving or being moved as it may have eight years ago. Either I'm very consistent or I'm still in the same place I was then.) This doesn't mean anything to me or bother me, because it's good just to be in an atmosphere that prompts or encourages me to look inside.

The liturgies and related activities here are incredibly varied and rich. Several times a week we go to a Jesuit residence for Mass at which on the average, ten priests will concelebrate. While there I get an incredible feeling of community. Then there's a different, more intimate sense of it when we have it here in the house where only six people live. I've been very impressed with some of the Jesuits I've met here. For some reason in my past, I've had a stereotyped image of the Jesuit as a glib sophisticate. I'm not sure how that was built up, but it's certainly being broken down here. The men I've met have great depth and seem to be very prayerful. So there goes one prejudgment!

About a 'title,' I respond to anything that's friendly, but I'm without any official label.

Well, back to the books. I'm at a slight disadvantage not knowing Greek, German, and Hebrew, but I admire it on the pages. The Greek is especially graceful.

Love to you and John,
Ita

27. Sometime in 1972

Dear Jean,

The expression that's used out here about a person who has so many things going that everything is getting out of hand is 'overextended.' And that's what I was for the two weeks in New York. I'm sorry I didn't meet you the second week, but by that time I think I was off in a whirlwind.

The courses this semester are very good, although one may be a little bit more than I can really chew. Three quarters of the bibliography is in French, and mine certainly isn't strong enough to grasp philosophy of religion and asceticism. It should prove interesting.

The director of the orientation program will be here for about a month, in which time I hope to find out how I go about the process of getting a place to lay my head for the next three years. Up to now everything has seemed so fluid. It was hard to know where to start.

We had a population explosion of one, a girl who was in the Peace Corps teaching in St. Vincent in the Caribbean. She wasn't exactly prepared for the −3 degrees on the day she came. As it warmed up, I think things looked better.

For you I wish the peace and joy that belongs to us children of a Father whose extravagance only begins with the creatures on the front of the card.

Happy Birthday, dear friend.

Love,
Ita

28. Week after Easter 1972

Dear Jean,

I thought I'd have the chance to talk with you last week. I took a quick trip in on Easter morning to see my father who has been in the hospital for a few weeks. But most of the time was spent seeing him or talking with Mom so I never got around to contacting a few people to say hello.

But come the first weekend in May, I'll be your neighbor. Classes end here the first week of May and then we take off. The summer will be taken up with workshops and classes in Ossining, but I think weekends will be fairly free.

As of this week next year may find me in Chile or the Philippines. Last week Korea was also on the list, but the first two have large pastoral institutes that develop catechetical materials for the surrounding areas and with my experience, I probably could get involved in some aspect of that. However, I won't be doing anything until I get a grasp on a language. So I'll probably be a student for a while yet.

During Holy Week I had my first private retreat, which was a contracted version (nine days) of the thirty days of the Spiritual Exercises. It was somewhat intense, but it was a good experience.

A few weeks ago I was told, considering that I had already fulfilled 'canonical'* requirements, I could make what is now called a promise of fidelity. After considering it for a while, because I hadn't been expecting to do it for at least another year, I've decided to do it before I leave St. Louis.

When I mentioned to Jennifer (Sullivan $7 \frac{1}{2}$) that I thought I might want to be a Sister, she was highly indignant. Her only reference is Aunt Bess and she didn't approve of that for me.

Take care. I should see you in a few weeks.

Love,
Ita

---

* The requirements set down in the Code of Canon Law, the official legal code of the Catholic Church.

29. September 24, 1972

Casilla 1003
Cochabamba, Bolivia

Dear Jean,

It occurred to me the other day that I wasn't sure just where you were, maybe frolicking somewhere in Europe. But wherever you are, I'm thinking of you.

The trip down was something of a merry-go-round, even for me, until I got to Lima and stopped for four days. On the one-day stopovers, it seems as though you spend almost as much time getting in and out of the country as you do catching up with the people you came to see. Lima I enjoyed very much, possibly because the four days fell around a weekend and several people had time to help me get a feel of the city, from the colonial palaces to the latest invasion site ringing the city where rural people have squatted and still have nowhere near the necessities of light, water, roads, for beginners. It struck me as I kept seeing things that I had only heard about that I wasn't reacting to them. I was only seeing and not understanding. There's so much incongruity that it's very hard to get hold of it. A person would have to be here a long time before beginning to understand.

I didn't know what to expect of Cochabamba but it has turned out to be a very pleasant place, not exactly a throbbing hub but large enough to have some diversion when I'm numb of tongue and brain. I think there may be about a quarter of a million people in the environs, making it the second largest city in the country. It also happens to have the best climate the country offers, being neither oxygen-poor mountaintop nor lowland jungle. It takes some adjustment to live at 8,000 feet but then it's not bad at all, only periodic havoc with intestines for some reason I still don't understand.

There are about fifty students at the language school at various levels, Spanish, Aymara and Quechua — two of the most common Indian languages in Bolivia and Peru and apparently, at least Aymara is very difficult. Off hand I would say almost everyone at the school is church-related in one way or another — priests, nuns, seminarians, the Christian missionaries or volunteers. Not everyone is a beginner. In fact, most come for refresher courses periodically, so I've gotten to meet many people who have been in South America for a while. In fact do tell your mother there is a Columban* here, Kevin O'Boyle who will be going back to Chile next week. He's a real delightful fellow.

The language course follows what is called the audio-lingual method. What that means here is a four-hour session each day — on a one student, one teacher basis (different teachers each hour) repeating and repeating until your jaw and tongue are quite stiff. I'm sure I've never talked so consistently in my life, and it can get quite wearying. It's supposed to work. Then there's usually at least an hour or more of tapes, then opening the book to discuss just what you've been parroting all day. It's a full-time job, but there are a great many people who help take the weight of the whole thing off your mind. There's much camaraderie and mutual encouragement. Those who have been here longer assure us that after a while you stop twitching! I'm looking forward to the time when I get out of the one-word-at-a-time-with-a-big-pause-in-between phase. At this stage if the person listening to me hasn't forgotten what I started to say, I probably have.

So I'm muddling along, actually in pretty good spirits, because I probably don't really understand what's going on. Let me hear from you, Jean.

Take care.

Love to you and John,
Ita

---

* The Society of St. Columba, originally an Irish missionary order, now with members from throughout the world.

30. October 26, 1972

Dear Jean,

Whatever it was that brought you to St. Michael's I hope the time there is life-giving for you. Right now I feel a little helpless about which way to respond because I obviously don't know the situation and I guess I haven't for a long time. When we'd be together I'd keep getting the feeling that you were stalled, on what, about what was never clear.

I don't know why I want to say something about expectations, but I'll blunder on. Many times in the last fifteen years you've said things to me that let me know you thought I was capable of some singular feats. In reality I'm probably not, but there are some ordinary tasks that if I grapple with them will probably be fulfilling and help me to be more of a human being. I don't have to be special or different, and when I'd try to say this, I thought in some way I was hurting you. Yet, I was trying to bring down to my size what your image of me was. If I was bigger than life to you, I couldn't be real or be me. And if we can be ourselves and accept ourselves obviously limited, weak, imperfect and [then we can] accept the mysterious fact that we are loveable, not in spite of ourselves but as we are. That was one of the biggest things I wrestled with in my '64 low-water mark. Why would anyone want to love me? It turns out to be a stupid, fruitless question. There's no factual answer, they just do and continue to even when you can't see or understand why. Love is healing, strengthening, integrating, accepting. You can be who you are, and become more. I know this is true because it's happened to me. Who I am now is due to many people who cared for me, and those who do now.

We aren't mirror images of each other and what I said about me I'm not applying to you. All I really want to tell you is I love you, and care about what's happening. I hope you'll soon be experiencing peace. For whatever it is that is now fragmenting you, I hope you'll find clues, an answer, an acceptance.

If I've run off the track, I'm sorry. Do take care of yourself.

Ita

31. November 28, 1972

Dear Jean,*

Thanks for the letter. Sometimes in letters things don't come across as they were meant. I was beginning to wonder if perhaps I had stepped on your toes inadvertently.

Again, this is not the best way to have a conversation, but there is something that struck me that might be to the point. If it isn't, ignore it. I guess, I've always known you as an idealist, as a person striving to become. Yet, it seems that there may . . . . . . your life who theorized the ideal, possibly beyond . . . . . . possibly beyond the point of humanly reaching it. That . . . . . . incredible conflict, what 'is' isn't good enough, and . . . . . . be is just out of reach. I think that's a very different . . . . . . to become what is in your potential to be.

I think I understand what you mean about the "we." . . . . . . the situation but I remember one occasion when you said so . . . . . . effect that really surprised me. I think you were talking about . . . . . . to John — but it sounded so restrictive of you. I really hope, ... you can get beyond that point to the freedom that should be yours, and to the peace and happiness that accompany it.

Last Thursday Bolivia was declared in a "State of Siege" which best translates to being under martial law, a not-uncommon occurrence in these parts. It is just about a month since the currency was devalued 60%, causing quite a suffering for most of the people. Last week two unions in La Paz had the temerity to consider striking as a protest to the economic situation, and out rolled the tanks. Things have been quiet here in Cochabamba, but the decree for the entire country, no meetings, no travel within the country without permission, no more than three people together on the street at night, etc. But life seems to go on, and many of our teachers say it really makes little difference and that eventually you become oblivious to such measures.

---

* Major portions of this letter have become illegible over the years. Beginning with line eight through line seventeen, the right quarter of each line is illegible. The paragraph appears here, as it does, because it helps us appreciate the intimacy and personal dimensions of Ita Ford that some may overlook who would cast her as, perhaps, more ideological or political in her make-up.

The Spanish is coming along. I guess I have the foundations and what I really need is much practice. But you just can't rush it. Most people say that after eighteen months or so, you begin to feel comfortable in it, but everyone goes at a different pace. I hope to put my rudiments to the test during the two-week break at Christmas. A few of us are going to visit the Bolivian-Peruvian *altiplano*, going as far as Cuzco, Peru outside of which are the ruins of Machu-Picchu, an Inca city rediscovered early this century by American archeologists. It's supposed to be an incredible site. From there I'm hoping to backtrack to Juli for Christmas with the Maryknollers who work in that part of Peru. Of course, most of the travel depends on the weather. It will be the rainy season, during which roads, bridges, etc., often disappear in landslides or become impassible. So we'll see. Also either coming or going in between countries, I would like to take the boat that crosses Lake Titicaca once a week. One thing, travel isn't expensive. From La Paz to Cuzco, a trip of about 30 hours at the least, is only seventeen dollars. Of course, accommodations are somewhat haphazard, but there's not much choice. You become very delighted with whatever moves.

Well, old bean, with the upcoming season I hope the Lord makes known to you his care, love, presence and peace. I wish that very much for you.

Take care and much love,

Ita

32. To Grace Monahan Niemeyer, January 15, 1973

. . . Did you get the *ruana*,* yet? It didn't go by way of Philadelphia, but through someplace in Massachusetts. It finally went up with one of the priests because the other pony express was filled up. Down here you'd think Maryknoll was a competing postal system. No one goes anywhere without mail and packages. We even call it a 'would you mind.' After someone walks in the door, people immedi-

---

* *Ruana* — a woolen shawl worn in the Andean countries.

ately start eyeing their bags. So much of it is actually forwarded mail. I guess people in the States who only write infrequently are usually one or two addresses behind the gypsies.

The Christmas trip was really good. It started off all fouled up, but worked out fine. I spent Christmas in the town of Juli, Peru, right on Lake Titicaca. That section of Peru is almost completely Aymara Indian who eke out a living in what at first appears to be the most barren spot on earth. The *altiplano* is above the tree-line for the most part. The earth would need pneumatic drills to make a dent in it, and for miles on end there's nothing, nothing. Yet after a couple of days you realize that it does have its own beauty — stark. Yes, life is very hard, but it's not completely depressing. I don't know if I could work there, but it was [a] very tranquil place to be for a few days. Christmas morning I went out with one of the priests to an isolated community for mass. It was the first time that I got the full impact of a village all wearing the same clothes. The women all had black shawls, decorated with red bands of design, fitted jackets to the waist, different colors but with the same designs and the same with the skirt. I got a kick out of the fact that they take off their derbies when they go into Church. Some wear shoes, others don't, and it was freezing. But for the most part I don't think they cover their legs no matter what the temperature. And in the rural areas, women never wear pants. You only see that in cities of a fairly good size. It's one of those things, in a place that to you would seem most appropriate for slacks, they just aren't accepted and you have to take that into consideration.

Tomorrow starts my last month of Spanish. During the trip, I think, I understood most of what was happening around me, but I'm glad no one was holding their breath for my answer. That's just going to take time. So after 5 $^1/_2$ months of studying, it will be time to put it to the test. The last two weeks of February there will be a general orientation course to Latin America. Then sometime after that, I shall gather a year's supply of toilet paper and head for Chile. Some shortages are more inconvenient than others!* But

---

* Ita was often lovingly kidded through the years about the supply of toilet paper she kept handy because of local shortages in the places in which she frequently found herself.

I'm sure people are coming up with ingenious substitutes.

Take care, and know that I love you very much and care about what is happening.

Love,

Ita

33. January 25, 1973, Chile

Dear Jean,

Tomorrow morning we hop a bus for nine hours, arriving in Talca Huano for our annual meeting of the region. This one should mostly deal with what went on for the six weeks of the community assembly in N.Y. There will be representatives from Bolivia, Peru and the community president. It will be good to hear what's going on in other parts of the world — sometimes you get so involved that you think the sun rises and sets on Chile.

I'm sorry to hear that the Reardons on Lockwood Road are all scattering. I hope they'll be able to look back later and feel that something positive had its roots in the present sorrow . . .

This will probably arrive after the second but it carries warmest wishes for your birthday and coming year. May the gift of life you received come to its promised fullness in the Lord's joy and happiness.

Love to you and John,

Ita

34. January 27, 1973, Chile

Dear Jean,

I've been thinking about the phrase 'kindred spirits' in your letter. Can it be that they only are in places such as New Mexico, Arizona or Virginia? It seems to me that there must be many people who, although they have other responsibilities to take up this time, still crave to feed their spirit and do acknowledge this side of themselves. There must be individuals or groups nearer for you. It's not selfish or bizarre to seek what gives you peace and joy nor should experiences of that for a short time have to carry you for years.

There can't be any reason strong enough for you to allow yourself to be 'imprisoned,' either in an apartment or in a relationship. If you are not growing and acknowledging who you are and what you need to be you, that's not being a good wife. It may be the path of least resistance and death.

Jean, as you mark another anniversary of the gift of life, try to see it more deeply. If you value it and want it, you have to continually struggle with what suffocates it. Don't give up on your call to be fully human, or constantly growing and coming to be.

I know what I'm saying is easier said than done and that it's hard. But to be able to have a sense that, at least, you are trying to get hold of that for which the Lord got hold of you, being in some kind of harmony, that's within our power to discern and act on. I don't mean to come on so strongly, but I do love you and would so much like to see you happy and at peace with yourself and then with others.

That this begins to really happen is my deepest wish for you this year.

Love,
Ita

35. To Grace Monahan Niemeyer, March 8, 1973

Cochabamba, Bolivia

Dear Grace,

Well, I'm all finished everything, Spanish, orientation courses, in one sense, and just beginning again in another and more real way. A new country with very different culture and traditions and God love them. Oh their own unique way of speaking the language, very fast and only the first part of the word gets pronounced. How's that for walking into a demoralizing situation as soon as you step off the plane! I must be a glutton for punishment.

Maybe I can put down how I feel about this. First of all, the only thing I can really say, in all knowledge, is that I'm expected. That's as much as I've gotten out of my letters from Chile. What the work possibilities are and where have never been mentioned. What the community situation is I can only gather from people who have come through there. Like most everyplace else, it's good and bad, maybe more on the hopeful side. So with all that lack of information, I'm going Wednesday (the 14th) not knowing what I'm getting into, but still it seems right to do it. It's just the next step along the way and it seems as though I should keep going, so I will.

Of course, this is a crazy life. Just when you get somewhat settled and comfortable in a situation — know your way around, make some friends and sort of feel at home — you uproot and start all over again. There are some really fine people here whom I will miss, but I guess you have to keep presuming or hoping there will be others along the way.

So that's the state I'm in right now, mailing books, sorting through things, and, if the sun comes out, washing before packing and girding myself for the *Latin despedidos,* the good-bye parties, which have casts of thousands. But I guess I'll survive them, though I'd rather avoid them. It's really an insult if you try to sneak out quietly.

So, I guess, it all adds up to my being happy and peaceful, as I said on the tape. Not ecstatic, because that's not my style, but as you are when things are in harmony. That's what I hope is going to be happening in you.

All those times we talked about 'learning' to love and what to do. It seems as though it's worked out to be very clear that your energies and intelligence are to go into the situation right now. It takes time and you just have to have patience with yourself. Believe me you're worth it to everyone who loves you. I say that from personal inside information — from me. Let me know what's happening and how you are, because I love you lots.

Ita

36. *March 10, 1973, Cochabamba, Bolivia*

Dear Jean,

Yes, I'm about to move. I'm flying to Santiago on Wednesday the 14th. To what and where I still don't know. I'm presuming that it will all gradually work out. Being in South America, I'm learning to live with a lot of unknown factors.

I hope your father is better by now. You're right. We have to let people make their own decisions, even if the outcome isn't going to be what you'd think smart or whatever. I think I've seen older people taking risks that may seem foolhardy, but I guess in one way, they think the time for being 'careful' is over and with only a certain amount left, they might as well try. They may have something there!

Last weekend I went with a group to Oruro, the center of Bolivia's celebration of carnival, where I saw hundreds of fellows like the one drawn above. Carnival lasts for at least nine days but the first few are marked with day-long parades of groups dancing through the city streets. The most popular seems to be the *diablura* with very elaborate choreography featuring the angel Michael, capital sins, temptations, and about fifty devils. During the course of the dance, Michael gradually subdues everyone. There must have been fifty groups performing this, in addition to others doing regional dances as well as others about historical events and animals. It was quite a show.

One of the things I've been forewarned about is that I probably won't understand anyone when I deplane in Chile. It seems they have their own abbreviated, speed version of Spanish in which it's perfectly acceptable to only pronounce the first part of a word. That could be demoralizing after five and half months, but I guess what I have is a good foundation in the language. I wouldn't say that I speak Spanish. That will just gradually happen.

In one sense, Wednesday's trip is a leap into the unknown. But it's one that I should make now. I don't know what it holds or what it really means, but with all the uncertainty, it still seems to sit right. This life is certainly crazy in some aspects. Just when you begin to feel comfortable, you uproot. I've met some fine people here. So I presume there will be others along the way. Although that doesn't take the edge off saying goodbye. But it certainly is good to know some of the people spread around who are involved in the same effort as yourself, who show some of the hopes. In that way, the transience is worth it.

I hope you are growing in peace and acceptance of yourself. I think we have a strong bond in our common becoming who we were called to be. It's not always easy to know the direction or be able to understand the signs. Maybe, we need more patience with our limitations and, then, go on what we do have. I wish for you Paul's prayer at the end of chapter three of Ephesians, especially the assurance that with the Spirit in us, more than we can hope for or imagine can happen. Take care, Jean.

Love,
Ita

37. 1973, Chile

Dear Jean and John,

In some ways I feel as though I'm on an extended tour, changing locations every few days. Now that I've tested the available beds in Santiago, I'm going south for about five to six weeks.

This is probably the only way to do it, but at times it can get to you. It's great to be back in a big city. Not that there's been much time to absorb it, but it's reassuring to know that when I do get my breath, there will be something to enjoy. My background is showing and I love it!

Jean, tell your mother Santiago is full of Columbans, mostly from Ireland, not by way of Brooklyn. I hope your father is better and that spring has promise for all. Take care.

Love,
Ita

38. To Grace Monahan Niemeyer, April 4, 1973, Chile

Dear Grace,

Your tape caught up with me yesterday before I left Santiago. In digging out the cassette to listen, I found two packs of cigarettes, which is like finding gold. There aren't any to be had here except on certain days of the week when you line up to get one pack. There's about five packs left now before withdrawal sweats!

I'm on something of a merry-go-round now, visiting all the Maryknoll houses in Chile, moving every three or four days. After two weeks in Santiago I arrived last night on the first leg of the southern trip. This should take a month, not only visiting but a few meetings thrown in along the way. Of course, there's the possibility I might just wake up one morning and refuse to pack the suitcase again, but there really is no other way to find out what's going on, what people are doing, and what the possibilities might be for me. Somehow I'm sure that I'll eventually know the situation or place to say "yes" to. If the Lord got me to Chile, I'm sure he'll provide the clues for what's next. So far it's a tease. A few places would definitely be out. One was great, but there's really no room and the plan is to leave in two years. So gradually it will get narrowed down, but no one is pushing me to jump into anything right away.

I hope spring sets all sorts of new life and hope growing in you. Trust in the love you have, peace and confidence. I'm still hanging in with you because I love you very much.

Take care,
Ita

39. May 23, 1973, Chile

Dear Jean,

I am just back in Santiago after roaming around the central position of the country for seven weeks during which I was supposedly getting some brief idea of what is going on and how Maryknoll is relating to it. I think what happened was that I just got very confused and tired.

What happens next is still somewhat up in the air but by the beginning of next week, it should be worked out. I'm going to do a little Chilean language study while living with a family or someone who doesn't change language every ten minutes. Right now I'm a little hesitant about taking advantage of a family's hospitality because of the great inconvenience in getting food. Another possibility that has just come up might be to spend a month living with a Chilean sister who does pastoral work in one of the areas with two Irish Columbans whom I've met.

During that time I'm to be thinking where I go next for a period of in-service training. You could begin to get the idea that I'm never going to put in roots, and that has had some effects but even if things seem to be short-term in the beginning, I hope to be getting something out of it and, maybe in a more general way, getting rooted in the country with the people.

Some people say I couldn't have come at a more exciting time, while others say this is a terrible introduction. I guess that's indicative of what's going on. Yesterday there started a strike for an indefinite period of all privately owned locomotion, most of the buses in the country. And there's talk of a repeat of last October's general strike that paralyzed the country. If it happens it will be a very difficult time because there already are great shortages of food and, if the trucks don't run to bring in what is available, its going to be a mess. Yet in spite of all this, I can't really say people are gloomy. There's an incredible adaptability to the circumstances and a great sense of humor. I must say I'm learning all kinds of lessons on where you put priorities — and just what are some of the basic pleasures of life.

How is your father doing? I hope he's continuing to improve.

Also please thank your Mom for her Easter Greetings. Since I've been moving around so much mail is catching up with me from all points, though I think I finally have gotten all the birthday cards that are going to get through. There's somewhat of a problem along those lines, but I think I get most of what's sent, considering I haven't been much of a correspondent. Maybe I'll improve if I do get to stay more than a week in any one spot.

Have you had any luck in your search for like thinkers or opportunities in which to insert yourself? I know you said you stopped going to the doctor, but then I can't remember if you said you started up again. Those two sentences don't connect logically, but a few things were going through my mind at the same time. I care for you a lot and really hope for you to experience peace and happiness, not just eternally, but also now. I hope you don't give up on you.

Love,

Ita

40. To Kathy Monahan Gregg and her husband Mike, June 9, 1973, Chile

Dear Kathy and Mike,

Greetings from *poblacion* Manuel Rodriquez. This month I'm living in one of Santiago's innumerable *poblaciones* that, I guess, could be described as resettlement areas — or areas that just become inhabited by people squatting on unused property. From beginning in tents or a one-room wooden affair, there gradually is construction of small individual homes. I would guess there are about five thousand families here and maybe a third have their permanent home, usually wood or brick sometimes, four rooms, small, considering the size of families, but a source of pride.

My temporary residence is with a Chilean Sister who's been living here these years. The main reason for my coming was for immersion in the language. I was switching every ten minutes before and so it was slow going. Also this gives me some time to get some idea of *poblacion* work, of which there is much now, since the movement is away from institutions and toward living with the people in their reality, working toward forming community among small local groups.

It's a far cry from Sheridan Square but comfortable enough, now that I'm getting the knack, knowing just how many layers of clothes I need to keep warm.

Where I'll be in July or so I still don't know. I'm drawn to Santiago as a place probably because my blood is urban but I might have more chances of experimenting with different type of work in the south. Wherever it is, I hope to unpack for a while even though it won't be a permanent situation. There are times when the image of pilgrim church gets to be a little too real!

How was the trip and the search for a new nest? I certainly hope you're doing better than I, though I don't have to take impending childbirth into consideration. How's the mother feel? I hope this is a time of shared joy and expectancy for you both and that all is going well. Take care.

Love to both

Ita

41. June 25, 1973, Chile

Dear Jean,

I called Brooklyn on Saturday and my mother told me that your father had died. After I hung up I had many remembrances starting with the warmth behind each "Howdy Pal." I guess what began with all the chauffeuring back and forth grew into the conversations on 79 St. and Scarsdale and a deep affection on my part for him.

I remembered, too, your observation just recently about how close the relationship seemed between your parents. It struck me how fortunate not only they, but you too were to have that time of sharing. Then, I found myself congratulating your father on his arrival to full life and also asking him to now do his part for your mother, yourself, the family and his friends so that you experience consolation, comfort, and strength in the void of his going.

I know this is a very difficult time for you, Jean, because you and your father had your own unique relationship. Having my own with my father, I feel very much with you. (In fact that was why I called. On Friday I received a letter that my father was in an intensive care unit. The heat and humidity were just too much of strain, but he seems to be doing better now.)

Words seem very inept at this time and the distance seems greater, yet you and your mother are very much in my thoughts. I find myself hoping that what your father is now living and experiencing will flow over for you.

Would you please tell your mother that I am remembering her now. Take care, dear friend.

Love,
Ita

42. *August 12, 1973, Chile*

Dear Jean

It's almost three weeks since I moved into a more or less permanent situation. (It's hard to be too definite about anything in Chile today). I am living in one of the many settlement areas that ring Santiago (and every other large South American city) with three other sisters like myself. Two others are recent arrivals, so it's somewhat like a new beginning.

Home is a small wooden house with three bedrooms and a living-dining-kitchen. Also indoor plumbing. It's comfortable and simple. The house is in *poblacion* La Bandera, approximately seventy to eighty thousand inhabitants who have been here about three years. At this point, lots have been assigned and construction of homes is proceeding at a very leisurely pace. In the interim the people live in long-range temporary housing.

What we hope to be doing here is building community among ourselves and establishing relationships with some of the people. Just what form that will take for me I still don't know . . . Because of the history and tradition of the people, there is not much of an emphasis on 'sacramentalism' or other institutional works. Rather it is the hope of the bishop of the area that through developing relations with the people there will slowly evolve a small base Christian community that reflects and prays together. Worship comes later. So we'll see what happens.

How are you? You sounded tired in your letter. I hope you've gotten some rest and some energy. I'm still hoping that you will find something to challenge you, something in which you can share and receive and from which you derive satisfaction. Are you still searching? Take care.

Love to John and yourself,

Ita

43. *August 12, 1973, Chile*

Dear Kathy and Mike,

I was just reliving part of your trip as the card from the British Museum arrived yesterday. I really can imagine how much you must have enjoyed London.

Well the bird has been in her nest for about three weeks now, and it still is somewhat of a novelty. The nest is a small wooden house with three bedrooms and a one room living-dining-kitchen — also indoor plumbing! Which is somewhat to scale, for there is a tub that is only large enough to stand in, but it has a 'seat,' about a six inch wide level. I've never seen anything quite like it . . .

There are four of us in the house, two beside myself being recent arrivals, so in many ways its similar to a beginning. What we hope to be doing is building community among ourselves and developing relationships with the neighbors. Exactly what form that will take for me is still not too clear. There are many neighborhood organizations and clubs as a start for contacts, or all the hours waiting on lines waiting for essentials or bread or kerosene. That is an experience, and unfortunately, almost a way of life. With the truckers' strike it really has been difficult for the people. There was another change of the cabinet on Friday, with all the military chiefs back in, and an ultimatum has been issued: back to work or face the military. So we'll have to see who backs down in this confrontation. It is leading to a situation where everyone's nerves are shot.

About the weather, yes, it is winter, but Santiago is having a very mild one. Winter here means rain and raw weather. There hasn't been much of either. Why it seems worse than it really is is the lack of heating in most buildings, so you never get warm. We have a kerosene heater which does a great job on one room and that's it. So you just wear a lot of layers. In fact, your ski underwear gets constant use as pajamas or [for wearing under outer clothes for] warmth outside, especially if you have to go to a meeting of any kind. Yet on a sunny day, it's very spring-like . . .

I see the Watergate hearings are still trying to unravel the truth. It's difficult to get too involved in it from a distance, but it just seems to be a reflection of the arrogance that has been shown to many of the countries in this area over a long period of time.

How's the mother-to-be, still doing well? You must be near retirement now. That must be a happy state. I'm sorry that I'm missing your pregnancy and the approaching birth, but I do share your joy and expectation, and delight in the happiness and peace that surround it. I hope all continues to go well. Take care.

Love,
Ita

44. To Grace Monahan Niemeyer, August 30, 1973

Dear Grace,

There were three letters from you in one week, one written to Cochabamba in February that just made it down!

. . . What am I doing? I amble around the *poblacion* at a very leisurely rate, and if someone looks receptive, I say hello, and try some conversation. I also go home visiting for a clinic nearby to check up on the babies who haven't been brought for the monthly control. Or I go to meetings or sit in on some adult education classes. Women, who never finished eight years of schooling, are now in a government program to get finished. I also wait on lines to get food, kerosene or whatever. It's altogether a very fluid situation. You can't exactly say what I'm doing, but the days go by. I guess, you might describe it as making myself visible and also trying to get to know some people. It's a very slow process when you have no specific 'reason' to contact people. It's more an idea of a being a neighbor.

Did I tell you where I live? In a new housing development that was formerly a large farm that is now home to about 80,000 people. We are in a wooden house with a yard that is now promising samples of lettuce, onions, beets, carrots, squash, cucumbers, and flowers. Not a lot of each but something if they come up. Most of the neighbors do the same all around their 'property' which is approximately 60'x 30' that includes the house, but it is enough to give a feeling of having something very tangible for themselves and their family, especially when the houses are constructed, but that's another slow process. So that's where I am and what I'm up to. Take care baby.

Much love,

Ita

45. *To the Ford family at the time of her father's death, September 10, 1973*

Reflection inspired by Leonardo Boff, The Sacraments of Life and the Life of the Sacraments

This letter brings you a beautiful message, news that when seen from the point of view of faith is truly marvelous. In these days God has asked of us a tribute of love, faith and deep thanksgiving. He came to our family, looked at us one by one, and chose for himself the most perfect, the most holy, the most mature, the best of all, the one closest to him, our beloved father.

> *Dear one, God didn't take him from us: he left him even more truly among us. God didn't take [Daddy], for himself, rather he gave him to us even more. He hasn't uprooted him from the happiness of our celebrations, rather he has planted him deeply in*

*the memory of all of us. God hasn't snatched [Daddy] from our
presence, rather he has made him more present. [Daddy] hasn't
left, he has arrived . . . he hasn't gone, rather he has come to be,
if possible, even more [Daddy], now to be present with us always
— here with us and there with you — (wherever anyone of the
family is).*

46. To Senator Edward Kennedy, November 25, 1973

Dear Senator Kennedy:

As North Americans doing volunteer service in one of the
refugee centers in Santiago, we would like to bring to your attention,
as well as to that of the Senate Committee on Refugees, the counter-
indication of our nation's offer of hospitality and refuge which is
effected by Form FD-510, the petition for an immigration visa.

This form, offered by members of the American Consulate,
solicits detailed personal information that for many of the refugees
is not only compromising, but also possibly dangerous. At stake is
not only their personal security, but also that of parents, family and
relatives in their country of origin.

After examining the form, several refugees explained their fear of
completing it. Their experiences have led them to doubt the confi-
dential treatment assumed for such documents. To list their activities
and associations on the same form with their relatives' addresses is,
for them, to ask for reprisals and retaliation against their loved ones.
In conscience they cannot consent to this information being stored or
available in 'data banks.' For them, this is a much more serious matter than the United States citizens' complaints of invasion of privacy.

In addition to the above, there is another strong reason for not
using Form FS-510 in our offer of refuge. Given the present set of
circumstances that have forced many foreigners in Chile to seek
refuge under the aegis of the United Nations High Commission for
Refugees, it would seem that the normal criteria for immigration
would not be applicable. In fact, many of the refugees would be
automatically ineligible according to the criteria set forth on Page 3,

section c. Depending on the interpretation of their past commitments to the rights, dignity and development of their fellow-countrymen, which in Latin America is often enfleshed in political activity of the left, they see themselves as being considered 'subversive' or 'agitators' who seek to undermine the United States government. What the refugees are really appealing for is a chance to reside in a country with a stable government, to be able to continue their lives free from fear and harassment, to be accepted for who they are and for what they can contribute to any society, their humanity, experiences, commitments and concern for their fellow men.

The question seems to be: does the United States consider the plight of the refugees serious enough to make the humane offer of refuge? If so, the offer should be made in such a way that it is understood. We fear with the refinement of the selection process, as it now stands, those in less serious circumstances, and with the possibility of several options, will be the only ones eligible for our hospitality.

Is that what we really want to convey to the people of Latin America?

Respectfully,
Ita Ford, MM,
Mary Tracy, MM

47. January 27, 1974

Dear Jean and John,

I don't know if you've gotten the rundown from mother yet, but I think she had a very good time, and certainly, we did. (Maybe you'd like to consider it for the next vacation . . .)

The report, on the other side, is my reaction to one of the searches here in the *poblacion*. It's quite an experience to go through. Last weekend arms were planted in a tabernacle in a small chapel in the same section of Santiago as we are. The priest was taken on charges of aiding the extremists. So it continues, but the church is taking a stand. Within a day and a half, a pastoral letter was out, denouncing the whole incident as a put-up.

The tension between the church and state helps keep us all honest. You have to make decisions, even though they won't be popular and can easily be twisted. So we muddle along . . .

Thanks for the reminder from Florence and your generosity during the year. May the promise of life in its fullness come to be realized in you both. Warmest wishes for the Lord's joy in the year to come.

Much love,
Ita

48. "Try to Imagine," La Bandera, Chile. An excerpt from a letter sent to several people.

Try to imagine a company of approximately one hundred soldiers and about two dozen FBI agents surrounding a working-class neighborhood of two thousand families at dawn. No one may enter or leave. All men and boys over fourteen years are summoned to a nearby football field, lined up according to alphabetical order to discover who might have a police record. Any man who has something recorded against him in the last ten years is taken. (Such notations include traffic accidents and not paying fines up to serious crimes.) Also taken are some with names similar to those with records, as are others for being 'suspicious.' All fall into a general category of 'delinquents.'

It is Friday morning, payday. Most of these men lose the week's pay if they miss a day of work. Yet they can't notify their employers. There's no telephone in the neighborhood, and no one is allowed to leave.

Try to imagine the wives and mothers milling around the edge of the field from eight in the morning until one in the afternoon (it takes time to question all those men), and being told from time to time to return to their homes. Will their husband look suspicious — unshaved, not fully dressed, maybe with only an hour's sleep after working a night shift? Is he thirsty in the sun, hungry from not eating breakfast? (There is no bread this morning. Deliveries were not allowed into the neighborhood.) As their husbands and sons enter buses to be taken to the city jail, put yourself in the women's place, asking the soldiers to allow them to send along something to eat or at least carfare to return. The soldiers refuse them because all the men are delinquents. "He's not a delinquent," one mother answers, "he's my son."

Try to imagine the children frightened by the soldiers with machine guns standing at the corners and accompanying the FBI men to each house. Some begin to cry, "Daddy, don't let the soldiers take you away."

Try to imagine FBI agents entering your home to do a thorough search without any reason given. One has an iron pipe in his hand. Imagine having the contents of your bookshelves evaluated, book by book, for their approval. Why do you have books by this publisher? Imagine the tension mounting as you talk to yourself, "I have a right to be informed, to read what I like, to read up on several sides of any issue so as to form an opinion. These men are making me feel guilty without any basis." Their attitude, however, conveys the idea that they intend to find something they don't like. And of course they do.

Put yourself in your own living-room with five FBI agents and a soldier at the door with a machine gun. Now explain who you are, why you live where you live, what you do. Make sure you produce the necessary documents to back you up.

Are you nervous? Why? You haven't done anything wrong. Everything is in order except the order of a society that takes this type of early morning visit in stride. Of course you won't object if some samples of your reading matter are taken along. Now what is your address, so it can be noted inside.

Try to imagine each of these things and make it as personal as possible because it is real. It has happened to us. What would you do? How would you react? From whom would you get the strength to face up to this evil, this terror? This is the third time that the soldiers have come.

Would there be camaraderie among the men in your neighborhood as they walked together to the field, sharing cigarettes and joking words to keep up each other's spirits? Would they be very aware of what was happening to the men down the street or around the corner? Would they fume in solitary rage or try to create an atmosphere of support, especially for those who possibly might have problems?

Would the women be equally, if not more, solicitous of each other? Would they be so outgoing in their fear as to say, "I'm not worried about my own family, but the neighbor's?" Would they encourage the more nervous to keep busy and distract themselves? Would their faith be the faith of the poor and oppressed who have no 'connections,' no 'pull,' but who must rely solely on the mercy and love of God? If you saw your husband taken away, could you say with complete confidence, "I have faith that God will bring him home?" Would your neighbors come to 'accompany you' as you waited to learn just what might be the charge against your husband? Would small groups meet a few days later to share how they felt, and then thank God for all those who had returned home and ask for his comfort and support for those still detained and for their families?

We hope so. The only way you and your neighbors could face up to and overcome arbitrary 'fishing expeditions' and organized terror is by being very concerned for each other and by having a deep faith, not in the judicial process or man's justice, but in a God who cares for his people. Of course, experiences like this among the poor and powerless run through the Old Testament up to today's headlines. Yet until you experience it, or somehow make someone else's experience your own, it never is truly real. We are privileged to have shared this, to know and feel a little of the suffering of the powerless, of those without voice. And we want to share it with you because our neighbors are your neighbors (Luke 10:29-37).

49. A talk given at a Maryknoll Assembly at Talca, Chile, January 1974

Thinking about Our Common Call

Five months ago when we started the discernment workshops, we talked about the ambiguity of the human and, therefore, the Chilean situation. One question posed was how do we interpret the signs of the times? Or how do we sensitize ourselves to the Spirit to be able to recognize the Lord's acting in events and in our own lives? Since then we have lived through and reacted to a condensed period of Chilean history. But possibly we haven't had time to reflect on the meaning of September 11* nor on many other things for that matter. Maybe now, with a little time and distance behind us, we can do that together. These four days are to share our experiences and to reflect together about who we are as a group, what are we doing, and where are we going.

Now even though it seems to me that we've done this before, I realize that what was covered in the workshops has not been the most present thing in your minds in the last few months. So I'll briefly review the main points that we touched and then hopefully clarify a little more the aspect of common call.

The talk on faith was directed to elicit our personal experience of Christ. We prayed about the question: "Who do you say I am?" And our answers varied. Some that I recall were: Christ was the challenger, the faithful one, the savior or liberator, the caller to relationship, brother, etc. Following this was the reflection on limitation and sinfulness. What happens when you stand before Christ, the same Lord whom you have named before? Our reactions were an awareness of forgiveness, of loving mercy, of being accepted as we are, knowing that we are loved, not on merit or what we do, but because of the Lord's love and goodness. Then we tried to surface and clarify our own personal history. How has the Lord acted and how is he acting in my life? What does this mean? (Israel was often reminded of her past for its meaning for the people at a later date.) Although we can look back on certain highlights, do we think of our basic faith

---

* September 11, 1973, the date of the military coup in Chile.

experience as continuing or moving ahead? Maybe a question that should have been included would be: How am I with the Lord *right now?* or what is he saying to me now?

Finally we looked at the communal faith experience or the inter-relationship between the personal or individual sense of identity in Christ and the community's on-going experience of God as well as its experience of union or the reasons for our continuing to remain together. We asked what is our communion, our common call? Each area drew up a statement, although this was done against the pressure of time in Talca and Santiago. Now because of the elapsed time and the intertwining of events, we have been asked to go into this again because of its meaning for what we will be doing these four days as well as its application for the future.

When we talked about common call before, the emphasis was on the fact that it was the underlying principle or the basic reference point used by a community when it was discerning how to respond to God's word to it in a particular situation. Maybe today we can look at it in a more general way.

To ask what is our common call is also to ask who are we? What is our common shared vision? Why have we come together, or maybe more importantly, why do we stay together as a group? What is it we strive to be faithful to? What is the overriding principle or philosophy of our lives? The question of common call is a question of identity and unity. And since there is no abstract thing called the Maryknoll community, but only a group made up of individuals, it seems that we have to look at the inter-relationship between the personal identity in Christ and the group's identity and its communion.

In responding to the Lord's call, each of us was led to the specific choice of becoming part of the Maryknoll community. This choice has shaped our lives ever since. To discover God's call and to respond to it is, on the psychological level, the discovery of personal identity — in the sense that we have made a life-commitment that gives meaning to our existence. In faith terms, this is a response to the Spirit within us, calling us to a specific life-expression or commitment in love of Jesus and his people. So in a very real way, our personal identity is discovered within the larger scope of community.

And how does the community understand its identity? I think this is realized through the personal commitment and fidelity of each member to her own call as well as through an awareness or, better yet, a deep consciousness that there is a commonality in our personal calls. We say we are not a group that has come together around the focus of work or issues; rather our orientation is based on Christ and the support of one another in faith. There is a paragraph in *Searching and Sharing* that expresses this very clearly: Each of us has been drawn to a life that is a process of realizing our relationship between God and ourselves. This experience impels us to take a stance by living a radical evangelical life with others who share this same vision. This vision, partial as it is, calls for expression in mission through the mystery of creation that is a life-long search, in and with the other, to discover Christ and the meaning of the gospel.

Historically the overall purpose of the Christian community as a whole has been . . . and is the establishment of the kingdom of God. And any means for doing this must be in accord with Christ's teachings. However, particular communities within the larger body have different calls to express and promote the kingdom, each community its own nature and purpose. How any community promotes the establishment of the Kingdom is in someway directly related to the charism of the founder, which is also shared by the members. Certainly part of our common call as Maryknollers is sharing in the Church's mission to all peoples, or as *Searching and Sharing* defines it: "participating in the outward thrust of the Spirit in the Church, sent to reverse the role of division in the world."

As we are very well aware, there are many different life-expressions of that statement which at times cause tensions, disagreements and real conflicts. Our differences in life-styles and expression possibly stem less from a 'generation gap' than from the radical cultural changes that man as a whole is experiencing. Also in thinking about it some more, I think this variety may not only be a good healthy sign but also the work of the Spirit. In chapter 12 of I Corinthians, Paul makes a strong case against homogenization. There is a variety of gifts but always the same Spirit; there are all sorts of services to be done but always to the same Lord; working in all sorts of different ways in different people . . . All these [gifts] are the work of one and the same Spirit who distributes different gifts to different people as he chooses. Following from this, we can say that our unity is not realized by reducing each of us to carbon copies of some idealized model nor by putting our distinctive gifts in opposition; rather it is celebrated through our variety and uniqueness. We can also say that we know the Spirit is with us when there is respect for the distinctiveness of his gifts and their complementarity.

We are a people who not only live in time but in an age of accelerated change, and we must always be aware of the pitfalls or temptation to fix ourselves in one historically or culturally conditioned expression of our common call. Those are all relative and subject to change. Understanding the true meaning of our call and reading the signs of the times will enable us to adapt to the word of God in a new and changing age, and to do so in peace and in union with each other.

However, looking at ourselves realistically, we are a group that has yet to arrive, and are still in process, carrying along with us our weaknesses and limitations, and now without the support of many externals that formerly helped form in us a sense of identity. As the habit, customs and fixed life-style were signs of our communion before, now we must look for other ways to achieve this mutual awareness. And I think we have them readily accessible. Two that strike me immediately are opportunities like this to share what Shirley called in one letter 'the meat of our lives' and also those times that we pray together.

When I was thinking about our sharing not only what we do, but how we have been affected by events and how we feel, it seems as though we move out of the realm of annual reports and into the area of making real our variety and uniqueness. Reflecting together on this level, in a very real way opening up and revealing ourselves to each other, would be impossible without an already existing bond of unity. Yet this sharing reestablishes and deepens the trust among us. It is also an expression of fellowship, one of the goals set for this past year.

This fellowship in love and trust is an important basis for our dialoging with each other about the events of the past year and how it is that we have been affected. Communion requires communication and a climate where each one feels accepted. One of our basic assumptions should be that each person here is trying to understand and respond to what the Lord is saying in her own experiences and in the events of our times. Can we say to one another: "I trust you. I believe in your good intentions. I know the Spirit works in you as he does in me?"

We talk about the Chilean reality, but not one of us here can say that she lives in the Chilean reality. We each live in a very small aspect of it. But because we live in different aspects, we have the opportunity to share what we've experienced and therefore to broaden each other's vision and understanding. This is another side of fellowship.

The other sign and strengthener of our communion is prayer. Listening to another pray, even though she uses words or phrases that I might not use myself, is a most effective way to come to recognize that she shares the same basic faith experience of being called by the Lord, a similar personal identity in Christ, and the same response of life-commitment as I do.

Clarifying our common call, then, just might be re-clarifying our own individual faith experience of Christ and our own response to the Spirit's call within us. The mutual sharing of this as well as the recognition that we do have a common vision is our communion.

50. *January 27, 1974*

Dear Jean,

The time seems to have flown since I've returned. Within a week I was working at one of the refugee centers in Santiago which at that time were all bursting at the seams. It's been a long, tedious and frustrating process for the refugees as well as for anyone involved. In one sense you could say it was a crash course in international and Chilean red tape. Now things seem to be going better, as most people do have a notion of destination, and it will be only a week or two longer. However, another group is entering: these are the people who were trying to seek refuge before but there was no room for them.

For the past three weeks I was taking a course in the mornings on the formation of small Christian communities. This is a big interest of the bishops throughout Latin America and is very suited to an area like ours where there is no institutional Church presence. How we might get going remains to be seen. But a few people have talked to us about having something. It's both a good and bad time for it. Some people are looking for something to fill the void that's left now that their commitments have no channel for expression. Yet many others in our area are really ground down just trying to get enough to eat for their families. They've been hit very hard by unemployment and the incredible rise in prices.

Two weeks ago we had a four-day meeting of the community in Chile and it was very revealing. We could arrive at no common outlook on the events preceding and following September 11th. What it showed is how we come to identify with the people with whom we live and work, and since we are in several different situations, we take on the colorings, even without realizing it. Maybe we are not as divided as a group of Chileans might be, but we reflect it to a certain point. One of the observers told us that we are in somewhat the same situation as the sisters in the Philippines regarding martial law.

When I was leaving you were about to start working. How has it turned out? I hope you've gotten some challenge and satisfaction from it. Why don't you take up a pen and tell me about it and other thoughts too.

In the meantime, I celebrate with you your gift of life and the continued promise and challenge of what is still to come. May there also be someone dear and loved to share that with you. Happy birthday, Jean.

Love to you and John,

Ita

51. *January 27, 1976*

Dear Jean,

Several times I have left Santiago with a stack of letters to answer and each time I return with the same unanswered pile. A few times I was just being optimistic, because life has been neither dull nor leisurely the last six months.

The news was getting so interesting that Bill and Mary Anne came down for a week's visit. They left this past Saturday much more at ease, now able to situate me in my habitat and the various mental-health refuges.

It was delightful having them here, and we milked every hour discussing what they saw until 3:00 a.m. By the end of the week, we were exhausted but very full from the sharing.

They left very impressed with the Chilean church's direction, which they said was light years ahead of the States. Probably there's nothing like very real urgent problems to get you down to basic issues.

The next time round they'd like to bring some of the children, but I'm sure I'll be back and forth before that happens. I'm scheduled for a year's study in '77 beginning in September.

Well, how's the adjustment to Paris? After all these years of being a possibility, how does it feel to be there? By now, your fluency in the language should be back, which is a big hurdle jumped. The first few months in Chile I had to keep reminding myself that I had studied five months in Bolivia and that the Chileans were speaking the same language. But gradually it came through.

How does John like the change? Is this just one three-year tour or can it be renewed? (How many times have you answered these questions?) Have you been able to do traveling?

Well, when you write, you can start anywhere because I know none of it. May there be much happiness for you and John during this time, and may the experience be a rich and full one. Warmest wishes, too, for a very, happy birthday.

Much love to you both,
Ita

52. *To Connie Pospisil, MM, November 1976*

Dear Connie,

It's the 'nutsy' whirlwind of the end of the year, we'll make it as usual, but pooped. This year we thought we'd be so clever and stagger things through November and December, but somehow you can't get ahead because something else always comes up.

I'm glad to hear that this year is a little bit lighter for you, and 'gladder' at the implied things that are going on within yourself. I ask with you that it keep continuing. That growing, accepting, and loving oneself is for me, a great gift of the Lord's liberation.

We were at El Quisco for a few days and I tried to reflect with you. I can't say, Connie, anything very original came out. But maybe it will reinforce some of your own musings on the subject, since you phrased it as "accepting a general assignment." It left it so open that it is hard to make comparison or be specific. What came out as 'cons' against a general assignment or in favor of returning to Chile were:

• The region needs the 'moral assurance' of a sister returning after being in the States.

• Although the Chilean Church leadership is strong, there's still a lot of work to be done on the base levels.

• It's a very important Christian testimony to be with and sharing life with the people during a difficult time.

• There are new work opportunities in Chile but we're short of personnel to respond.

•The curtailment of medical services and personnel leave a lot of people without proper health care, and especially health education/prevention.

For you, Chile and the Sisters here are known. Returning refreshed and with new *animo* [energy], you can get going much faster than in adjusting to a new region, country, etc. Then, there are all the personal reasons — ties with people, friendship, community, etc.

The pros of a new assignment were:

• Being sent where the congregation thinks the need is greatest: the disposition of openness to new experience, service.

• Sharing with others what was received in Chile.

• Trust in the Father and His leading you in the unknown.
Question: Have the year and a half in the States prepared you for
something else, changed your perspective? You and your
talents/services might be lacking in another region. As I said, these
aren't original, but what came to me. The new assignment seems
more of a call of faith and trust; the return to Chile, to service (and
given the situation, faith and trust, too.)

Carla is running out the door to the P.O. So I'll end here. Take
care, Connie.

Much love,
Ita

53. *An article in* Orientation, *Maryknoll Sisters, vol. 3, May 1977*

Recently I received a letter that contained one of those flowery
exaggerations that people who romanticize our lives and work tend
to write — "you who live daily on the front line of the Christian life."
I glanced out the window at the front line — dusty after six months
of no rain, rocky, a drunk righting himself on the fence that joins the
cantina next door, children running with the bread bag to buy the
Chilean staple, others coming home from school, one woman hanging up the wash, two neighbors talking over a fence. At a quick
glance the front line looked very peaceful.

Yet that mixed-up image does say something because in many
ways Chile is a front line that is a constant challenge to a Christian.
At least I find that has been my experience.

There's no need to repeat the long list of news items, outrages,
horrors, reprisals, etc., that you read in newspapers that say more of
our national news than do the ones printed here. But the ramifica-
tions of the headlines get lived out in the hidden daily drama of the
poor — the poor to whom I have been sent to bring the Good News;
the poor to whom Jesus said — I have come that you may have life
in its fullness. And there's the challenge!

For three years we've watched a situation go from bad to worse
and we've tried to respond. In collaboration with the hierarchy and

with outside financial support, various types of programs have been created to meet needs — children's dining rooms, health programs, cooperatives, cottage industries, legal help, programs for the families of political and disappeared prisoners. Yet in analyzing these programs, it is always admitted that they are temporary measures that don't touch the source of the problem. At best, they serve as a means of denouncing a situation of sin and injustice as well as having the people affected group together in solidarity and to be more aware of the situation. The Church cannot, should not, take on responsibilities that belong to organized government.

And where is the Good News in all of this? In reflecting about it alone and with others, I see Chile deeply experiencing the paschal mystery, with the light of Easter still to come. We can't wish away the suffering. Like Christ, how many times have we asked with the people, "Father, if it's possible, let this pass." Yet it seems that the cup cannot pass without our drinking it.

The challenge that we live daily is to enter into this mystery with faith. Am I willing to suffer with the people here, the suffering of the powerless, the feeling impotent? Can I say to my neighbors — I have no solutions to this situation; I don't know the answers, but I will walk with you, search with you, be with you. Can I let myself be evangelized by this opportunity? Can I look at and accept my own poorness as I learn it from the poor ones?

The front line is real and hard, though at times it has a peaceful face. Yet I see it as an opportunity to become more human, more Christian, more dependent on the Lord, my community and the people placed in my life right now.

54. To Maryknoll Sister Janice McLaughlin, October 6, 1977

Dear Jan,

It's probably all been said a thousand times, but I add my voice. Thanks for being with the little people. Thanks for hanging in. With so many others, I give thanks that the Lord spared you to keep working for and with those struggling for justice and brotherhood.

These days Carolyn and I are in a course, which, among other things, is looking at the 'national security' state and the collision course the Church is on with it, once it steps out of the sacristy. Reality backs up the analysis as we have several *expelles** with us. I was thinking of you. The reference is different yet the experience is similar. Another common denominator is the Third World!

Pray for those who care enough to trust in the Lord and live the risk. Let's keep going ahead, supporting each other's efforts and deepening commitment.

Much love,
Ita

55. *November 28, 1977*

Dear Jean,

Your files might be in disorder but, at least, they tell me you wrote a letter that never arrived. March-April were months of little or no personal mail. My mother later wrote a summary of five letters that never reached me, so much for the inviolability of the mail.

It sounds as though you have your own *pensíon* going, with all the relatives and friends coming to visit. In all your escorting are you finding favorite places or things that are meaningful to you? Have you and John had time to make nearby trips? How are you, Jean? What has the move to Paris meant for you? That interests me.

This has been a full year here. For four months we were just two, and the other sister had just arrived to live with us, when one went on her home vacation. Besides the work, which will never be accomplished, but it is a reality we have to live with in forming a new community, I got involved in a group therapy to work on some of my quirks. It was very helpful, even though I can't say I readily volunteered for my times in the frying pan.

---

* *Expelles*—ejected ones. Sister Janice McLaughlin was arrested and expelled from Rhodesia (now Zimbabwe) by the white government because of her work with the church in support of black majority rule.

You asked about my dates for next year. They still are not firmed up. I'm waiting for the community vice-president to visit next month. I'd like to discuss with her the possibility of alternatives in next year's program. A year seems a very long time to reflect about something I'm already convinced of. However, if my stay is four months or a year, I should be arriving sometime in June or July. I hope from here to make stops in Peru, Nicaragua, Guatemala and Mexico to get a glimpse of what the Sisters are doing in different areas. When I have it worked out after the New Year, I'll give you surer dates.

You mentioned that your mother has angina. Mom's been living with it for twenty-two years. To a certain degree it can be treated medically and then, paying attention to the doctor, of course, age makes a difference, but both our mothers will probably live very full lives until the Lord calls them.

I'm glad to hear Jim is doing well. From all my mother's reports, Rene and Bill's families are thriving. I feel I'm going to have to be reacquainted with most of the children. For the youngest I only exist in pictures and for some of the others, five years is a long time to keep up memories. That's also true of other acquaintances. Many lives have had radical changes, perspectives have altered, etc. I know I certainly have been affected in many ways by my living here among the very poor. For some people I'll probably be a mad radical, but experiences alter outlooks. It should be interesting.

It's doubtful that I'll be writing in the next few weeks so I wish you and John a very joyful Christmas (and also a good trip). May the Lord of peace and justice fill you both with his love and his fullness of life.

Much love,
Ita

56. March 3, 1978

The major portion of this personal letter to Jane Buellesbach was dupli-
cated by Ita and sent to a number of others. The duplicated portion
excluded only the first four and last three paragraphs of the letter as it
appears below.

Dear Jane,

Greetings from hot, dry Chile. Though you've probably had enough of the white stuff, I'm looking forward to the first snow next year; I think I still prefer it to the rain and mud.

Sorry this letter is arriving at the last minute, but after the assembly I went south and only got back the first. Yesterday Carla, Connie, Gerry, Helen, Mini and I batted around your question, but we wound up talking more about the poor than what it means for us to be with and work with them. Carla has written up that aspect and I, without much time taken for deeper thought, will try the other. Where to start?

On the intimate and personal level, for me, it has meant being evangelized. Living with the poor has made me face up to my creatureliness, my impotence in many situations, my own poorness and limitedness and, therefore, having to face (and trying to develop more) the real dependence on the Lord, community and others in my life. Maybe it's been a personal luxury to have come to know and accept myself more among the poor where life is more real and where, possibly, there is less pretense of being other than who one is.

You mentioned our evolving understanding of mission. Though intellectually we understand the necessity of changing from 'doing for' to 'working with,' in practice it's often frustrating. What frustrates is not the principle but the challenge to our own learned cultural values, interpretation of reality, and ways of getting things accomplished. Our concepts of time, efficiency, providing for the morrow, a certain 'calculating' side of us doesn't jibe with the culture of the poor. When we 'work with,' we constantly have to be open to the others' possibilities and adjust our own expectations.

Working with the poor calls for a great restraint and modesty on all levels so as not to overpower, overcome, or take over the situation. It certainly has been a great advantage working in La Bandera which from its beginning (which predates my arrival) has been a modest presence. There's no church 'plant,' there's no 'power structure.' There's nothing to protect or defend. Money coming for projects such as the dining rooms, is channeled through the deanery or zone to be pooled among the other *poblaciones* of the area. The modest scale is important, I think, for several reasons.

• It makes a statement about the Church. The Church of the poor is economically poor. If we set up something else, it's not their Church.

• It's situating ourselves at the level where the people feel comfortable and able to approach.

• It lends credibility to promoting solidarity.

Working with the poor means promoting and then allowing the person to be subject of his own destiny, instead of forming him in our own image and likeness. It calls for a deep understanding of another class or state of society — worker, *campesino* — as well as understanding that being a member of a class is part of a man's identity. (I never had a class consciousness, but I've come to see how strong it is among the exploited workers.)

Being with the poor means overcoming our distaste of getting dirty literally and metaphorically: the literal dirt, mud, excrement; caring for and supporting the sinner, the underdog, and unpopular causes; entering into messed-up lives; running the risk of being misunderstood, misinterpreted, of being accused as subversives, etc.

Though we'll always be somewhat different, somewhat 'other,' our experience of trying to live simply, 'unclutteredly,' available to whomever, has allowed the possibility of being 'just a neighbor' with whom one exchanges recipes, cuttings of plants, [from whom one] borrows extra dishes or chairs when visitors arrive, invites to family events. The 'being with' on this level, the most human and warmest, crowns the privilege of being and working with those who because of their values and solidarity will eventually evangelize the rest of the world.

These are very scattered thoughts, but I hope they'll be of some help. Possibly, too, *Enfoques Chilenos* of last June, which has an article by Segundo Galilea, "How the poor evangelize us."

As I'm typing I realize there's so many areas I haven't touched — the political situation, the people's aspirations, the whole aspect of injustice in the economic order, etc. Hopefully, Carolyn and others will go down different paths. When you're trying to beat the clock, it doesn't turn out as one would like. Sigh . . . Thanks for being in touch. I'll be seeing you in a few months.

Love,
Ita

6.

Year of Renewal and Reflection: 1978–1979

Introduction

It was difficult for Ita Ford to leave La Bandera and Chile for the year of Renewal and Reflection at Maryknoll, New York. She questioned the necessity of a vow of final commitment, thinking it superfluous. But, at Carla's urging, she made her departure for Maryknoll, traveling through Bolivia, Peru, Guatemala, Nicaragua, and Mexico as she made her way back to the Motherhouse. As she visited many Maryknoll missioners along the way, she gathered perspectives on the work of the community in Latin America. She arrived home eager to share her perspectives on justice and poverty at the 1978 Maryknoll Sisters' General Assembly.

Back in the United States she experienced great culture shock, not least in her reentry into the institutional life of the Maryknoll community. Friends and family recognized the stress and anger she experienced at the waste, indifference, and apathy that characterized American culture. Chile's ongoing nightmare was unreal and locked away from most Americans. The suffering of people in Latin America, particularly the poor, was a distant, unheard cry.

While Jimmy Carter's presidency did offer a new emphasis on human rights, his voice was muted in relation to the travails of Latin America. In the United States, inflation was high and economically the country was going through its own struggle. The press was not interested in the Latin American context, as such, and Ita found very limited news coverage of the events in Chile. Three weeks after her

106

arrival at the Maryknoll Motherhouse she wrote to her friend from La Bandera, Sr. Connie Pospisil, of her concern for the Maryknoll Sisters there and her longing to be with them as they embarked on a hunger strike to protest the conditions under Pinochet. In her letter she reflects on the meaning of the Mystical Body, and her insight that they are all joined through Christ as they put their bodies on the line in solidarity with the poor and their suffering.

Ita was able to design her own program of studies at Maryknoll and she used the resources offered to help in struggles with the large questions before her. The rector of the Maryknoll School of Theology, Fr. John Meehan, agreed to be her spiritual director. Realizing too that she bore scars from the trauma of her years in Chile, she decided to see a psychiatrist. So Ita's year of Reflection encompassed spiritual, psychological, as well as intellectual renewal at Maryknoll.

At their General Assembly in 1978, meeting from October through December, the Sisters sought to clarify their mission as a commitment to social justice and a preferential option for the poor. Ita took part in the meetings of the General Assembly and edited papers of the committees. Her voice is represented in the sections highlighting social justice and in the final statement of the Assembly that crystallizes this expanded horizon of religious commitment:

> *The saving mission of the poor is becoming visible to the Church and offering hope to our world. Solidarity with the poor is not an option but a sign of the Kingdom that must be made explicit in our day. We commit ourselves to the cause of the poor through the witness of our lives, our words, and our ministry.*

In an interview with Maureen Flanagan, who was on the staff of the Sisters' Communications Office, Ita evidenced increasing insight into the mission of the Sisters in Chile and on what she had learned from her years in La Bandera. Intertwined with her review of their ministry was Ita's own awareness of how it impacted her sense of vocation and self-identity. From the poor of Chile she had learned of her own poverty, i.e., of the limitations of a life that is dictated by individualism. The poor of Chile lacked much control over their outward circumstances, but their lives were marked by hospitality and interdependence. The Chilean poor gave readily to one another and took up each other's burdens. The Kingdom of God was powerfully at work in these efforts. This was a model of church on a smaller scale: pastoral, unstructured, and connected to the fabric of the everyday crises of life. This smaller scale, she believed, represented a model for the new direction of mission and of the future for Maryknoll. It challenged Maryknoll no longer to measure its success or identity by the number of its members or the size of the institution. Among the poor of La Bandera, she felt she was much more engaged in life and that it was a place energized by the Spirit and the building of God's Kingdom.

Ita's "Retreat Notes" from her spiritual direction with Fr. John P. Meehan reveal the interiority of her search and the spiritual development that occurred during this year. She yearned to know the love of God from inside out. Her "Retreat Notes" show her struggles with her own inability at times to love and forgive herself. Years before, she had resonated with Thompson's "The Hound of Heaven," especially the depiction of God's powerful pursuit and offer of grace to a "divided self." At this stage of her life, Ita reflected upon the poetry of T.S. Eliot's "Ash Wednesday," and such phrases as:

> *Teach us to care and not to care*
> *Teach us to sit still*
> *And I pray that I may forget*
> *These matters that with myself I too much discuss*
> *Too much explain*

She progressed. She was capable of greater intimacy with God and an interior liberation from her particular demons and idols of the past. Her spiritual journey was one full of detours. Wrestling with the need to acknowledge God's love, progress was not a straight line. She knew more fully the love of God that had been there for her and she was once again ready to allow herself to know that love. She quotes Simone Weil: "God's love for us isn't the reason for loving him — but for our loving ourselves." Through her reflections we see her wrestling with scrupulosity as she attempts to free herself to accept God's love and to acknowledge her own worthiness.

Ita experienced a deep call to interior dialogue with Jesus during this period. She broke through to a deeper level of acceptance of Christ's love with a freedom that she had not experienced before. On May 24, 1979, in her end-of-the-year self-evaluation letter to Sr. Patricia Gallogly, the Sisters' Orientation Director for the Renewal Year Program, Ita evidenced the achievement of a new sense of joy and serenity. She was ready to return to Chile, possessed of greater awareness and a greater clarity about the meaning of her vocation. But there was to be yet another detour. The following day, May 25, while driving with friends in Rhode Island, she was seriously injured in a car accident. She found herself in the hospital for a month with a broken pelvis and torn knee. Determined to regain her strength, she threw herself into an intense regime of physical therapy and made rapid progress. Her humor and wit were undiminished. At the same time she was struck by the fact that, once again, life was not in her control. As always she pondered what God's plan was and how she might understand this latest episode and detour.

Letters, Writings, and Interviews

57. To Sister Connie Pospisil, June 21, 1978

Maryknoll, New York

Dear Connie,

I'm cutting the morning session to write. We have been so caught up, vicariously, in the strike that it just occurred to me that I haven't written to anyone since I hit the Motherhouse, almost three weeks ago.

You mentioned 'mystical body' in your letter with a new meaning for you. Maybe I had a similar experience from a distance. One day at Mass here the words of the consecration went booming through me — "This is my body given for you." The connection was instantaneous, all those giving their bodies, the possibilities there are for us to give our bodies. It was all made so possible and powerful in Jesus' having given his because he loved, new meanings open up as we experience different things even from a distance.

Was that ever hard being here! My only urge was to get on a plane and be with you all. There was next to nothing in the newspapers here, but Jan McLaughlin sent me whatever came out in Washington D. C. It seems that in the free press here, people's attention is shifted periodically to different sections of the world. For the past month it's been Africa, so there's not much on any place else. (Pat Edmonston's brother is publisher of *Newsweek* and he told her that Latin America doesn't 'sell.' People aren't that interested, so it doesn't get much coverage.) . . .

Jeanne is coming tomorrow night for a week. Monday, she, Carol Hassey, Gerry and I are going to Watch Hill [a Maryknoll retreat] for a few days. It will be a chance to catch up without being bombarded here. I still can't manage the Center between missing Chile and all of you, over-stimulation and various culture shocks (I think there's a Maryknoll shock), I'm just about hanging on. Right now I'm down in Mayfield alone — and it's beautiful.

I'll try to be better at writing when I get myself together.

Much love, dear friend,

Ita

58. *Interview with Maureen Flanagan, 1978. This edited transcription is heavily dependent on the earlier work of Judith Noone, MM.*

MF: You mentioned that in '73 your work was making friends with your neighbors and being there to share with them in their troubles. That's understandable to people here (Maryknoll) but I don't think that people in the States would understand it in those terms.

Ita Ford: I think [that's] just probably because pastoral work is so hard to define, but the basic thing is being with the people. The whole concept of Church as it's evolving in Latin America, away from a structured hierarchical model to other models — service, small communities of anywhere from 20 people to 20 or 30 families . . . What many of the bishops have asked us to do, first of all, is just be with the people, be a presence, let them know that the Church, as one man once said, "has now come down to us; we no longer go up to the Church."

MF: Do you work within a parish structure?
IF: No, we're in what they call a pastoral sector that has been removed. In Santiago where I am — that is, in the ring around the city — about 70,000 people came in and just squatted on the land, [which] was formerly a dairy farm. They were added onto a very old parish that was on the edge of the city. There was one priest for the people and all of a sudden there were 150,000 people. It was an unworkable concept, so the vicar just cut this group off from that parish and we're not going to worry about parish or anything. This would be an ideal time, we thought, to begin to work on forming small communities among the people. But it is very slow and deals with a very small number of people. But many of the people had rural roots. Their contact with the Church might have been once a year on a mission or something. They are not very church-going people. They don't clamor for the services. There are some sacraments that are important to them and, at [those] times, they go to other places to get those sacraments. So there isn"t the pressure to offer the mass and all that stuff.

MF: How many people are you living with?
IF: The Sisters? The work started in 1970, at the time Allende's socialist government was elected. I got there in 1973 and at that time a new community was forming with three Sisters, one from Chile, one from Santiago, and myself.

MF: Has the area's population changed the same way? Or are these people to stay?
IF: The population is pretty constant. The people would be market people, construction and odd-jobs workers; women would be maids,

housekeepers. The level of education . . . I think, I've met three people who have finished high school. Most women have gone to about
fourth grade. Some never went to school at all. I've met a few women
who taught themselves to read. Many people say, "I did learn how to
read but I've forgotten." They've never practiced. They've never had
the chance. They have no books or anything. They learn skills but, by
not using them, they have lost them. They are very unsophisticated,
but very open. The hospitality level in Chile is incredible.

MF: *That's all you hear from people who come back.*
IF: Which, I think becomes slightly contagious. It's a characteristic
that is so attractive that you're drawn to it and what it does for the
person. You go to someone's house and they get a chair on the dirt
floor and they'll take a rag and dust the seat of the chair and say, "Sit
down." And it's like it could be a throne. And it's just like a wooden
bench.

MF: *And they haven't lost that in spite of all the trouble?*
IF: No. They might say all they have to serve you would be a cup of
tea when they would like to give you something else, but you never
go into anybody's house where they do not want to serve you something and it offends them not to serve. Whatever. They have to serve
you something. They're not calculating. They don't give to you
[expecting anything back].

MF: *You spoke a lot about what it means to live the life of the poor in
that sense.*
IF: With people who have much less income, life is simpler; they
have fewer things to protect . . . The effect it had on me was in the
personal reverence of being in such a situation. It affected me in the
sense that I went deeper into myself. Because I lived among the poor
I came to know some of my own poverties. [When I worked in the
States] I pretty much controlled my own life. But in Chile, the poor
are so dependent; they do not control their lives, they are so affected
by possibilities of getting or not getting a job, not being able to get
the attention or service they needed.

MF: Yet it doesn't turn into any kind of bitterness or resentment?
IF: No, it's like a stance, a person's stance in front of the universe almost, in front of society, a consciousness of who they are. I think the poor say, "We, the poor." Even if a man has a job, he's so conscious that in the spectrum of society he stands with these people, which is I think so different than [we Americans]. We see ourselves very individualistically. We are individuals and it's, "I do this," " I go here," "I don't do what the group does."

MF: Somehow it's a sign of weakness here [in the U.S.] to move with a group of people.
IF: And there it's different — an understanding of the individual and solidarity. I've come to understand what solidarity means. You [or I might] put the emphasis on community, individual rights, and privilege, but the poor person doesn't. It's not that the individual doesn't exist. The focus is on the group, because individuals are never going to make it.

MF: Do you fit within that kind of group? Or will you always be something of an outsider? Are you accepted as an American?
IF: I think our nationality is not the biggest aspect. We fit within the group in some way probably because we live in community so that there is something by which to identify us. Chile has always had a lot of foreign influence. Recently, there was a lot of anti-American feeling during the coup, but they always exclude [friends and acquaintances] because they are very person-oriented too. They could say something against the Americans, "but we don't mean you." Among the poor, at least, we are seen as the "Religious." The concept allows the people to react to Religious as being other. Almost any North American woman who walks in, the people say, "There is a nun." My brother and sister-in-law were down and spent a week with us and they kept talking about "the nun with the husband." Because the concept was that she was slightly taller, fair, i.e. North American, she had to be a nun.

MF: And yet they are so close to the city.

IF: But the basic involvement, at least among the Chilean Religious at this point is in the institutions. For the children who know us, whatever a nun is, that's what we are. Two times, at least, there have been Sisters with habits that have come. One time a kid said to me, "They're gypsies." And another time another kid was talking about "the grandmothers who were all in black." And we were saying, "No, those are Sisters" and the kid said, "No, the nuns are nuns who walk around in slacks." The bishop thought it was hysterical. It was a very silly thing, but the kids don't associate nuns with the long black dresses.

MF: What do you do day-to-day?
IF: There are a few basic activities and most of the other things evolve out of just being there. The basic activities would be in forming small Christian communities, which would be weekly meetings with couples, often at night, 8-10, 9-11 or midnight, reflecting on the events of the week, the relations one with another. And because of the events of the week there is usually some type of crisis which we respond to, and a prayer or scripture reflection.

We're involved in preparing people to be catechists, or preparing people to respond to their neighbors, helping people develop the natural gifts and services that are needed there. It's trying to bring out and discover with them the possibilities of service, so that they become independent of us in a way, so that they become a community that serves itself instead of looking for people to come and do the services for them.

MF: This is kind of a difficult question to ask, but in the U.S. when you explain the presence such as the one you have there, many people say, "What are they doing there not supporting themselves and yet not having any organized activity?" What is the strength of not holding a job per se — a financial job?
IF: Well, we get a small stipend from the archdiocese of Santiago. That is, the bishops consider what we are doing work. And so they pay for it. It's . . . you can't really live on it. We pull together four salaries to allow for our food, shelter, heat, electricity. We earn

enough together to make a go of it. But what we're doing is actually considered work. It's hard to understand. Sometimes I understand our work in terms of what we used to think of as [the work of] Protestant pastors: caring, being concerned about, being involved in [people's] lives.

We've also many times thought about holding down jobs. Usually one person in the house is holding down a job like maybe in the public health clinic. But in the last couple of years, with the economic situation in Chile, the few times when we've really thought about it, the type of job we could get, if it wasn't teaching in a Catholic school (because a foreigner cannot teach in the public school system), might be lower. We could maybe be a waitress or a housekeeper. There are even religious who do housekeeping, but at this point, there is such competition on the job market, taking it from people who don't have jobs would be tragic. It's one of those dilemmas that you have to live with.

MF: Maybe another way of looking at it would be how you are accepted by people as kind of existing in their neighborhood.
IF: They'll ask, "How do you live?" And I say, "We don't." What we have would be a little less than the minimum salary that most of them earn. But we try to just lay it out and answer. We live a very fishbowl existence. Everybody knows who is in your house, what is going on, if you don't answer the door or come to the window. I've been in bed with bronchitis and wanted to stay in bed and people would come and say "Why didn't you answer the door?" And they'll throw stones on the roof for half an hour until you're out of your mind. We live next door to the local bar. The head of my bed is about 3 feet away from the head of the couple who live next door. You're into their fights, you're into the joys, you're into the disagreements, into the struggle. There's a role I think we have, for good or bad, so when something is going on, people will come to us as leaders, referees, facilitators. That is a constant all day. And many people come thinking you're the big magic answer: "I need a house, I need a job, I need clothes, I need food, I need . . ." And all we can say is, "I can help you in what you're trying to do but we don't have a big warehouse."

Where there is no dough there is no financing for that. And I guess our point there is to turn people back again to their natural group to say, "There's a problem here. How can we altogether look at it? . . .

I'm always at a great loss to say what we do. To define what we do is very difficult.

MF: To me it's always been good to hear that — almost an uncertainty in how to express it, because nobody else in the world can express it.
IF: I can't give a job definition to what we do in reality. We're there to be with, to discover with the people the coming of brotherhood and justice and trying in some way to be part of that with those to whom it's maybe more real . . . those who have been really put down, oppressed in various ways, who haven't had possibilities. I don't think we are there to tell people, "Here's your answer." It's an incredible privilege and opportunity to discover this happening with people who are interested.

MF: Was this your expectation of what would happen when you entered?
IF: In 1961 I think that I went in very distinctly with the feeling that I had received a great deal and wanted to say thank you. What it means now — I'm not sure what it means anymore. What's more important to me now is building the Kingdom, trying to understand just what the future might be, if there really were bread for all people, if there really were justice.

There're a lot of things that are very uncomfortable about being there [in Chile], but it's like the right place to be. It's like you intuit a place. This is your place right now. I can't say it's my place forever and ever. Right now, I recognize this is where I should be.

MF: I think people have been brought up to believe that somehow you come upon this vocation and you're very certain, and talking with the younger group, the first year people, and now the second year people, they said that it is one of the most refreshing things to find — that people were still questioning — even though they happen to be in for fifty years.

IF: I just know that my own history has a lot of detours in it, that it isn't a straight line.

MF: *What kind of women, consequently are attracted to Maryknoll? Has that changed?*

IF: People are very different. There are timid people, there are strong people, but maybe there is a constant. To me, Maryknoll is a vehicle, in the sense that each individual has a particular instinct or call or [sense that] what they should do with their life is bigger than Maryknoll. I see Maryknoll as the enabling vehicle. I come across people who somehow have a common, shared faith, and this sense of going out and being with other peoples and other cultures, a type of searching for what is still to come, but at the same time [a commitment to] being very involved with the whole man right now. That dualistic type of thing — "I'll take care of that man's soul" — doesn't say anything to me. And I think if you become involved with this vehicle, this group of women, then there's a responsibility to it, too, to support each other. If I look for support I also have to support. If I'm looking for the strength to continue, I also have to strengthen others in that sharing of faith and friendship. I was just trying even to get into the language of that, or understand maybe this women's lib, or I don't know, that [sense of] sisterhood, or something like that. Maybe there's some element of that now that could be understood. I don't know. I mean it's bigger, certainly bigger than that . . .

59. *Article by Ita Ford in* Maryknoll Magazine

"La Bandera attacks mental health crisis"

"I didn't know what came over me. My nerves just got out of hand. Carlos asked for another piece of bread and I slapped him." Señora Teresa is very composed as she shares her thoughts with eight women seated around the room. Those listening also have experienced the anxiety and helplessness of not being able to stretch a small amount of food to meet the needs of growing children. On many occasions, as they recalled, their nerves had 'betrayed' them. However, on this sunny afternoon in *poblacion,* La Bandera on the southern end of Santiago, Chile's capital, the women are trying to support each other in the daily drama lost behind the statistics and proclamations of six and a half years of oppressive military rule and an economic model that excludes most of them. (A recent sampling of 340 families showed that only 153 had some member with a full-time job.) Each woman listens intently to Señora Teresa, who recently finished training as a group leader in a new community-based program of mental health.

As in so many Third World countries, Chile's health problems are widespread and its resources are unequally distributed. The situation is more acute when one focuses on mental health. According to government statistics, 10 percent of its 11 million population suffer from neurosis. This number is often higher in urban sectors with a large concentration of rural people. Having migrated to the cities in search of work and a better life, they all too often face unemployment that eventually exacts a high toll: the breakup of families, neurosis, alcoholism, and school dropouts. Chile's 80 psychiatrists and traditional mental health facilities were proving inadequate for this growing need. A new approach to mental health, stressing prevention, was necessary.

During 1976-77, a community-based mental health program was started. Similar in design to what health promoters found in other Latin American countries, the program is based on local leaders, who work with groups for three months. They provide the theory of neurosis and its various symptoms and manifestations, teach relaxation exercises, and help the participants to share their problems, and face their emotions in an accepting atmosphere.

Serving as a bridge between the neighborhood and the professionals are the community leaders. In La Bandera, that bridge is Maryknoll Sister Connie Pospisil, of West Hempstead, New York. Almost fifteen years in Chile, she has had a variety of nursing experiences – in a rural hospital, in an urban public health clinic, and with the Rural Institute of Education. After updating her studies, she returned to Chile in 1977. The new program was presented as a great need so "I jumped in," she says.

Collaborating with a social worker from the National Health Service, Sister Connie and a few volunteers completed the three-month program and additional training as group leaders. Since then she has been promoting the program and training leaders. "I see my work as helping people recognize their dignity in the eyes of God and other humans so as to be able to live more humanly — to be more fully alive," she says.

The long-range plan is a Mental Health Center developed by the people themselves as they feel the need. The future services would be extended to treat alcoholism, drug addiction, and human relations problems. As the community experiences its own potential for caring for and serving each other, its solidarity grows. It begins to look beyond symptoms to find the causes of problems. "It's a slow process, but an advancing one," Sister Connie explains. "I am privileged to be part of these beginnings of a new life for downtrodden people."

The Latin American bishops, meeting in Puebla wrote, "Many of the poor have achieved the evangelical values of solidarity, service, simplicity and readiness to receive the gift of God." For Sister Connie, Señora Teresa and the other group leaders who serve the community, the gift of God is an integral liberation, a freedom from sin, oppression and illness. The promise of Jesus, "I have come so that they may have life and have it to the full" (Jn. 10:10), is taking on deeper meaning for many in La Bandera.

60. Ita's Retreat Notes, August 1978-August 1979

These "Retreat Notes" are a remarkable look into the interiority that was so basic to Ita Ford's life and vision. It would have impoverished this collection not to include them. Nonetheless, they are difficult reading, as we would expect of personal notes jotted down in the course of a week. They have undergone the most minimal of editing so as to preserve Ford's own stream of thought and to avoid losing anything as a result of the editor's

interpretations. JPM are the initials of the Retreat Master, Fr. John Mee-
han, MM, referred to often by Ita Ford elsewhere in her letters.

JPM It's like the analogy of 'territorial imperative' — you're claim-
     ing yourself. It's good!
     As you keep reviewing what has been happening, you'll be
     moved to Hellel psalms — with all stop.
     Like tears of fullness and joy . . . Also, another thing even
     though I was tempted to say, the process is wrong in the sense
     that I'm not doing my part — I resisted for two reasons: . . .
     The Lord is bigger than my idea of scheduling and hang-ups;
     and also — how I can really put myself down when the gifting
     is happening, as he's saying you're loved, precious, cared for
     — not because of what you do — but because I love you.
     I have to begin to like, cherish, love too — and being comfort-
     able is already happening. The other left over reflex that has to
     slowly relax.
7/V 2 months or so:
1-6 Potter reworking clay to his liking
Jer. 18:5-6   Can I not deal with you, Israel, as the potter deals with
     his clay? You are clay in my hands as the clay in his.
Mt. 11:28-30   Come to me, all whose work is hard, whose load is
     heavy; and I will give you relief. Bend your neck to my yoke,
     and learn from me for I am gentle and humble-hearted; and
     your soul will find relief. For my yoke is good to bear and my
     load is light.
Gal. 2:15-21   We acknowledge that what makes a man righteous is
     not obedience to the law but faith in Jesus Christ . . . no one
     can be justified by keeping the law . . . the life . . . I now live in
     this body I live in faith: faith in the Son of God who loved me
     and who sacrificed himself for my sake. I cannot bring myself
     to give up God's gifts . . .
5:1 when Christ freed us, he meant us to remain free. Stand firm,
     therefore, and do not submit again to the yoke of slaves.
Ps. 46   Be still and know that I am God.

Acts 11:1-18   What God has made clean, you have no right to call pro-
fane.

(What God has made loveable/whom he loves — you have no
right to call unlovable).

Jn. 10:10   The thief comes only to steal, kill and destroy. I have come
so that they may have life and have it to the full.

15:1-9   You are pruned already by means of the word I have spoken
to you. Make your home in me or I make mine in you . . .
Whoever remains in me, with me in him, bears fruit in plenty;
cut off from me you can do nothing . . . Remain in my love.

It's in this I've come full circle back again to the invitation and
basic fact of life — survival. Remain in me — keep the life line open
— and you'll live, bear fruit, give glory to the Father, be a disciple and
have your requests granted.

JPM: Remembering the gifting of this year: from where you started
— to coming to know you're loved greatly — just as self — that
this should be communicated — you've been there to the
mountain and the veil has been lifted. The Christian memory
and spiral: death/resurrection — Christian in that we recognize it and ascend up the spiral.

This is the second sabbatical experience 71/72, 78/79

The "Be still and know that I am God" is important — especially
its authority over the neurosis. A call to acknowledge his Magnalia
Dei (the marvelous works of God) and give lie to the 'but' — squirm-
ing worm. Of course you have weaknesses, defects — without them
there would be no need for a savior — they are your "happy fault,
necessary sin" (Augustine) for the love, power and mercy of God to
touch. Yet all around, spring is bursting forth with signs of new life
in yours is there too. Lay aside, once and for all, the unloved demon
— let go and experience all the love that is in and surrounds you.
Accept the filling and healing — it's been done . . . . Don't submit
again to the yoke of slavery. Go out and see what's happening with
all those blossoms. This passage seems to have all the elements of
what's been happening lately.

A reconciliation, the old creation gone — a new creation here — so in Christ we mingle become the goodness of God and pass on that good news — So don't neglect the grace — because now is the favorable time — the day of salvation.

Okay and here's the challenge. There have been favorable times — other days of salvation that have been glorious — and I coasted on them, dried them out, wrung them and did nothing for caring, cherishing, protecting and nourishing them. So now here I am again and I want it to be different. I don't want to neglect what I've received. If the new creation is on its way or here, I don't want a malnourished, deformed neglected self — but one that's alive — that hands on that good news, that lives it, that has it as an integral part of self. — As on the emotional psychological level, so too here — I have to rewire the circuits.

JPM: Find your way — times — places – that are good for you, that resonate. No one can do it but you — or tell you. Try different approaches until you're on to it.

2/XIII Thes. 5:19-24 Do not stifle spirit. Do not despise prophecies. Grace. Test everything; retain what is good . . .

JPM He who calls us is trustworthy, therefore he will do it.

Also/ God is faithful — I Cor. 10:13, 2 Cor. 1:20 To think about/ 2 Thes.3:3; 2 Tim 2:13; Heb. 10:23, 11:11

I Thes. 5:24 He who calls us is trustworthy (he will not fail you)

Phil. 4:5-6 The Lord is near, dismiss all anxiety from your minds. Present your needs to God in every form of prayer and in petitions, full of gratitude

I Cor. 1:4-9 I continually thank God for you because of the favor he has bestowed on you in Christ Jesus . . . He will strengthen you to the end . . . God is faithful, and it is he who called you to fellowship with his Son.

Is. 25:9 That day it will be said: See this in our God in whom we hoped for Salvation.

2 Thes. 3:3 The Lord is faithful. He will give you the strength. Help me to open this word you let me see. Increasing faith and trust in it. It is your work

(2 Cor. 5:18) — what's happening. Like the promise in Is. 25 out of

the banquet — I want to draw strength from that — from your promises — Not to coast on them, but to hope in them, be in touch with you. Please keep showing me. Thanks

XII Vespers   Happy are they who believe that the promises of the Lord will be fulfilled.

Reflection day: Waiting . . . wait for — sometimes we get wrapped up in Obligation of waiting — that we miss it in another form — miss an opportunity to wait upon — hanging loose, patience, vulnerability, openness . . . wait with — accompanying "upon."

God's love for us isn't reason for loving him — but for our loving ourselves. (Simone Weil)

It's just getting quiet and deep/rich: The message of Advent is — "I am faithful"— in those patterns of life I will come . . . Pay attention.

8/XII JPM I Thes.5:17-24   Be happy, pray constantly, give thanks, don't suppress Spirit, he who calls us won't fail.

JPM Looking back — at what has happened — from desert forward . . . there is much to give thanks — in fact it would be good to keep some kind of journal record — for help of others — because you've been there. It's God in the fullness of time to look ahead and build into life times and places that are sacred so as not to let the well run dry. Times that are important to you and a place that you associate with prayer.

If ministry aspect also jumps out to you, even more important to do so.

"He has entrusted to us the news that they are reconciled" (2 Cor.5:19).

2/I 2 Cor. 12:7-10 "My grace is enough for you: my power is at its best in weakness."

It is when I am weak that I am strong.

2/II Ps. 40, 1st point   I waited for the Lord and he bent down to me and heard . . . he brought me up out of the muddy pit and gave me a firm footing. And on my lips he put a new song — of praise to

our God . . . Thy wonderful purposes are
all for our good . . . Thou, O Lord, dost not
withhold thy tender care for me; thy unfail-
ing love and truth forever guard me.

What seems to be slowly happening is an acceptance of the truth
of who I am: coming to know it, see it in relation to the whole — and
accepting the knowledge of who I am and where I am — the Pauline
image of parts of body. It's a gradual, non-violent, non-threatening,
non-disappointing experience — coming to be comfortable with who
I am, how I have been gifted for others. It became clear I couldn't
forgive myself — though of course Jesus had. — So to will to enter
into that aspect of the gratuitous love of the covenant. You've been
forgiven — can you forgive yourself? Yes, — "woman, you are rid of
your infirmity" and he laid his hands on her. And at once she
straightened up and she glorified God.

The most amazing thing is to recognize your sinfulness — in
the light of being loved — it's not a horror but insignificant. Almost
as though that was such a dumb thing to keep you from the knowledge of being loved and accepting it.

What a liturgical experience!

Over from Phil 2:6-11   (Christ emptying himself)—what has to
be emptied is me — what do I have to let go of?

15/XI-Liturgy for new CGB [Maryknoll Central Governing Board]:
asking to be open — to be shown what was in way. I was the idol —
Maryknoll. How I had created my own no-win situation — sacrific-
ing to it for what vindication? Acceptance? — ruled by fear. And the
idol was dead of course — had no life or power except what I gave it.
If I stopped, it was a paper dragon.

17/XI— with Grace.   Something's coming — imminent — it's palpable. You're about to be born. The idol is a lie — guilt —
There's nothing you could ever dig up that would account for
it. You're good — Be with what's happening. I left with a
natural high.

19/XI

JPM Deut. 30:15-20.

I set before you life or death . . . Choose life, then, so that your descendants may live, in the love of Yahweh your God, obeying his voice, clinging to him: for in this your life consists . . .

I want to choose life — I do — I reject the death — the idols: I look to being born. To experiencing the wow. It is good.

Deaconate   Sign of Peace: a new image of Maryknoll came as all the celebrants embraced the deacons, the wishing well, blessing, sending off with support. It doesn't matter that there are things on which we disagree — the sending of one to be faithful to his call is the main thing — what we're about — a truer image than the sword of Damocles.

A lot of things are falling into place — it's good.

1/XII JPM 2 Cor. 5:17-6:2   For anyone who is in Christ, there is a new creation. It is all God's work. We beg you once again not to neglect the grace of God you have received. At the favorable time I have listened to you — on the day of salvation I came to your help. Well now is the favorable time; this is the day of your salvation.

6/10— John 15:4-5   Invitation to share life: fact that if not rooted in Christ you can do nothing.

JPM experience of aridity not to be run from our strengths can become our weaknesses Irish heritage can militate vs. going down to find the waters already there present. Be patient — take time with self, others, Lord. Like — respect self. God saw all that he had made and indeed it was very good (Gen 1:31)

Love your neighbor as yourself. To like/love self doesn't mean being satisfied with yourself. But must discover what's you and there is good there, more than you probably acknowledge. Accept your salvation history — it's the only one you have.

20/X Isa. 45:9-11   creature to creator — clay to potter . . . me to Lord.
    Is it for you to question me about my children and to dictate to me what my hands should do?

    My first reaction — no, of course not — when I do, I'm rebelling. — Submit.

    Second reaction — anger — why does it have to be this way? It doesn't. Let's wrestle about it.

Third reaction — OK, let's wrestle to come to understand what's happening, where am I going or being led?

JPM We have to come to know why the desert — because all has been drained — or a given state. Also look for roads in desert — Sometimes we can't see for the dunes and so have to 'vision' roads — What for us is life-giving, fulfilling, joyful — can be all signs to move in that direction . . . What re-creates, rejuvenates, re-wows? Dream in presence of Lord — with no limits or givens or 'have-to-bes.' Base line is self as good, worthwhile, loved — moving toward fulfillment. Again — the positive — what is the good for me — get into that — move toward that — let it be possible — for joy, peace, serenity.

3/11 Lk. 13:10-17 Healing of woman on Sabbath — eighteen years enfeebled, bent doubled and unable to stand upright. What do I have to be healed of — what weight oppresses me that I am bent?

Homily In God's presence let us look at that for which we can't forgive ourselves. What's *that*? Difference between contract (each party fulfilling their part — or contract void) and covenant — (forgiveness — gratuitousness)

30/VIII Jn. 15:4-7 "Make your home in me as I make mine in you." The invitation — Call to relationship and more than that, or which means — life, fruitfulness, intimacy to life — anyone who doesn't remain in me — withers and so is burnt. (Jer. 8:13) "I would like to go harvesting there," says Yahweh, "but there are no grapes on the vine, no figs on the fig tree: even the leaves are withered!"

To fruitfulness: productivity — enabling — Whoever remains in me, with me is him, bears fruit in plenty!

To intimacy — make your home in me as I make mine in you. All the times I've tortuously gone over and yearned about this and then backed off neurotically and/or selfishly. You say it so simply, invite so directly. I want to respond and to the degree and in the areas that I need help to do so, I ask you to help me enter consciously into the relationship — to make my restless self's home in You. With Dr. Moorehead:* Radar problem not result of God, people, but comes out of blocked denied feelings — especially sadness (and possibly anger). How to surface past feelings that never came to head or were spent and also what to do with them when they've surfaced — two questions and big challenge — hard work. To jump in and see what happens — is probably the best thing now. I don't want to go through life with these weights anymore. I want to be freed. Like a lot of other enslaved people — I need to de-mythologize the oppressor, the darkness, the past. I feel optimistic that this time I'll get there. It's a roll-up-your-sleeves type of job — You'll need lots of energy besides patience and understanding.

29/VIII   Acts 1:4 "Wait for what the Father has promised."

Acts 8   "Then you will be my witnesses . . ."

Wait — be patient, be quiet — for what has been promised. Wait in the surety that you're loved, that what (you) will be receiving what this year is meant to hold. You don't have to force it, manage it. Instead tune in to what is promised so you'll be able to recognize what's happening. Without the Spirit — one doesn't witness to Christ. How many times have you witnessed to yourself, to another or to an ideology? Maybe this year is to tune into where the Spirit is leading you — you with your own history and future. Possibly it's also to come to accept your own history and future, yourself — not as it conforms or doesn't to 'norms' — but as the individual loved and led for larger purposes. There's no use wishing the history were different, because then you wouldn't be you. It all adds up to something — so look at it, live with it — see the mistakes, your own detours — and what in spite of yourself — or because of yourself — was a move ahead. Let it all be lighted up to see what comes next. Then you will be a witness.

Spirit is a favorite theme of Luke; he talks mostly about Spirit as a Power sent from God by Christ to broadcast the good news:

1) The Spirit gives the charismata that guarantees the message:

---

*Dr. Moorehead was the psychiatrist Ita saw during her Reflection Year.

the gifts of tongues, miracles, prophecy, wisdom.

2) The Spirit gives strength to proclaim Jesus as Messiah in spite of persecutions and to bear witness to him.

3) Spirit guides Church in her major decisions — admission of pagans without obligation to observe law, Paul's mission to pagan world. Acts also mentions Spirit as received in baptism and forgiving of sins.

From John 14. In place of departed Christ, faithful will have Spirit. He is the *parakletos* [Paraclete], who intercedes with Father and whose voice is heard in human courts. He is the Spirit of truth, leading men to the very fullness of truth, teaching them to understand the mystery of Christ — his fulfillment of the Scripture, the meaning of his words, of his actions, of his signs, all hitherto obscure to the disciples. In this way Spirit is to bear witness to Christ and shame the unbelieving world.

8/VIII30 Retreat Days with Lilla Hull

Hosea   11-2   God's personal love for sinning unfaithful Israel.

      11:9   I am God not man: I am the holy one in your midst and have no wish to destroy.

      2:14ff   I am going to lure her . . . and speak to her heart.

      21ff   I will betroth you to myself forever, betroth you with integrity and justice,

  with tenderness *(hesed)* and love

I will betroth you to myself with faithfulness, and you will come to know Yahweh. (*Hesed* and knowledge of God=2 concepts united in Hosea.)

Knowledge of God: not merely intellectual. God 'makes himself known' to man when he engages himself to him by covenant and shows his love *(hesed)* for him by the benefits he confers; similarly man 'knows God' when he loyally observes God's covenant, shows gratitude for God's gifts and returns love for love. In Wisdom literature 'knowledge' and 'wisdom' are practically synonymous. 1st words — tender, faithful love — stronger than all my limitations, tepidness — the reality, 'giveness' of the love because 'I am God, not man.' Did I have to have Chile ties cut to really come to 'know' it? The love, belonging, comfortableness, — maybe were — not obstacles because

I believe they were gifts — but were preparatory; And just in case I'd
be prone to absolutize them — I have to let go of their immediacy and
so as to 'know' the Father. There's something so appealing and invit-
ing about the process of "You will come to know Yahweh."

>From *Ash Wednesday* by T. S. Eliot [Ita's version]
"Teach us to care and not to care
Teach us to sit still
And I pray that I may forget
These matters that with myself I too much discuss
Too much explain.
  . . . Suffer us not to mock ourselves with falsehood

  . . . And I pray that I may forget these matters that with myself
I too much discuss, too much explain . . .
Teach us to care and not to care.
Teach us to sit still . . .
  . . . Suffer us not to mock ourselves
with falsehood
all back and spend it with and for others.

18/II/VI   Barnabas — son of encouragement
Mt. 10:8   "You received without charge; give without charge."
Life, abilities, personality, good news, friends, this year and
relationships with You.

16/V II Cor. 5:14-21   The love Christ overwhelms us.
Anyone who is in Christ is a new creation . . . God in Christ
reconciled the world to himself, not holding man's faults
against them, and he has entrusted to us the news that they are
reconciled and we are ambassadors for Christ; it is as though
God were appealing through us.

18/VI II Cor. 6:1-2   "Do not neglect the grace of God you have
received . . . now is the favorable time this is the day of salvation . . ."!!

7/VIII   Grasshopper stuck on tar
Check Eliot's lines.

Is 50:2   "Is my hand too short to redeem? Have I not strength to
save?"

How often have I measured God by my own puny scale? Because of that — not only was that a block to my knowing His love but in some crazy way it was a block to His being known by me . . . That's probably why the experience of this year had to be on a big scale — one that I couldn't control — and keep down. I had to come through all the neurotic barriers that He was so much bigger and loving and accepting. It's awesome to realize that God has revealed himself to me — because he wanted to, because he loves me.

9/VI Mark 12: 41-44 Widow's Mite

"Some put in what they have over — she from the little she had put in everything she possessed, all she had to live on "

As Jesus was so single-heartedly directed and identified with the Father that meant, his fulfillment was to do the Father's will, so I would like to get beyond the keeping back something for me, and learn his and the widow's giving and giving over of myself — especially since all I have has been given and I've been showered with much in love. May I learn to offer it.

3/VI Judith Ch. 9

4/VI Mark 12:17   Render to God what is God's — you

5/VI Luke 5:1-11 — Peter's recognition of sinful self when faced with Jesus' power and boat load of fish and subsequent call. The more we can come to truly see ourselves — as sinners and creatures in front of Jesus' power and love and forgiveness and acceptance — the more we can be enabled by him.

I don't think before today that I considered it a miracle that we got out of the car as we did — that we weren't killed or badly hurt — or that more weren't hurt. I feel like I deserve the rebuke — "weren't 10 made clean — where are the other 9?"

Ps. 46 "Come, think of Yahweh's marvels, the astounding things he has done in the world"

JPM Don't forget — remember what's really happened to you.

6/VI Mk 12:24   "Is not the reason why you go wrong, that you understand neither the Scriptures nor the power of God?"

29/II/79   whiteness from where light came walking — woods or along beach in harmony with the ocean

> Ita: I hope this is the first of a continued conversation. I've wanted it for so long as you know — but in some way, I wasn't ready.
>
> Jesus: I know, that's why I had to help you get ready. I never rush a person.
>
> Ita: I know you've always let me take the time I need to get to each point. And now something new is going on — some empowering — and I would like it to be centered on you. The personal relationship, discipleship, mission. Will you help me?
>
> Jesus: Of course I will. Where do you want to start?
>
> Ita: I'm not sure. Since for so long I've related to you in so many ways — somewhat very formally, ritually — other times in my quite neurotic way — I feel a little awkward — although I know that it's all right — I guess in some way I'm where John and Andrew were — desiring to know and enter into intimacy with — and don't know the "right" way to proceed. Yet it seems to be the right moment — so can we presume some kind of hurdle-jumping?
>
> Jesus: Come on, Ita — the hurdles are clear — I've done that for you too. I've been waiting for you and I'm glad you've come. We have a lot to talk about.

24/II/79
Father, I will to say yes to your new deed that's coming to light. Given all my limitations you have led me slowly here. It's peaceful — it's good. I give you thanks.

61. *Letter from Ita Ford to Connie Pospisil (New York to Chile), April 20,*
1979

Dear Connie,

I hope the *jornada* went well. The agenda looked very interesting. Thanks for asking about the family. On the surface things seem
better, but it's hard to tell.

You asked how things are going at the Center. I'd say well
enough, given the whole set-up. The group with Pat has worked out
well — in that we enjoy and support each other. But we're never that
close so as to rub elbows or have a conflict that has to be worked
through, so in that way, it's a little unreal. I guess institutional living
in itself just has that kind of drawback. I find it functional, but 'hot
house.' The economics is a bit of a back breaker and I'm just skim-
ming the surface, but I think it's important to keep at it in the future.
The other courses, Prophets and Luke are a pleasure, but I'm not
putting much work in. In fact, psychologically I think I've finished
the year and now I'm waiting for the year to finish.

I'm writing this letter from a friend's house and I realize I didn't
bring the letters that all of you wrote after your day of reflecting on
Bandera and my possible return. So I hope you don't mind if I wait
on talking to you about that until I have you 'in front of me,' at least,
through your letters, since I have the feelings of your responses, but
I don't trust my memory on exactly what was said. Hopefully, sometime next week I can respond to that, even though, just as you
seemed to experience before returning, it's almost impossible to definitely decide before returning and there's also something of a feeling I have about being open to what the region asks of me as much
as I would like the region to be open to what I ask.

Well, friend, take care. I'll write soon.

Love,
Ita

62. Ita self-evaluation, May 1979, for her Reflection Year at Maryknoll

Looking back on it, the best thing about the reflection year program has been the year, the time to unwind, to let the dust settle, to look at and assimilate the experiences of the past six years and some 'left-overs' from further back. Linked with this has been the group itself with whom I have shared friendship, faith, struggles, hopes and laughs.

Time and loving support have been the foundation for healing, growth and integration. In addition, the other resources available gave me the opportunity for a custom-made program — studies, spiritual direction, and psychological help that responded to my situation and needs.

Given the limitations of institutional living, the community experience this year has been very positive. Within the group I was able to give and receive love and support. I also felt a great mutual trust and respect. The group spirit that emerged was due as much to the others' as to my own openness and cooperation. I don't think there was any great distinction made about the roles within orientation. Pat Gallogly has been an integral member of the reflection-year community and my relationship with her has been very much the same (although in lesser degree due to differing schedules, etc.) than with the other members.

My general health has been fine and my emotional adjustment has been very good, after passing through the uprooting and separation-from-Chile stage.

Complementing these basic elements have been several courses that have helped me articulate and integrate my past experiences. "Theology in Situations of Conflict" was particularly helpful for reflecting on Chile. The Overseas Training Program debriefing and seminars sparked a good exchange of experiences and increased my sensitivity to the problems in other parts of the world. It also made the year more enjoyable through friendship with the seminarians. The missiology and scripture courses I consider as part of a continuous process of reflection; the economics courses provided a basic tool for future social analysis.

My faith commitment has been greatly strengthened this year through the conscious experience of the Lord's love for me and his active role in my history. I am becoming confident with my own spirituality that is shaped by being in mission and in relation with others, seeking together the fullness of life expressed in Jesus.

As I have expressed to Pat, I don't relate to 'final' commitment, except as a canonical requirement. My own history within Maryknoll probably shapes this attitude. By the time I made my commitment in 1972, I had been through an eleven-year period of clarifying what my call was and how it should be expressed. Being reasonably sure myself and more confident in God's faithfulness, my commitment was for life. Since then, many different experiences have helped flesh out and make this choice clearer and more meaningful.

I believe I am responding to the Lord's call to me in the best way through the areas of Maryknoll, . . . in the Church's evangelizing mission to the poor and oppressed and living simply in a celibate community. This is where my life has meaning, challenge, and fulfillment, besides I'm happy and like it. I'll be glad to fulfill the final requirement on my return to Chile.

63. Evaluation of Ita Ford by Sister Patricia Gallogly, MM

This was an official evaluation of Ita's Reflection Year, prepared by Sister Patricia Gallogly, the Director of the Renewal Year Program.

Ita arrived from Chile in June 1978. During the summer she studied Liberation Theology at Maryknoll Seminary and began her Reflection Year at the end of August. When the group came together we formulated our program for the year based on the goals for the Reflection phase. Each member of the group then worked out her own individual study program. During the first semester Ita studied Scripture with Dr. Finkel and OTP [Overseas Training Program] seminar with Fr. Terry Cambias. In January at the time of the winter session Ita participated in one week of the Mission Institute. During the second semester she studied Scripture with Dr. Finkel, Biblical

Anthropology with Mr. Keber, and continued OTP seminar at the Seminary. At this time Ita also took a course in Economics at Pace College and Economic Ethics at Union Theological Seminary.

Early in the year during the debriefing sessions with Sr. Maria Rieckelman, Ita became aware of some of the effects of the trauma she experienced during her early years in Chile. She sought psychological help and found it helpful in enabling her to face areas of her life she had not looked at before.

Ita has also sought individual spiritual direction this year and found it really helped her touch the reality of God in her experiences. She sees her personal prayer as developing to the point where she really can express with God just where she's at. I have noticed too in sharing her experiences of God in her life, Ita expresses a very open, honest and vulnerable relationship with God that has really touched me deeply. Her prayer life has definitely grown and developed out of her experiences particularly from her life among the Chilean people these past few years. How often she has expressed that her own sense of needing Christ as Savior has come through sharing in the faith-life of the people.

As she has often admitted, Ita found it difficult leaving Chile to come for Reflection Year. I felt her resistance early in the year but saw her always so open and honest in acknowledging it and saying just where she was at. As the year progressed however, Ita relaxed more and more. Within the group I see her as a very warm, sensitive person — one "being with you." In her own self-criticism, Ita has said that, perhaps, she lacks discipline in allowing immediate situations to take over some of her priorities, such as studies. I have seen these immediate situations as people who Ita responded to at times of need by just *being* with them. This, I see as her particular gift in community — sensing where a person is at and ready with an outstretched hand.

Her relationship with her family has been a concern for Ita this year. How close was she willing to allow herself to grow to them, knowing she'll be leaving shortly? Then with her brother-in-law's illness in March and the burden this presented to her sister, Ita has felt the pain of standing by and seeing those she loves suffer. These have been difficult and frustrating months for her as she has just tried to somehow be with them in their sorrow.

I have already told Ita that one of the ways she has especially enriched my life this year has been through sharing her own faith-life and what it has meant for her to be among the very poor in Chile. Her commitment to Christ and His mission is so evident in everything about Ita. It just flows out from the core of her being.

Ita plans to make her Final Commitment after returning to Chile. She doesn't feel this is a big step in her life as she sees her commitment already as a reality. She knows, however, that the decision opens her to moving in faith, trusting in Yahweh, the Faithful One. She may stumble and, perhaps, make a mess as she says but she's sure of His Faithfulness. I wholeheartedly recommend that Ita move in this direction and I truly rejoice for her presence among us in Maryknoll.

Sister Patricia Gallogly

64. To Sister Rachel Lauze, MM, July 17, 1979

Dear Rach,

As I read your letter, I couldn't help smiling who's in control, who's in charge here? has been part of the dialogue I've been involved in during these days at Watch Hill. I don't know why it's such a struggle or that there are so many levels of letting go, but I keep coming up against it a lot.

Today I especially missed the ol' group. After a year of talking, praying, being wrapped up in Nicaragua, it was so strange not to be together today when Somoza finally left. I pray that true peace can be made now by those who are left behind to rebuild.

Have you gone on the road with Agnes yet? Are you giving any talks? I hope all goes well. I would almost say, I don't think that would be my cup of tea, but then again, I wouldn't volunteer for a car accident either. So I guess we just manage as things come along, wisdom of my venerable Chinese grandmother, expect the unexpected.

Take care. I bet you're enjoying the 4th floor work.

Love,
Ita

Ita with her brother Bill and sister Irene.

Ita with Bill's children.

Archbishop Oscar Romero, whose plea for help inspired Ita's move to El Salvador in April 1980. Her arrival followed his assassination in March.

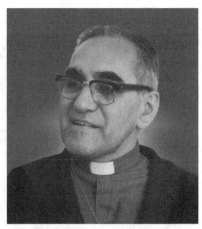

Wreckage of the Jeep, following the accident of August 23, 1980, in which Carla Piette drowned.

Ita with Maryknoll Sister Maura Clarke in El Salvador.

A gathering of Sisters in El Salvador in September 1980, including Maura Clarke (third from left), Ita in front, and Ursuline Sister Dorothy Kazel, far right.

Lay missioner Jean Donovan and Sister Dorothy Kazel from the Cleveland mission team in San Salvador.

Sisters and peasants pray as the bodies of Ita, Maura, Jean, and Dorothy are disinterred from their shallow graves.

Ita Ford's grave in San Salvador.

7.

El Salvador: 1980
Final Witness and Accompaniment of the Poor

Introduction

ta Ford's letters and writings from this period track the last stage of her life, while providing an extraordinary perspective on the unfolding tragedy of El Salvador. Her writings trace a number of stages on her journey, from her return to Chile and almost immediate decision to go to El Salvador; her struggle along with her friend Sister Carla Piette, once in Salvador, to find an opportunity for service; the Refugee Project in Chalatenango that they both embraced; Ita's survival of a Jeep accident, in which Carla Piette died; her recovery from this trauma, and the decision to remain in Chalatenango, working with Sister Maura Clarke, despite increasing death threats; the regional meeting in Nicaragua of the Central American Maryknoll Sisters (PANISA) at Thanksgiving, 1980, just before her return to El Salvador on December 2, the day she and three other North American missioners, Maura Clarke, Sister Dorothy Kazel, and laywoman Jean Donovan, were murdered by Salvadoran security forces.

In this period of terrible oppression, brutality, and denial of human rights, Ita wrestled with the questions of how to serve and actualize the Maryknoll Sisters' commitment to the poor. She struggled with the demands of living a life of accompaniment to the poor of El Salvador, fully aware of the threat this situation posed, a threat that would be dramatized most directly by the assassination of Oscar Romero, the Archbishop of San Salvador, in March 1980.

The earliest letters from January through early March 1980 convey the questions Ita put to herself about whether to stay in Chile or respond to Archbishop Romero's call for Sisters to help in El Salvador. She was deeply impressed by the leadership of Romero and his faith and courage in giving voice to the voiceless in El Salvador. His theme of accompaniment and his recognition that the Kingdom of God is planted in the lives of the poor spoke to her experience in Chile and La Bandera. However, Chile's brutality and repression both prepared and didn't prepare her for the intensity of the violence and the even greater brutality in El Salvador.

The early letters written from Chile illuminate her effort to converse with the Chilean Maryknoll Sisters and discern her future. On her return route to Chile, she had stopped in Nicaragua in November 1979 to visit Sr. Julie Miller, just a few months after the Sandinistas' successful ouster of the Somoza dictatorship. Ita's letters witness to the ongoing conversation within Maryknoll as the Sisters struggled to respond to the extraordinary demands of the war-wracked region, and, specifically, the challenge of Romero's call for more Sisters. Those who had survived the war in Nicaragua needed to repair and rebuild, and they understood their primary commitment as working to help Nicaragua reconstitute itself with the hope of greater social justice.

Friends advised Ita that after her experience of Chile, despite a year of Renewal, she did not need the added challenge of El Salvador. They thought Ita should consider other alternatives for ministry in Chile rather than another nation debilitated by civil unrest. But the Sisters of the Central American Region, meeting in May 1979, had made a plea for Sisters to help in El Salvador. Carla Piete, seeking to rejuvenate her ministry after years in Chile, had already decided to respond to this call. This, combined with Romero's appeal, struck a chord in Ita, and exerted a powerful pull. After many months of discernment, Ita decided in early March that she wanted to serve in El Salvador.

It was at the Panama airport at the end of March, after she had committed to ministry in El Salvador, that she learned of Romero's assassination. Twelve members of Maryknoll attended the funeral and witnessed the extreme violence that erupted after the funeral mass outside the cathedral. They gathered with the Salvadoran clergy after these events to work out a statement to counter the false news reports issued by the Salvadoran government about what had occurred.

Unfortunately, U.S. policy, in the name of national security and the fear of communism, was firmly committed to the Salvadoran government. The specter of the Cuban Revolution of 1959 had established a pattern that shaped American policy in opposition to any form of socialism and in support of right-wing governments, regardless of their violations of human rights and the principles of democracy. In contrast, the Catholic Church, in a departure from history, was undertaking an active social ministry on behalf of the poor, even when this entailed opposition to the ruling elites. In El Salvador, as in other Latin American countries, the church's solidarity with the poor led to persecution. A collision was building between the church on the side of the poor — represented by Archbishop Romero and his allies — and those who called themselves Christian, even as they resorted to torture and brutality to protect their wealth and power.

Among the countries of Central America, El Salvador was in some respects the least developed. Agrarian and feudal in its economic and political make-up, it was a sharp contrast from Chile, with its large middle class. In 1979, 50 percent of the population of El Salvador was illiterate. Three out of four children suffered from malnutrition. Three out of five families had no access to water. One percent of the population owned 40 percent of the arable land, which they used largely to produce export crops, such as coffee. This social structure had endured with little change since 1932, when thirty thousand peasants had been slaughtered after they protested the loss of traditionally communal lands. As the size of plantations grew and grew, it was widely acknowledged that a mere fourteen families controlled most of the country's wealth, while the overwhelming majority eked out an existence. The military bolstered and served this elite, as had, for centuries, the Catholic Church, until the Second Vatican Council and the bishops' meeting of Medellín (1968) and later Puebla (1979) charted a new course.

Archbishop Romero himself had undergone a personal conversion since his selection as archbishop in 1977. He had brought to the fore a new vision of the church identified with the poor and speaking out for justice. He wrote to President Jimmy Carter on February 17, 1980, asking that he send no more arms to El Salvador, but to no avail. Many of his fellow bishops did not agree or support the direction he took. But the Archdiocese of San Salvador was alive with this new vision.

Sr. Carla, who had traveled to El Salvador from Nicaragua the evening of Archbishop Romero's murder, was among those present at his funeral. On April 15, 1980, Ita joined her.

The shift from Chile to El Salvador brought a new experience of culture shock. Ita read voraciously to help her understand this new situation and to acclimatize herself. Together, she and Carla worked to understand how the Salvadoran church could best use their talents. At first they visited with Sr. Maddie Dorsey in Santa Ana, a community very much like La Bandera. Despite these parallels, they found the church in the town of Santa Ana less open than the church in San Salvador. Though they felt at home with Sr. Maddie and her urban ministry, they believed the greater need was with the growing crisis of refugees. Since the declaration of a state of siege in May 1979, an undeclared civil war had been unfolding, particularly in the region of Chalatenango, the northern border between El Salvador and Honduras. It was to deal with the growing number of displaced persons, uprooted by this increasing brutality, that Romeo and his successor had called for volunteers.

In early May, Ita wrote to Sr. Regina McEnvoy of the Maryknoll Sisters Central Governing Board:

> *Since Salvador is a priority, Carla and I thought it might be helpful if we shared the information we are gathering as we go around. We're starting off with monthly plans until we finally get settled somewhere, the first of which I'm enclosing. In speaking with Monseñor Urioste, the Vicar General of the archdiocese, he repeated the same priorities that Monseñor Romero told you last fall. What we hope to arrange within a week or so is a live-in experience with some Sisters who are working in the rural pas-*

> *toral in Chalatenango. Neither Carla or I have* campo *experi-
> ence and given the situation of the country we'd prefer to break
> in with experienced people rather than jumping into something
> alone. (#76)*

Ita and Carla committed themselves to develop a plan to help
refugees in the Chalatenango region, although it meant working in
a rural terrain and amongst a population with which they were unfa-
miliar.

Ita was inspired by a meeting of sixty Salvadoran catechists who
related their stories as catechetical leaders in base Christian communities. She had been disappointed not to have the opportunity to
work with Romero, but she was deeply moved by the testimonies of
these lay leaders. Ita and Carla found it difficult to establish themselves with the *campesinos* however, due to the latter's distrust and
fear of strangers. They pressed on, nonetheless, seeking advice from
religious and clergy, who worked with the poor.

Carla and Ita's presence in El Salvador brought the number of
Maryknoll Sisters in the country to five. To offer mutual support and
to build a sense of community they tried to meet with Sr. Maddie
once a week, and with all the Sisters as a group for twice-a-month
meetings. Gradually through the Salvadoran Religious and the archdiocese they managed to find housing in the city of Chalatenango to
commence their work. The Asuncion Sisters agreed to share their
housing with them as they developed a Refugee Center in Chalatenango.

At first Ita and Sr. Carla looked upon this refugee work as a
short-range project. As the violence and the numbers of displaced
people continued to mount, however, they grew to realize that it
would require a longer commitment. Many *campesinos* were pushed
off their land by the violence. Others were conscripted and forced
into the military. Fear of paramilitary death squads was rampant.
There was no one in the justice system to whom they could appeal
for either justice or protection. Because the civil war remained undeclared the International Red Cross was not able to provide protection
under international law. The area along the Honduran border was

particularly dangerous. Under Romero's leadership, the Church had tried to fill the role of the Red Cross by establishing refugee centers. One of the first was on the grounds of the seminary in San Salvador. But lacking international protection, people in hospitals and refugee centers were constantly vulnerable to seizure at the discretion of the military government.

The first three-month report that Ita sent to Maryknoll chronicled the development of their Refugee Project and their frustrations as they tried to see their way in the dark. At one point they seemed to argue that it was beyond their resources and wondered whether it would be better to serve with Sr. Maddie in Santa Ana. They questioned whether anyone else should be sent to El Salvador, given the difficulties they were encountering. But eventually the tide began to turn and they felt a new level of acceptance and trust. By this time, they had moved into their new quarters in Chalatenango and their funding requests had been granted.

But then on August 23 tragedy struck. Ita Ford's tape recording on September 6 and the letter on September 7 to her mother and the Ford family convey the power and tragedy of events surrounding that day and the following night.

In Chalatenango they were living in a convent next to the church, which was not far from the police and army headquarters. As people disappeared, they would make lists and press for information at the police station. On August 23, Ita was told there were some prisoners needing help to return to their homes. One of them had been on the list she had submitted earlier in the day. In the afternoon she collected a nineteen-year-old man and brought him back to the Refugee Center. There some of the refugee women reacted with alarm, recognizing him as a member of ORDEN, a right-wing paramilitary organization. Given their discomfort over his presence, Ita and Carla thought it best to return him to his village immediately. But it was the rainy season, and the roads were treacherous. They decided, nevertheless, to risk a quick trip in the Jeep with two seminarians accompanying them. Tragically, after delivering the man to his village they were caught in a flash flood that took the Jeep before they could all get free. Sr. Carla died in the accident. Ita survived an extraordinary ordeal. She had floated downriver and managed to struggle to land by grabbing the root of a tree. She was discovered the next day by peasant farmers and brought back to the center in Chalatenango. By then the body of Sr. Carla had been recovered.

Ita describes the tremendous support she received from the Maryknoll Sisters, the Cleveland Mission Team that included Sr. Dorothy Kazel and Jean Donovan, as well as the Salvadoran people, including Religious, peasants, and the refugees with whom they worked. The decision was made to bury Sr. Carla in Chalatenango where she had worked and lived. It was in keeping with a tradition of the Maryknoll Sisters. Ita forced herself to be there for the funeral, but she was physically and emotionally drained by these events, and afterward was hospitalized for several days. Despite invitations from the Chilean Sisters to return to their house, she was determined to remain and carry on the Refugee Center's work and continue on the road of accompaniment. She believed she had survived for a purpose.

After leaving the hospital Ita spent time in San Salvador in the house of the Asuncion Sisters, where she was able to reflect and reintegrate. Sr. Ana Graciela wrote about her experience of Ita during this visit in a letter to Mrs. Ford:

> She spent ten days with us here in the house, praying, thinking, strolling around the corners of the garden where she used to chat with Carla. From this time on she was the one who carried the conversation; she enlivened things with her jokes. She was a different Ita. I think that when she saw how we felt about Carla she put confidence in our friendship. Maura was like a silent presence, who surrounded Ita with tender kindness. The Maryknoll Sisters were concerned about Ita because she was so slight physically, and the death of Carla and her own physical ordeal might have serious consequences.
>
> But the grace of God was working in her and she got back her health and worked tirelessly, helping many persons, saving them. She went to their homes, even far distant ones, and she brought them to refugee camps. So many people remember Ita

and Maura as the angels who saved their lives. When she was here in the city, she never stopped doing projects to get money from outside the country and getting help from beneficent institutions here to bring food and clothing to refugees. One time when I said to her to be more careful on her trips, she laughed at my fears: she felt safe because she was an American citizen . . . When we used to ask her when she was going to take her final vows she answered very seriously that she had made perpetual vows when she took her first vows — otherwise she would never be living in Chalatenango. That was her answer. But we understood the rest of the phrase — living in a dangerous place where she risked her life each day. The Lord took her at her word and she made final vows in heaven. You should all feel very fortunate in the great grace the Lord has given you in such a daughter, in such a sister who was so exceptional, so full of love and concern for everyone, especially her poor. We will all continue to consider her a part of us because she offered her life to work for the most needy people in our country, the campesinos.*

Sr. Maura Clarke moved to Chalatenango from Santa Ana in August. She was an experienced missioner, having spent many years in Nicaragua. She had a gift of warmth and a great capacity to face the brutality around her with grace and compassion. While Ita was exhausted but determined, Sister Maura was fresh to the situation, having just returned from some time in the United States where she had been giving workshops in Global Education. Maura wrote of her experience in Chalatenango in this period:

The other day passing a small lake in the Jeep I saw a buzzard standing on top of a floating body. We did nothing but pray and feel. We don't know how long this can continue but the pain goes on and there are many hungry people hiding and struggling . . . The courage and suffering of these people never ceases to call me. †

---

* Letter of Sr. Ana Graciela, August 1981, Maryknoll Sisters' Archives.

† See Judith Noone, *The Same Fate as the Poor,* p. 129.

Ita and Maura benefited from a retreat in Guatemala in mid-September where Ita met up with Sr. Carolyn Lehman from Chile. She needed contact with people who had known Carla for many years, and she appreciated the support of Sr. Carolyn and the Chilean Sisters. In October Ita wrote to the Sisters in Chile that she needed to stay in El Salvador to absorb what happened, and especially the fact of her own survival that night. As regards El Salvador, she did not see a solution close at hand but rather much suffering yet to come for the people.

In October, two members of Salvadoran Human Rights Commission were murdered and there were increasing threats and intimidation of those working with Ita and Maura in Chalatenango. In early October Ita gave an interview to Peter Helvarg of Pacifica Radio about the situation in northern El Salvador and the increasing displacement of people. He described her as "a thoughtful and attractive woman; small, light-boned and watchful, casually dressed in blue jeans and cotton." Her interview described astutely the situation and the desperation of people subjected to increasing violence and ever more sophisticated weapons, part of the United States' support for the Salvadoran military.

In the interview she recalled the death of Sr. Carla and the circumstances of the accident. Helvarg wrote:

> She showed us the smashed remains of the Land Rover that had been pulled out of the river and towed back to the refugee center. "When I got out of the water after the accident and had to walk for hours through the forest to get to the town, it was so cold. All I could think of was, Why her, God? Why did you call her and not me?" She tried to smile. "I don't know. Maybe I've been chosen for another purpose."

At the end of November, around American Thanksgiving, Ita, Maura, and the other Maryknoll Sisters in Central America attended a regional assembly in Nicaragua. Ita arrived a few days early to rest and visit with friends before the meeting. She evidenced strain, and yet great determination. She responded to the kindness and care of the group, particularly old friends like Sr. Julie Miller. She especially appreciated the care of those who had known Sr. Carla, and who shared her loss.

Although new to the group, Ita offered her views of the need for more Maryknoll Sisters to come to El Salvador in its time of great suffering. But she agreed that those volunteering would have to know that they were risking death.

For the closing liturgy, for one of the readings, Ita translated an excerpt from "The Poverty of the Beatitudes" by Archbishop Romero.

> *Christ invites us not to fear persecution. Believe me brothers and sisters, he who is committed to the poor must suffer the same fate as the poor. And in El Salvador we know what the fate of the poor signifies, to disappear, to be tortured, to be captive, to be found dead.*

The last postcard Ita sent was to her mother on December 1, celebrating the birth of her brother's son: "So here's to three generations of Fords thankful for the gift of life."

The next day she and Maura flew back to San Salvador, where they were met at the airport by their friends from the Cleveland Mission Team, Sister Dorothy Kazel and Jean Donovan. The next time their friends saw them was several days later, when their broken bodies were exhumed from a shallow grave in a remote cow pasture.

Though she never failed to celebrate life, Ita, as much as Maura, Dorothy, and Jean, was keenly aware of the possibility of death on the road she traveled, the road of accompaniment. On December 2, 1980, Ita and her companions followed that path to the end. However, it is not just the memory of her death that lives on, twenty-five years later, but the example of a life given over in dedication to the God of Life and the abiding vision of a more just and compassionate world.

Letters, Writings, and Interviews

65. January 3, 1980

Dear Mom,

After spending Christmas in Coelemu, I came back up to Santiago and have spent the last five days in Bandera visiting the people and catching up on the news of the past year and a half, births, marriages, deaths, changes, etc. It's been delightful going around on New Year's Eve and Day and later listening to the stories. Carla is very much missed, but she left behind a lot of solid work and the groups continue.

While we were in Coelemu, we went out to a rural chapel for an early Christmas Eve liturgy. The manger scene was something very typical, besides the traditional figures, the people bring gifts for the baby and family. So there was a sack of tomatoes, beans, fruit, rice, tea, and detergent (I guess to wash baby diapers) as well as toys for the baby.

This evening we will be getting together for five days of retreat, followed by a one-day meeting. At the end of that, I guess, there will be a 'send-off' party for Carla. She plans to leave on the 14th, via Lima and Panama and arriving in Nicaragua around the 22nd. I'll miss her a lot. We have a lot of colorful history in our past.

I don't think that I'll have a settled place for a while, for a couple of reasons. First, I should get around to the various houses [of the Maryknoll Sisters] and new works and second, there are still some Sisters to arrive. It might even mean opening another house. Meanwhile, I'll probably somewhat base myself in Bandera when I'm in Santiago.

I know all this sounds rushed, which it is. All the time here has been squeezing the days until two or three catching up. So I've done no letter-writing at all. Maybe after Carla gets underway.

Love to all,

Ita

66. *January 11, 1980*

Dear Mom,

As I move around, its nice to know there's one thing certain —
that you faithfully get out the news. Sorry I've been so erratic — it
seems as though I'm spending my time catching up with different
people here — and then another day is gone.

During this week I've been at Los Leones and there are about a
dozen of us here — taking vacation or whatever before returning
north or south. If Carla gets going on Monday it will be by the power
of some faith she has. First I was going to leave her passport at the
travel agent on Tuesday when I discovered it was expired! She just
presumed she could get another one in a day and she did. Now all
that is lacking is a seat on the plane. She's on the waiting list. I
myself would like things a little more sure!

There have been some lovely testimonies to Carla for her 15
years in Chile — especially from one of our friends, Eduardo Alevar,
a Franciscan priest with whom we worked in Bandera. He came this
morning and gave a beautiful homily on how Carla had touched his
life and priesthood . . . .

I finally checked in with the regional board yesterday. Pretty
much as I expected, they suggested that I take these two months to
visit and catch up on what's been happening, a sort of re-entry program. After that we'll get more specific about where I'll be hanging
my hat.

We get major international news — so we're aware and concerned about what's happening. It seems very sticky.

I guess before you all got together on the 25th the younger
Fords all duly reported to their far-flung aunt. Whenever the letters
arrive together, I get the image of parental persuasion in the background!

As you get the snow, we get the heat — but good. It's not so bad
here with all the trees, but one roasts in the *poblacion* from noon 'til
four.

I have to go do some errands for the traveler — so I'll stop.
Hopefully the next two weeks I'll get some letters written to Rene

and some friends at Maryknoll. I've been getting around to it since I came back but maybe I'll be stationary for a few days and will get down to it. Take care.

Love to all,
Ita

67. *Sometime in late January 1980*

Dear Mom,

As soon as I got back from vacation, Carolyn put me to work on helping doing the annual report for NY. The last few days' meals have been the first I've earned since I've been back in Chile . . .

I've heard from Carla along the way and she seemed very unconcerned that most of the connections didn't work out. So she was a day or so behind her original plan — and was waiting for a visa for Nicaragua and Panama. I presume she's been in Nicaragua for a week or so by now, but I haven't heard yet . . .

I'm not really sure of what I'll be doing for the next couple of weeks. At first I was going to go north and visit one of the new works but the sister there says it's not a good time to come. I may begin to nose around in Santiago to look at different areas because it's looking more and more like we'll probably be opening another house in a *poblacion* — because after 7 years of having no new people, this year Chile got 4 and may get another. I think some of the region is in a state of shock.

Well, I've watched Carolyn wash everything she can get her hands on — just to express relief from getting the paper work out of the way. The afternoon is hot enough to dry most things in less than an hour. In fact, for a while I had a lovely awning of sheets — but now she's on towels. So time to stop. Take care.

Love to all.
Ita

68. *February 10, 1980*

Dear Mom,

This is a non-pass-around note to you. I want to share something that came up on retreat, which was based on the beatitudes. In explaining what was behind "blessed are they that mourn," the director brought out the idea that the mourning that Christ did was for others — for situations that weren't whole or healthy or right, like when he cried over Jerusalem.

When I went out for a walk I was asking myself, What do I mourn over? The answer right away was Rene's situation and everyone involved in it. It's not a situation I can do anything about, except hold them all up to the Lord, but it's also one I suffer along with. It seems to me a no-win one, in the sense that someone or more persons will be hurt, if they aren't already. In some ways it was hard to leave Rene in that situation, but my staying wouldn't have affected it much.

The other thing I wanted to share has been in the air since last September and is still there, but it should be taking shape in a month or so. Around the time of the operation, I began to get interested in El Salvador. I talked to one of the board members a couple of times, but it still wasn't clear how the region was going to organize itself. Since then, after meetings in different countries, its now been decided that Nicaragua and Salvador — for different reasons — are both congregational priorities for Latin America. As a person in between jobs at this point, I've had to look at that priority and say I'm open to consider it. Right now, there are meetings going on in Salvador to establish priorities and job descriptions. In a couple of weeks, I should have that news, and then I'd have to see if I fit into what they want or need. Also they want me to keep looking in Chile. So there will be a few things to be juggling at the same time. In some ways, there's no difference between the needs of Chile and Salvador. There's plenty of work to be done in both. What even makes Salvador a question is the Congregation seeing that it's very important at this time to support Archbishop Romero and a few others who are very important as church leaders.

So pray with me that I make the right decision when the time comes. I'll let you know as it develops. Take care,

Love,
Ita

69. *To Sister Rachel Lauze, MM, February 10, 1980*

Dear Rachel,

Thanks for your letter and the news of the comings and goings of many. After you leave a place, so many people come to mind — and you wonder how they are.

I'm really glad the year at Marymount is turning out so well and not being much of a burden. I hope you'll have the time to perfect your cartoon potential, even though the professor doesn't hold it in high esteem. I see it as a great expression of your sense of humor.

Did you ever get in touch with Beverly Malone at Sadlier? I'm sure she'd help as much as she could.

Coming back to Chile in summertime really allows for a pleasant re-entry. Most people are slowed down and relaxed so the catching up is fun. I've crossed paths with Patrice a couple of times. This month she's up in the north getting a taste of desert life. She's delighted that Pam's coming, so am I — for Patrice and the rest of us. Mary Ann Flanagan's arrival is pushed back now, because of her father's illness. That was really so sad and must be terribly hard on the family.

I don't have my hat hung in any definite place. I'm in the strange position of searching within Chile while waiting for information to discern about El Salvador — that sounds bizarre, but that's where I am, especially since Salvador, along with Nicaragua, are seen as priorities by all the Latin American regions. I hope you'll pray with me that I'll know which road to take.

In the meantime, just for novelty I'm back to weights and the lethal weapon. It started to act a little funny and the doc here thinks it's a stretched ligament. Oh well, an unstable knee isn't as bad as instability from the neck up!

Take care and keep in touch.

Love,
Ita

70. *To Sister Regina McEvoy, MM, February 11, 1980*

Dear Regina,

Greetings from the southernmost precincts!

I hope all is well with you. Since we talked twice last fall about the possibilities of El Salvador, I'd like to share with you where I am on that. On the way back to Chile, I spent 2 weeks in Nicaragua and had the chance to understand what went on in the PANISA assembly [regional assembly of the Maryknoll Sisters in Panama, Nicaragua, and El Salvador] and to ask a lot of questions. I am also very challenged by the South American world section: taking on — at least in spirit — the needs of Nicaragua and Salvador.

From what I understand, there should be some solid information on needs and priorities in Salvador coming in a week or so.

I would ask that you pray with me as I discern if I'm to respond to that need or if I should remain in Chile. I appreciate your support very much.

I have also shared my searchings with the sisters in Chile and they have been very supportive.

As it gets clear which road is the one to follow, I'll surely let you know. Should you have any input now, I'd be glad to have it.

Many thanks, for now,

Love,
Ita Ford

71. *To Jean Reardon Bauman, February 12, 1980*

Dear Jean,

Belated birthday wishes as you celebrate the gift of life and all that it holds out to you!

Re-entry into Chile during summertime is slow and lazy. There are various possibilities in the air as several houses have opened, since I've left, and there may be a need for another in Santiago. After seven years with no assignees, this year Chile got four — so we'll be juggling for a while until they all get settled.

Hope you and John are happy.

Take care, much love,

Ita

72. *March 2, 1980*

Dear Mom,

The last week or two — on my part — have been mostly spent letting the El Salvador possibility roll around inside me. Then I went to the new House of Prayer — changed from El Quisco to the edge of Santiago. I went through the old Ignatian process of the pros and cons, besides reading my guts. What I came to and feel good with is a decision to go. I've been talking off and on with the board here and Friday we'll get together again. I think within a week or two it should be finalized. As a guess, I'd say maybe I'd be going in mid-April.

I realize this isn't the greatest news I've given you, and in fact, one of the cons was that the family wouldn't be overjoyed, but I think it's a good decision. There are more reasons for going than not. Besides, since it first came up last August, I've been toying with the idea, but couldn't do anything about it except discern it with some people because the region wasn't organized on how they were going to face personnel problems because most had just gone through the Nicaraguan War. In the last two months they've been working on it and also getting responses from other Latin American countries.

Though as I say you may not be delighted, I know you'll accept that I've given it a lot of thought and have looked at it from a lot of angles — as well as having been challenged and supported here.

I'll also be a continent nearer!

I'll be waiting to hear from you.

Love to all,

Ita

73. *April 2, 1980*

Dear Mom,

I don't know how to begin this letter; how to react to the last week and a half. Archbishop [Romero's] death started a continental examination of conscience about how each local church was or wasn't being faithful to the gospel. The Masses, in Chile, at least, were moving testimonies.

Then Monday morning as I was walking through the Panama airport, the radios in the duty-free shops were full of flashes from Salvador. Jenny McDonald, who met me at the airport, is the administrator of the archdiocese here. We went straight to the bishop's house. There we talked with a bishop from Ecuador who had also been at the funeral. Then, Julie Miller called to say that all who had gone from Maryknoll were all right, and that some were in a meeting with the bishops after the Mass when they drew up their statement contradicting the official version of the events.

For myself, I have all sorts of reactions — from feeling robbed of not having had the opportunity to know Mons. Romero (we're to work in his diocese), to horror at the paranoia and fear of the right and their brutality, to wonder at the gospel message and the impact for acceptance or rejection that it has on people; to feeling with the poor of Salvador and their loss of someone whom they knew cared for them.

But we believe that his death will bear fruit. It's part of the Christian mystery we celebrate this week; in that same Christian tradition we'll go to Salvador.

Tomorrow I take off for Nicaragua. The plan is for all of us from Nicaragua and Salvador to be together for meetings during Easter week. That's all I know right now, but I'll let you know as it develops for there.

Christ's crucifixion is a continuing reality and so is the power of resurrection. May the resurrected Jesus empower us all to be loving and faithful. Happy Easter,

Love to all,
Ita

74. To Sisters Connie Pospisil and Carolyn Lehmann, MM, April 2, 1980

Dear Connie and Carolyn:

The enclosed clipping will probably just be the beginning of news and reflections that will filter down. Besides the sisters from Nicaragua and Salvador, it seems that Regina and Jo Kollmer were at the funeral. Some (including Regina) were at the several hours-long meetings that followed to draw up this statement.*

Julie called Monday afternoon to say that they were alright, but that they will probably limit themselves to simple things for awhile. The experience must have been something else, but she didn't want to talk about it on the phone.

The poor, poor of Salvador! God help them. God help us too.

The other thing to say is that to get through *aduana*/customs I had to go through a bod[y] search. I guess there was a tip-off about drugs coming in (and they did a lot) and I guess they thought I was a carrier. So I had to wait until everyone was cleared, then go into a room and take off my shirt and pants. I asked what the problem was and the woman said, "There isn't any." So even though the plane arrived on time, Jenny McDonald had to wait almost an hour for me outside — so I'm still not a predictable arriver!

Tomorrow I'm off to Nicaragua. God only knows if the ladies [Maryknoll Sisters] from Salvador will come to the meeting.

Remember us sinners.

Much love,
Ita

75. To Mike and Kathy Monahan Gregg, April 13, 1980

Dear Kathy and Mike,

Greetings from Sandino territory — *patria libre,* as they call it

---

* The reference is to a statement by a number of Religious leaders following the funeral of Archbishop Romero, which was interrupted by sniper fire from security forces.

now.* I arrived on Holy Thursday and for the past week have been at a workshop, which actually did take place although half the group was still working out their feelings of the past two weeks in El Salvador. (10 Maryknoll ladies, who were there, had gone to the archbishop's funeral.) I came to the workshop, because as of Tuesday evening my address is El Salvador.

My timing couldn't be worse, I know, but this is the culmination of a process that started last August when the need was seen to reenforce the group there. Actually I am still reeling from Romero's death because we were prepared to work with him in some way. I guess I feel that part of my future was robbed. Then it wasn't until I got off the plane in Panama early Monday morning that I heard about the funeral scene. (Since then I've heard much more because of participants who were at the meeting. Some were outside, others inside and their version is markedly different from the government's statement.) So my free-floating anxiety has been intense.

I'll be one of a sum of 5 Maryknoll sisters in the country now, though we're hoping for one or two more in June. The original plan to start something new in the archdiocese is on hold for a while as we begin to learn our way and also give the church people the time to recover and pick up the pieces. Another friend from Chile, Carla and myself will join one loner in an area called *Santa Ana*, a sister from Panama is joining the other loner in a port city called *La Libertad*. (With two people in the country — in different cities — you could appreciate the calls for warm bodies!) Since the country is quite small the distance between us is only a couple of hours by bus. So we'll be able to get together fairly regularly.

I appreciate that many people will be concerned about us. We're also concerned for each other and will be doing our best to support and care for each other.

Keep in touch, Much Love,
Ita

---

* Augusto Cesar Sandino—the Nicaraguan nationalist who inspired the revolutionary Frente Sandinista. *Patria libre*—free homeland, the Sandinista motto for post-Somoza Nicaragua.

76. To Sister Peg Merker, MM, April 14, 1980

Dear Peg,

Last November you mentioned that you might like to hear from me in Nicaragua. And so now you are, but not exactly in the way you meant! I'm here *de paso* [in passing] on my way to El Salvador tomorrow and Julie Miller is pressing all warm bodies to help clean up loose ends of regional communities.

Right now there seem to be three types of materials we are wading through.

1) A description-reflection of the experiences in El Salvador from the time of Archbishop Romero's murder through the funeral.

2. A reflection by the sisters of Nicaragua on their participation in the national revolutionary process.

3) Assorted descriptions by Sisters in Nicaragua and Salvador of their present work or experiences.

The last is what I'm enclosing for you, because we feel it may serve more for background; the first two I think will be circulated congregationally-wide and, of course, you'll be getting copies, too.

I've been asked to remind you of a dilemma between communications and the sisters in countries like El Salvador. We will try, as feasible, to get information and reflections up to you to circulate or use as you think fit, but for prudence or safety reasons — there are many times when the Sisters do not want to be named directly or have information attributed to them personally.

Now that I've done my "job," a few personal lines. My straddling of Chile and El Salvador got resolved by the PANISA Assembly and other sisters volunteering to go to El Salvador. The archbishop's murder was quite a blow — for me in part a robbery of some of my future (as I had thought) since we were to have worked with him. So tomorrow we set off to join a suffering people who have, on top of that, lost a friend, advocate, and pastor. It's a journey in faith and trust in the Lord's presence, guidance, and strength. Pray for us.

Love,

Ita

77. *To Sister Connie Pospisil, MM, April 14, 1980*

Dear Connie,

On my plane ride from Chile to Panama, I realized we never returned to the conversation we shared that night in your bedroom. In the "nutsyness" and flurry of the past week, we never got back to it, but I'll be remembering you as you work out what's right and good for you.

It's been a week of free-floating anxiety here, but I think I'm pretty grounded now and with fear and faith, I get on the bus tomorrow for Salvador.

For right now, Carla and I will be making our base with Madeline Dorsey as the archdiocese recovers from the past few weeks and we begin to look around.

At a meeting here on Saturday, Peg Healy came to her decision to work for Salvador in Washington, DC which many people recommended. I'm going to miss her not being with us. So for now, we're five. Let's pray for each other.

Love,
Ita

78. *April 21, 1980*

Dear Mom,

Carla and I are making our base in Santa Ana, the second largest city of Salvador (an hour's bus ride from the capital). We're living with Madeline Dorsey, who, in a lot of ways, reminds me of Margaret Casey — manner, enthusiasm etc. The area is called *colonia Lamatapec. Colonia* is the equivalent word for *poblacion.* This one started about three or four years ago when, through a parish co-op, money was gotten together to buy the land from coffee growers (the biggest industry here) and about 1200 families came. They are slowly constructing brick houses and all around the shells of the houses are piles of brick for weekend work The lots seem smaller than Bandera's and the houses are attached. To our eyes, bricks look expensive, but here there's not much wood, so the bricks are cheaper. The project is designated as "minimum housing."

Madeline has a lot of activities centering around the chapel here and is in the process of phasing over, hopefully, to a group of Salvadoran Sisters, by year's end, because the region has named the archdiocese a priority and because the sister who was with her last year stayed in the States to care for her sick parents.

So for the time being, as we look around and get a sense of the country and church we're also accompanying Madeline.

We arrived last Tuesday night. Why it takes 13 hours from Managua to San Salvador is that at each set of borders (Nicaragua-Honduras; Honduras-Salvador) the delay for customs and revising buses and luggage is about three hours. So the trip itself is more like 6 hours. Due to the situations in each country, the searching is extensive. I even had to hand over some cassettes to have them checked for content!

Wednesday we went to an all day meeting of Sisters who are involved in pastoral work in the Archdiocese (which includes 4 departments of the country — city and rural) and Thursday morning there was a meeting of priests and sisters where we made appointments for the week to talk to vicars and begin to present ourselves. Then we had to scurry to immigration to ask for more time in the country. (At the border they gave me five days.) They gave us 30 more and now we have to start collecting papers to start the process to stay.

For the last few days, we've been working on trying to plan a month at a time (which is tricky since you really don't know who you are going to meet or what they'll suggest). We're trying to arrange live-in experiences for a couple of weeks with other communities who do rural work, because neither of us have that experience and we have no idea if we'd like it or go crazy or what. Also it will be a time of getting a feel for the country and people and also catching on to their words, so many of which are different from those used in Chile.

The newspapers are rather poor here, especially for international news. The only thing that seems to be happening is the Cubans arriving in Costa Rica. That's good for four to six pages. As if you'd miss the point! Maddie gets some magazines in and so for now, we won't start duplicating subscriptions. We'll wait until we get started somewhere.

Though I haven't been there yet, the other house of the Sisters (2) is about 1 1/4 hours away. Wednesday we're all getting together in San Salvador and will return here for a meeting on Thursday. The distances aren't that great. We can go from here to the capital in the same time as it took from the center of Santiago to La Bandera. The difference here is you're traveling on a good highway, there through city streets.

So the first week was fairly full, but calm. The heat is something else. I guess you gradually get used to it. People keep saying this is the "cold" season, as the sweat rolls out of all the pores (mine). I guess it's relative — as so many things are.

As our clothes blot our bodies, our minds are trying to absorb everything coming at us from all angles. Such are the beginnings of life in El Salvador. More to come. Hope you are well. Take care,

Much love to all,

Ita

79. *To Sisters Carolyn Lehmann, MM, and Margaret (Peg) Moran, MM, April 22, 1980*

Carolyn and Peg, friends and support across the miles,

We're sitting in a coffee shop writing letters furiously, asking for birth certificates, antecedents, etc. We're a block away from the cathedral where we've stopped and sat alongside the archbishop's crypt for quite awhile. The simple people keep coming to visit him. Some crying, some just taking 5, 15 minutes to pray, visit, tell him their story. It's a very touching experience.

Salvador, being tiny, the distances aren't so great, so commuting between Sta. Ana and the capitol is equivalent to the ride from La Bandera to the center of Santiago.

So taking the bus 2 or 3 times a week for meetings or appointments is no big deal.

Tomorrow we're going to mark my rolling into 40 with the entire area (5 of us in Salvador and Peg Dillon who's coming from Nicaragua for an area meeting on Thursday). The area has grown from 2 to 5 in the last three weeks, so I guess we have to set up a minimum of organization (ha!). Mostly I think we have to figure out how to look for work in the archdiocese and reconcile that with someone alone at this time. Because Peggy Healy decided to return to Washington, the division of warm bodies is tricky for a while. So there are no absolutes. We'll keep you posted as we move about. We know you're hanging in with us and we appreciate it a lot. *Saludos* to the *Santiaguenas.**

Much love,
Ita

80. April 28, 1980

Dear Mom,

Best wishes on the birthday of your #1 son.

The last letter I wrote was in a coffee shop across from San Salvador's main Post Office, asking for birth certificates. Do not send them yet. Today I was told that all documents that come from another country have to be declared valid by the Salvadoran Consul in that country ("authenticated"). So since three of us have to have this done (and I also will have a statement from the Ossining police) and NY, for sure, has a Consul, you will be receiving Carla's and Theresa Alexander's birth certificates. Then, maybe Bill can go, or send one of his runners, to the Consulate to get their seal or ribbon or whatever. Then, they can be sent down. (I asked for two copies of my birth certificate — but only one has to go through this process.) Lest you think that's the end of the Byzantine paper work, once they arrive here, they have to be validated by the foreign ministry, then officially translated, and then turned in to immigration. In the

---

* Hello to her friends in Santiago, Chile.

interim, as of today, I can stay in the country three months. I was given five days on entering so we had to scurry for letters from the Archdiocese and doctors' certificates, etc., so as not to be on the Guatemala border within a week. (It seems that persons arriving by plane get thirty days without much trouble; coming in by bus must be less acceptable.)

This past weekend Carla and I went to a mini-workshop given for rural leaders of liturgy (called delegates or celebrators of the Word) and catechists. There were sixty men in all — farmers, mostly — with an extraordinary faith and simplicity. It was awe-inspiring to listen to them talk of their experiences. They come from one of the parts of the archdiocese where we may be working. What we hope to set up within a week or so is a live-in experience with some Sisters who do rural pastoral work.

From the workshop, I came to the house in La Libertad. There were five letters waiting, including the swinging groups' birthday greetings. By the time we finally get settled, we'll have had a slew of addresses all over the country. Maybe we should just keep the Sta. Ana address until there's a definite one. Even if we're four or five hours away, someone will probably go see Maddie regularly.

Thanks for the birthday gift. As yet, I don't know how it works. We officially belong to the Chilean region, so every gift and sponsor is sent there. In the next couple of weeks we'll have to write and figure out the internal business.

I'll eventually get hold of a good map and mark it up for you, so you can visualize our wanderings. In the meantime, take care.

Love to all,
Ita

81. To Sister Regina McEvoy, MM, May 3, 1980

Dear Regina,

Greetings from the most recent arrival in El Salvador. In His own time the Lord got me here, although since His ways aren't ours, the journey wasn't all that clear at times.

When the news of Monseñor Romero's murder hit Chile, one of my first feelings was that of being robbed of the opportunity of having known him, of having had the opportunity of working with him. I guess I felt that part of my future had been robbed with those bullets. However, once getting here and having the chance to meet and talk with a number of people, I feel differently. It's a privilege to come to a Church of martyrs and people with a strong committed faith. Though I'm here only two and a half weeks, I have a strong conviction that I'm where I should be, though the particulars of the future are not very clear yet. I thank you again for your encouragement and prayers that helped make my coming here a reality.

Since Salvador is a priority, Carla and I thought it might be helpful if we shared the information we are gathering as we go around. We're starting off with monthly plans until we finally get settled somewhere, the first of which I'm enclosing. In speaking with Monseñor Urioste, the Vicar General of the archdiocese, he repeated the same priorities that Monseñor Romero told you last fall. What we hope to arrange within a week or so is a live-in experience with some Sisters who are working in the rural pastoral in Chalatenango. Neither Carla nor I have *campo* experience and given the situation of the country we'd prefer to break in with experienced people rather than jumping into something alone.

Also for now, we're making our base with Maddie Dorsey who has been alone. As an area we're going to have to make some arrangements for supporting and accompanying each other. However, this diocese doesn't offer leadership, testimony or possibility of teamwork, which the archdiocese does, so looking ahead, we'll be eventually working in the archdiocese.

I hope your visit to Guatemala and Mexico was enjoyable and fruitful.

Love,
Ita

82. To Jean Reardon Bauman and John Bauman, May 4, 1980

Dear Jean and John,

Greetings from El Salvador! (Did I mention to you the possibility of my coming here?) It's been a journey that began in theory last October, and got concretized in February and decided in March. What basically got me here was to re-enforce the community (in Jan. there were two, now we're five) and work in Archbishop Romero's diocese. I'll still be doing the latter, but not in the same way as projected from Chile.

The first impressions here are within the framework of an incredible climate of violence. According to the new bishop, from January 1 to April 15, there have been 1,102 assassinations in the country. It boggles the mind but it's the reality here.

I've been very impressed with the pastoral agents I've met. Last weekend I attended a course for rural liturgy leaders ("celebrants of the Word"). There were 60 men participating, the majority farmers. Their testimonies were right out of the Acts of the Apostles. It's awe-inspiring and humbling to come into a Church like this.

Love to you both,
Ita

83. April 15-May 15, 1980, Santa Ana, El Salvador

THE ONE MONTH PLAN AND EVALUATION

Objective I: *To orientate ourselves to the country and church of El Salvador.*

This is an on-going process, which we hope to deepen in the months ahead. This evaluation will focus on how we did or did not fulfill the targets we set to help accomplish our first month's goals.

Goal I: *To be active members of the Maryknoll Sisters' El Salvador area.*

Target 1: *Share community with Maddie.*
For the first month our home base has been in Colonia Lamatepec, Sta Ana with Maddie. One or both of us were here for 20 of
the 30 days. The quality of our being together has been rich and
mutually supportive.

Target 2: *Share our financial situation with the area.*
At the April 24 area meeting, we reported to the area the amount
of money we had. In discussion, it was decided that we would
use that for our moving around and investigation expenses.
When we get to the point of a definite work possibility, we will
submit a request for funding from the Center. In the interim,
Maddie offers us her hospitality.

Target 3: *Spend time with Joan and Terry as their/our schedule
allows.*
On April 24 we decided that the 5 of us in the El Salvador area
would get together twice monthly in addition to other meetings,
spontaneous visits, etc. We have been faithful to this and see
these days as important in forming relationships of support and
friendship.

Target 4: *Come to know the people of Colonia Lamatepec and the
city, Sta Ana.*
While in Sta Ana, we have joined in the liturgies and some of
the other activities that center around the chapel. Carla has
made the weekly sick-call rounds three times; both of us have
gone to wakes of family members of the community here. We
have made the normal contacts that come from living with a sister in pastoral work. Carla has followed up on the contacts more
than Ita has.

The *colonia* is on the outskirts of the city of Sta Ana, but dis-
tance-wise, it is quite close. We are both getting a feel for the city
by doing the usual errands of post office, food shopping and

going to the Asuncion Sisters' school for a little "space" and reflection.

Goal II: *To contact members of the archdiocese of San Salvador.*

Target 1: *Attend meetings of clergy and religious in pastoral work.*
We attended the meetings that have been held, and appreciate the opportunity they provide to meet and come to know the personnel of the archdiocese.

Target 2: *Visit and share with sisters in pastoral work.*
Except for what will be mentioned in Obj. II, Goal II, we, as yet, have not been visiting on any extensive scale. However, the religious in pastoral work use the afternoon & evening between the clergy and religious meetings for sharing and input. We joined them on May 6.

Target 3: *Search out persons who can orient us to the political-socio-economic situation of the country.*
This target is also an on-going process. Through meetings, talks and interviews we are getting input and will continue to look for it. Concretely, at both meetings of religious and one of the clergy, there have been speakers on the political and economic situation of the country. Also we have met individually with some of the resource people of the archdiocese.

OBJECTIVE II: *To investigate job possibilities in the archdiocese that promote the decisions of Puebla and our G.A. documents.*

Goal I: *Gather data on pastoral needs, priorities and religious personnel in the Archdiocese.*

Target 1: *Meet with vicars and bishop.*
April 22 we met with Mons. Urioste, Vicar-General of the archdiocese to talk about priorities and pastoral needs. The priorities continue to be those that were mentioned by Mons. Romero, the

vicariates of Chalatenango, Cuscatlan and Soyopango (con-cretely, Ilopango, an industrialized sector). Cuscatlan, although a priority, is not feasible due to the lack of cooperation by the priests there. They are not open to sisters there. We also dis-cussed the archdiocesan pastoral line, the political situation of the different priorities, the level of repression, etc., the possibil-ity of a salary, and other matters.

April 22 we also met with Fr. Fabian Amaya, Episcopal vicar of Chalatenango and pastor of Ilopango. He gave us an overview of both priorities, what is happening church-wise now, and the on-going needs of the areas. He invited us to a workshop at which we could meet people from both areas of need. In addition to other conversations with Fr. Amaya during the weekend of April 25-27, we met again with him on May 8 to discuss our process of investigation.

May 2 we met again with the vicar of La Libertad, Fr. Benito Tobar to discuss a possibility in his area.

May 6 we spoke with Mons. Rivera Damas, Apostolic Administrator of the archdiocese. He reiterated that Chalate-nango was the priority.

Target 2: *Read archdiocesan communiqués, documents and pastoral letters of Mons. Romero.*
We are in the process of doing this.

Goal II: *Arrange dates for a live-in experience with sisters in pastoral work in* campo *and city.*

Target 1: *Visit areas of Soyapongo, Chalatenango and Cuscatlan Soyapongo.*
We had contact with members of the Christian community of Ilopongo the weekend of April 25-27. Chalatenango May 7-11 we stayed with the Sisters of the Asuncion and experienced some of their work. We also visited the Belenitas (Sisters of Bethlehem) in El Paraiso, Chalatenango. We did not go to Cuscatlan, due to the input of Mons. Urioste.

Although our goal was to arrange a live-in experience with other sisters as a time of orientation and apprenticeship since neither of us has rural experience, we have come to realize that this goal is unrealistic at this historical moment. Due to the sensitivity and confidentiality of many of the sisters' contacts with the people, new and unknown persons with them can hinder their effectiveness. We are now in the process of investigating another way to proceed so that we will not be on our own nor without guidance and possibilities for reflection during this transitional time.

2 week plan: May 15-June 1, 1980

OBJECTIVE I: *To reach a decision regarding a definite place to work and live within the priority zone of the Archdiocese — Chalatenango*

Goal I: *To obtain data and keep informed on changing events in the Department of Chalatenango.*

Target   1: To visit the area on May 18-20.
          2: Present pros and cons to the religious meeting on May 19 of the Chalatenango area for critique and input.
          3: Converse with the Vicar on the information gathered.
          4: Share the finds with the Sisters of the Maryknoll area on May 27 and if possible visit area with them.
          5: Commit ourselves to a certain place by June 1.
          6: Arrange for on-going evaluation with the Vicar after commitment is made known.

OBJECTIVE II: *To continue to orientate ourselves to the country and Church of El Salvador.*

Goal I: *Visit contacts made during the first month for updating on national situation.*

Target 1: Visit priests who are informed.

2: Converse with the people as much as possible.

3: Attend the Church meetings and Confers, May 31.

84. To Sister Rachel Lauze, MM, May 17, 1980

Dear Rachel,

I love the latest edition — or maybe new edition — of applied Scripture. Thanks so much, and for the rooting too. I think we may be counting on that very much during the summer.

Peg saw me in and also marked the first month anniversary with a two-day visit in between other work north and south of here. She's quite a lady — doing her job, but wishing she were here.

The first month has really flown, as we're trying to get a feel for the country and church as well as looking for a place to hang our hats. Historically this is not the ideal time to arrive on the scene — but the Lord got us here for some reason.

My friend and fellow pilgrim from Chile, Carla Piette, does her mental health by copying some of the stylized folk art that comes from a town called La Palma. This card is one of last night's clear-the-brain time. It also carries warmest wishes as you celebrate the gift of life and the possibilities for love and caring that it holds out to you. Happy Birthday!

I must say that my life has been quite different in between your last celebration and this one. There was no way of even imagining as we were cracking lobster shells last year that I'd be sending you wishes from El Salvador this year.

There's much I'd like to share. It's probably not realistic to think that things will calm down, but within the next few weeks, we should have a definite job and maybe we'll stop and get down some reflections of what this time has included and meant.

Please give my love to Lil (?) and Julie.

Much love to you, too.

Ita

85. *May 18, 1980*

Dear Mom,

We have one month under our belt, but with the pace of moving around visiting and trying to investigate job possibilities, it seems longer. Up to now, there's almost been no time to stop and think what it all means. However, we're getting to be experts on what would be equivalent of interstate or inter-provincial buses, as we trot off to our different appointments.

Last week we were in the department of Chalatenango, which is a priority of the archdiocese, looking at different possibilities. It's still a little difficult for me to get a framework around the rural situation, as you have several small towns and then scattered groupings of houses that make up a parish, as opposed to the concentration of people in a *poblacion*.

We've been offered several options, but some don't seem to be appropriate for these times, either too isolated, too conflictive or other things. What I think we're coming to is to be based in the city of Chalatenango, where there's another group of Sisters, seminarians and three priests and work out from there. As all now seem to do.

As a "city" Chalatenango might be a little larger than Licanten, the major market where rural people come and go all week to buy and sell and mill around. It's 1 3/4 hours from San Salvador and buses are fairly frequent. Tomorrow we'll be meeting with the Vicar and five other groups — so about thirteen, I guess — to give our impressions and get their input. We're hoping to have something definite by June 1.

Ron Potter is also in the Chalatenango area — but so far we haven't seen each other, except at clergy meetings and then only to say hello. (I don't know anything about a Center House, because as far as I know there are only four Maryknoll men here, two in Chalatenango and two further east. Maybe they have something to fit into when they come to the city . . . but I don't think so/or at least so far. I haven't heard anyone speak of a bustling Center.)

Peggy popped in this week for two days, in between other work.

It was great to see her and she'll probably be calling to say hello. (As of last weekend, Julie and two others were still in Cuba. They should be back soon though, because she's due for furlough the beginning of next month.)

Yesterday's mail brought two Christmas cards, one from Eleanor Sweeney. They both were sent to Maryknoll, forwarded to Chile, but because of postage, went by boat, then to Nicaragua and on to here. Maybe I'll get birthday cards in August! It's all so relative!

I'm going to give you a taste of Latin *tramites* (red tape). First, the birth certificates have to be brought to the City Clerk's Office where they "authenticate" the signature of the city registrar, that is, they attach another piece of paper (or whatever form they use with a city seal, saying — this is the true signature of Irving Mellon). That's for NY. I hope Carla's will be approved, as is with its lovely gold seal. Then, when you have that (mine) plus Carla's and Theresa Alexander's birth certificate and my police record from Ossining, the whole shooting match gets presented to the Salvadoran Consulate in NYC, which adds another paper and seal, saying — yes, these are true and authentic documents of the states involved.

We're hoping that's all for your end. A few years ago the certificates went from country to state to Department of State in Washington, DC. So everyone could certify the authenticity. Once here there're about four other steps, so that, finally, your birth is signed, sealed and delivered.

Someone who has been through the process — for which you're allowed three months — is convinced that the whole point is to raise some revenue, because you're fined if the papers aren't presented on a fixed date and, of course, no one has them ready because at the beginning they never tell you all the steps you have to take. We used to lose our minds in Chile, but here I think we've met up with the epitome of making it complicated. So I won't be surprised if, after you've done the errands and sent these back, they come back for another seal or stamp.

I was paid $100 for the article in the Maryknoll magazine. How about that! I'm told that we're heading into winter. That means it often rains all night and sometimes there's a short cloud burst during the day. However, the only time I saw a thermometer, it said 96 degrees, so much for winter.

Most churches have a bat ballet during Mass. I'm slowly coming to terms with tropical nature. (Roll of eyes, roll of drum, scene fades). Take Care.

Love to all,
Ita

86. To Rene Ford Sullivan, May 29, 1980

Dear Rene,

I'm taking a day off today to be alone, to think. I'm super saturated with horror stories and daily body count to the point that I thought I'd hit the next person who told me that someone else was killed. I'm not sure how you get "acclimated" to a country that has an undeclared civil war going. But sometimes you have to have a break.

Carla and I now have a job. We're the full time workers of the emergency committee in the Vicariate of Chalatenango. What that means is that the Church of San Salvador is facing reality and getting ready to help with food, medicines, and refugee centers. Actually, there are a couple of refugee centers already in operation, as people have had to leave their homes because of threats, close by steady skirmishes between the army and the popular organizations that want to form a new government, as well as family members having been killed and a lot of fear. I don't think we could have dreamed this job before we came. But we came to help and this is what we're being asked to do.

There're a lot of bizarre things that go on in this country including the help from Uncle Sam. It's pathetic that there're millions for army equipment, but nothing for humanitarian help until war is declared. Groups like the International Red Cross cannot or do not respond until the point is catastrophic. Carla keeps asking how many dead make a war? What's the magic number? However, I guess, the groups don't feel they're ready yet. They have to put a government together and gain international solidarity and some sort of recognition. Meanwhile, there're a lot of displaced people and disrupted lives and that's what we're focusing on.

As of now, we still don't have a place to live in Chalatenango. We've been promised two rooms in an old rambling rectory, which will soon be unoccupied. Until then we spend a couple of days a week with some Sisters who have been quite good about our descending on them at all hours unannounced and giving over half their house. To explain that — most houses are constructed so that there's accommodation for out-of-doors living. So they have two rooms with doors, then a covered porch or gallery that is the kitchen, dining area, laundry etc. All this is behind the façade on to the street that is also another room like an office. (That's probably as clear as mud.) Anyway, the three of them sleep in one room; and we have the use of the other.

The city has electricity and, a slight wrinkle, water four hours a day (5:30 a.m.–9:30 a.m.). Needless to say, the activities start early! I've gone to meetings that start at 6:30 a.m. Like it or not, I'm going to have to change my sleeping habits or drop from exhaustion. I'm more of a night person, but at least for here, I have to adjust to another clock. In many ways we hope this job is temporary, in the sense that this situation not be prolonged. But it's hard to look ahead and imagine what will follow because we don't know the outcome of what's to take place. It depends on whom you talk to. And the predictions are different. The one thing that seems sure is that there's going to be a food shortage because a lot of farmers feel caught between groups that are training in the mountains, etc. and need food so come to ask for it or rob it if it is not given. The armed forces retaliate because the farmers are collaborating with "extremist" or "subversive" groups. It's not what you call the most tranquil situation. After awhile a lot of people just leave the house, their belongings, animals, etc. because they can't take it anymore.

There're a lot of other aspects. It's really a complex situation. If only it were as simple as good guys versus bad, but it's not. And a lot of groups don't have their act together and aren't in agreement about what to do and when. I think a lot of lives are lost that way.

This must seem a bit heavy. Sorry about that, but this is my reality now. I was thinking before about my entrances into Bolivia and Chile — the first taste of South America — every detail strikes you, especially as it's a new experience. Then Chile — entering in at a time of political chaos — what Carla always calls "the days of madness." I remember how I tried so hard to figure out what was going on before the coup and then suffering with the people afterwards. Now Salvador and, yet, another historical moment with violence that my reason still refuses to accept as credible. And in the midst of that, we still try to get hold of the country and culture, etc. It's like forming friendships in a psychiatric hospital. It's real, but crazy.

And how are you, now that I've dumped? I think of you a lot and ask for your light, peace and happiness.

Take care.

Much love to you,
Ita

87. *To Sister Regina McEvoy, MM, June 1, 1980*

Dear Regina,

Warmest greetings and love to you!

This morning I set out to try to get a handle on the last six weeks, since my arrival in El Salvador. After praying for a while, I started to talk to myself in one of my notebooks and the attached is what came out.*

Since you have been so closely associated with my coming here as well as your great interest in the Church and people of Salvador, I decided to type it up for you. (Then, I stuck in a carbon for Chile, the region here, and my family.)

---

* Reference to the form letter attached (#88).

Carla and I have been asked to work on a committee that is being formed to respond to the present refugee problem in Chalatenango as well as to prepare for humanitarian help as the inevitable comes about. Within the next week or so we should be based in Chalatenango, but we will work out something with Maddie so that we'll have frequent and regular contact.

We'll keep in touch as we can. We all also could use your prayers as we walk this road in faith.

Love,

Ita

88. To Sisters Jessie Poynton, MM, and Laura Magallanes, MM, June 1, 1980

Dear Jessie and Laura,

Greetings from the Chileans in *diaspora* — much love to you both!

I've been meaning to write to you both (as opposed to sending plans, evaluations, funding proposals, etc. — it's a bitch this accountability to half the world because you're on loan and the buck doesn't seem to stop anywhere, but keeps going round). It's really been hectic. By living with Madeline Dorsey in Santa Ana, we've been doing about a four hour commute a couple of times a week to the area we'll be working in. So a lot of time gets eaten up that way. I was getting to feel that I was on a treadmill, so I got off for two days to sleep, read a novel, and take some time to get a hold of what's been happening. The enclosed reflection is what came out this morning after I prayed a while and opened a notebook to talk to myself.

Jane Kenrick, the Mercy in Santiago showed up here last week and even more remarkable, she found us — and she was the representative or embodiment of all the people we care about in Chile. Seeing her gave me such joy and also made me realize how much I miss you all.

We spent the first couple of weeks here checking out priorities and job possibilities. A couple of times we were literally a spit from the Honduran border and kept thinking, we're going to be cut off completely when the crunch comes. Besides the people on the whole are terrorized. So it's not the ideal time to appear on the scene and think you're going to start some lovely group work that's very much a no-no now. Then one day at a meeting of Sisters the problem of all the refugees, the people who have fled their homes because of persecution, nearby fighting and fear, came out. The need for places to house them, for food and medicines, etc. as well as looking ahead as the situation worsens. Within an hour or so the idea of a committee came about. And since we were the two without full-time work, we got that part of the job. The others, about eight or ten, will help us plan, reflect, make contacts, etc.

For the time being we'll be living in a couple of rooms of the rambling rectory of Chalatenango, a provincial capitol, a cross between Licanten and Coelemu, with a constant market going. The department of Chalatenango is itself one of the Vicariates of the Archdiocese of San Salvador. It's two hours northeast of the capitol by bus. Since a lot of contacts and agencies are in San Salvador, we'll still be busing, but not as far.

Just after a short experience, I have some reaction to decentralized governance. Of course this situation isn't the norm because there have always been very few Sisters here. In January there were two, but now we're five and pretty much all decisions are made here. A weakness I see is the limited number and three of us new on the scene. Maybe, I miss the give and take of a larger group, because I find a small group, especially if one (or even more depending on the situation) is naturally quiet. It would almost be like the area of Talca-Licanten,* handling everything from annual reports, finances, job descriptions, personnel, etc. On top of that, we have to bat around what we might do in case of war. All this and we're getting to know each other! As a group we try to get together every two weeks just to do that — know each other.

---

* The area in Chile where Ita served.

On the whole, God has been very good. We still seem to be fairly well glued together in spite of the daily horrors and all the rumors of imminent insurrection. My baptism into the violence was sponta-neously arranged by some local thugs (I'd guess thirteen or fourteen years old) as we were coming in one evening around 7 p.m. Coming up behind me, one put a knife to my ribs, another a machete to my neck. Being New York City trained, I said, "I'm a nun. I won't hurt you," because a truck was passing by and they got scared. So they got my bag, watch, and Carla's watch because she turned around when she heard my voice. In those cases, it's usually the inconvenience that gets to you, like having to get another [illegible], loosing agenda, notebooks, etc. once the shock wears off. I really prefer being pick-pocketed, if given a choice.

Well, the Lord be with you both. Pray for us sinners. Write and put a stick under the others too. This is *cosa seria** and we count on support, but it is nice to see it in writing too.

Love,

Ita

89. To Sister Peg Hanlon, MM, June 1, 1980

Dear Peg,

Did Jane Kenrick turn up at your door? She's really a great gal and fun.

This morning I sat down to try and get a hold on the time since I've been here. Things are moving so quickly that there hasn't been much time to sort out what's been happening. After a while I started to talk to myself in one of my notebooks and the attached is what came out. As I read it, I thought it might be something to share so in went a carbon for Chile, PANISA,† and Regina [McEvoy]. So for what it's worth . . . .

Probably within a week or two we should have a base in Chala-

---

* A serious matter.

† The Central America region of the Maryknoll Sisters.

tenango, some rooms in the rectory. In some ways, I think I look at the refugee committee as a short-range job, but who's to know? I guess we just have to live this process a day at a time and keep strengthening our group sanity.

When you least expect it, I'll be over to check on the paint job and the garden and other touches.

Much love to you and Patti,
Ita

90. *June 1, 1980*

Some reflections — six weeks after arrived in El Salvador and at the beginning of working on the Emergency Refugee Committee at Chalate-nango.[*]

Phil. 1:21: "For me, Christ is my life" — As usual the scripture is not only appropriate, but right to the point, not just that Christ is the Lord of Life, in charge of the day and the hour, something which has to be thought about in this country of forty to fifty and sometimes a hundred assassinations a day, but that he is the meaning all along the way and in the fullness. His kingdom of brotherhood, justice, peace and love is what my life is given to — right now, here in Salvador.

I don't know if it is in spite of or because of the horror, terror, evil, confusion, lawlessness, but I do know that it is right to be here. That may be the only surety as, with Carla, I start a work that is going to put us in contact with some of the hurting, homeless, hungry, and who knows whom else!

How to go about it? Organize it? Whom to consult? Whom to believe? Will events just run us? Will history take over? Will it be helpful? Can you be effective in war? Those are a lot of questions, sound ones, and I don't know the answers.

---

[*] This is the mimeographed reflection Ita refers to in several personal letters.

Today's gospel (Jn. 16:12-15) says, "I still have many things to say to you, but they would be too much for you now. But when the Spirit of truth comes, he will lead you to the complete truth . . ."

I arrived in El Salvador during the liturgical reading of Acts which seemed so appropriate; coming into a church that had just lost its leader; listening not only to testimonies of him, but also to the personal testimonies of the delegates of the word and catechists, those simple persons who have risked and have been threatened because of their association with the Church, because of their fidelity. Priests and sisters have had to leave the country, some after having lived for a time as fugitives. People are making choices and are being killed for those choices, as others look on approvingly. Defenders of the "true religion" get letters of permission from the authorities to go after apostates.

Now it's the cycle of Pentecost. Although it all overlaps and intertwines, the reading of Acts was my point of reference to enter and plug into Salvador. Pentecost is the time of my own empowering to participate in it. The gift of the Spirit is very real and important to me, especially His teaching, enlightening, leading me/us into the truth.

"Each one of you has received some spiritual gift, use it for the good of all; activate the different gifts that God has distributed among you" (I Pet. 4:10). To activate our gifts, to use them in this situation, to believe that we are gifted in and for Salvador now, that the answers to the questions will come when they are needed, to walk in faith one day at a time with Salvadorans along a road filled with obstacles, detours and sometimes washouts. This seems to be what it means for us to be in El Salvador. And it is good for us to be here (Lk. 9:33).

91. June 7, 1980

Dear Mom,

I was right about your new bathroom décor. Obviously you're going to have enough birth certificates, police records, etc. to paper one side. Isn't it wonderful? There's nothing like your own little dabbling in the Byzantine process to give you some idea what "getting papers" means here. Thanks for all that you are doing. There's really no way to tell you if the final steps are taken because of two reasons: 1) the ministry here doesn't tell you what you need; they only reject it if it's not right. So what you have to do is ask the last person who went through the process what it was that they needed. 2) The ministry keeps changing the requirements, so even if you faithfully imitate the last person's papers, the rules may have changed. And we won't know that until we present the papers!

Also the reason why I returned the birth certificates (and police record) from here is because they needed the clerk's and Salvadoran consulate's authentication. That's what we do in our spare time. But it was something else coming back after a week and have three envelopes from Bill, plus a letter. The certificates generate family news, so that's a plus.

Carla and I have a job, but as yet no place to live. So she swings the week between three places and I sometimes four, depending on which city we're in for the night. Officially we're working for the area of the archdiocese called Chalatenango in a job that may be short-range or longer. We're the coordinators of the emergency committee to respond to the need of the refugees/or displaced. As yet it's not at the scale of the recent year's film footage of Vietnam, Cambodia, etc. of civilians on the road, but that's now part of the reality here. We're into food, medicine, clothes, shelter, plus financing. So we're back and forth to San Salvador constantly and, at least if possible once a week to Santa Ana to check on Maddie, since she's alone again. Sometimes, I go down to the port, La Libertad, to check in with the ladies there (Terry and Joan). Otherwise we stay with some nuns in the capitol who have a shower. They think we're crazy, but take us in for the love of God or the good of the cause.

We've been promised two rooms in Chalatenango, but they have to be "conditioned," one's a meeting room, the other smaller. They lack things like doors and, maybe, a wooden frame or two to make partitions. Right now the plumbing is being fixed, we'll have water for only four hours a day. I think an outhouse would be better, myself. So while all that's going on, the three nuns in Chalatenango have moved into one room, so that we can have the other when we show up. As I say, everyone is very accommodating. Why they think we're weird "birds" is because most Religious here are very "conventual,"* that is, with a very ordered schedule, local superiors and more or less stable in one place. Since we're none of that and are creating a job mechanism that can't be fully done from one place, they don't know quite what to make of us. But possibly they just think all North Americans are slightly crazy.

I don't think there's any problem about sending the "news of the week," because news magazines and clippings seem to go through fairly regularly. Either we'll get it or we won't. But on the chance that we won't, I wouldn't add lots of extras — because you'll be spending money in vain. It's like Chile in certain ways. Sometimes the most unlikely things come through and harmless news everyone knows anyway is withheld. To know!

I had a letter from Mary Tracy remarking on your get together on Mother's Day. I scored once again by missing it, but you know you're remembered and loved.

You said you're in touch with Pat Haggerty. We've never met and I know she's now home for the same program I was in last year. I also understand she's collaborating with the ecumenical groups who are working for solidarity here, which is a great work. If I keep moving around, you're going to have some of the same incredible contacts around the world — Bangladesh, Chile, Central America. We'll have to work on the Asian and African connections and you'll have your own international news service. Speaking of which, Carolyn Lehmann should be at her mother's house about this time. I think we'll have to put a moral obligation on her to stop here on her way back, after all she's one of our duly elected leaders!

Well, so much from here. I'm glad all the budding actors and actresses are doing well. I hope their agents are too.

Thanks again for all the legwork, paper work. Take Care,

Love to all,
Ita

---

* Ita refers to a more traditional — convent-centered — style of Religious life.

92. *To Sister Melinda Roper, MM, President of the Maryknoll Sisters,*
June 11, 1980

Dear Melinda,

Greetings from the "floating loans."

This is a copy of a letter to Annette, Dan Driscoll, USCC Latin America Bureau, and the National Episcopal Conference.

The Ecumenical Humanitarian Aid Committee at a meeting today urged us to present two petitions to Maryknoll and the U.S. Church at large: that pressure be put on the International Red Cross which is hearing testimony on Salvador these days; also that some Church representatives (Maryknoll and others) "come and see" the situation so as to help inform the American public, who, as a whole, are ignorant of U. S. policy in El Salvador — and the real danger of intervention.

Since the death of Monseñor Romero the news coverage on Salvador has declined to almost nothing. The committee fears that decisive action will be taken by the government under the guise of "stopping subversives" or "containing communism" — and that all of Central America will be involved if this happens. It's a heavy scene — but if we have a preferential option for the poor as well as a commitment for justice as a basis for the coming Kingdom, we're going to have to take sides in Salvador — correction — we have. Please help us from there if you can.

Ita and Carla

93. *June 11, 1980*

Dear Melinda [Roper],

We two Maryknoll Sisters, working on the Emergency Committee for the Vicariate of Chalatenango, Archdiocese of San Salvador, El Salvador and in collaboration with the Ecumenical Committee for Humanitarian Aid and witnesses of the repression suffered by the people of El Salvador, present the following petition to your office:

Given the political situation of El Salvador, which is nothing less than an undeclared civil war, we urgently ask that your office petition the International Red Cross, Geneva, to recognize the existing state of war in El Salvador, so that International norms of behavior in times of war be respected and supervised: concretely — that hospitals and refugee centers be respected as neutral centers and that humanitarian aid of food and medicines be allowed to enter the country.

Without a declaration of war, the victims of repression or of the war itself cannot receive help from international humanitarian agencies.

Gratefully,
Ita Ford
Carla Piette

94. To Sister Annette Mulry, MM, Administrator of the Maryknoll Sisters' Office of Social Concerns, June 11, 1980

Dear Annette,

Greetings and love!

This is a quickie to travel [sic] almost immediately after a meeting today of the Ecumenical Committee (CEAH).

In their analysis what's most needed at this moment is an international declaration and recognition of the lived reality here. Hospitals are being invaded—with patients being kidnapped or killed; no guarantees have been given for the existing refugee centers. The internal refugee problem is growing as the people are fleeing from (1) deaths threats; (2) areas of continuous military operations; (3) destruction of their homes, crops, and animals.

The coordinating committee of CEAH urged us as Maryknollers and North Americans that we ask you to pressure the International Red Cross that in these days is hearing testimony on El Salvador.

They also urged that someone from Maryknoll "come and see" because the news coverage is so poor, and what there is, is often slanted or inaccurate. If we have a preferential option for the poor, we have to take sides in El Salvador. At this point, there is no "third way."

More to come later.

Love,
Ita
Carla

95. *To Sister Marie Giblin, MM, June 18, 1980*

Dear Marie,

The last two times I saw Peggy Healy, I asked for you, so maybe it's time I send my own greetings. How does it feel to have one year behind you? It must be a great satisfaction.

Our reflections here in El Salvador these days might not be too systematic, but they are very basic and gut level and purifying. The ambience doesn't lend itself to beating around the bush sort of talk, yet it does seem to be a good place to be, in the strange Christian paradox.

There are loony moments, too. We were writing up a project for food for refugees, and to prove local support, we had to give ourselves a salary on paper. I asked Carla what she thought would be adequate. After a minute she said, well, if I was getting paid for this, I'd want $150,000 in advance! I thought that was sort of low myself.

If I remember correctly, Peggy said you were involved in some project with Spanish speaking folks in Westchester for this summer. I hope it was a good experience.

Greetings to Maureen, Megan and Terry! Take Care.

Love,
Ita

96. *To Sister Jane Gregorich, MM, July 7, 1980*

Dear Jane,

Carla and I received a letter from Marge Lyons the other day and the second paragraph stopped us short. Jane, I'm so sorry to hear of your brother's death. Having heard you speak of him often, I know you felt close to him, being bonded in the family and in the Lord.

In the face of this mystery, I join with you and your family in offering your brother's life and priesthood back to the Lord. At the same time I ask for you, your family and friends, and your brother's parishioners and friends — that the Lord generously console and strengthen all at this time.

What comes to me now, too, is that part from [Leonardo] Boff's book that I gave you so short a time ago when your father died. The Christian belief of unending life, of continued presence and relationship is so meaningful and helpful.

I hope the time with the family is healing, restoring and comforting. Know that you are remembered by us.

Love,

Ita

97. *To Ana May, an old school friend, July 13, 1980*

Dear Ana,

Greetings from the active side of an active volcano in never-never land! At least once a week, if not once a day, I fantasize and forget everything. It's my safety valve because twenty-four hours of reality here could tempt you to take up a gun and turn it on someone else. What a zoo! It's a suffering country of bad news and law of the jungle. There are so many things that outrage our sense of humanity and decency that just ordinary fear gets to be funny and absurd. One day last week I was in the coffee shop with a few people when all around us everyone started toppling to the floor and crawling under tables. Of course, instinctively, we did the same and while I'm under the table I congratulate myself that I meet threats quite nicely and after a few minutes we all crawl out and sit down and continue our conversations. It seems that someone was running past with a machine gun and no one cared to be the target. Then, life goes on. The nightly shootings and the daily 'hearing tests,' "Did you hear that?" "Yes." One night I burst out laughing as well — "Yes, our ears seem to be okay."

Besides taxing our nerves you might wonder why we are here and what we are doing. Periodically I let that cross my mind and I don't always have satisfactory answers. There is not a great deal of your ordinary [pastoral] work going on in an undeclared civil war; a large portion of the population is displaced. That is, they have left their homes, their little plots of land for what they think will be a safer place. Some have gone to refugee centers, most have gone to other parts of the country to relatives and friends, etc, and others from other areas have come to this area. It would be as if one-third of Tappan went to Yonkers and one-third to Jersey City, and the rest stopped and stayed put. Then, depending upon your sympathies you look for people you thought you could take in. For a country that is basically agricultural, the short range reality is a lot of people are just fleeing and their food and belongings are left behind and because a lot of land is not being sowed there is going to be a food shortage in part of the country next year.

Having dropped off the moon into the middle of this, it wasn't too long before we realized that an ordinary bag of tricks was not appropriate for this setting. So we're into emergency work, trying to locate the very frightened people who have no food but are too scared to be visible. And since we are very visible we have to delegate a lot of the food work. It is not the most satisfying job. It seems to be the most appropriate for the moment so we amble along trying to minimize our frustrations, just like everyone else here.

Today I think I'll visit Bermuda since I've never been there. Ana, I'm glad I can be absurd with you because most of the time I can't even vent in letters because it makes people nervous. They shouldn't be nervous. It's my turn, and my way of coping is to develop a weird sense of humor. At first I thought the sisters in Nicaragua were off the wall after the war — now I understand where they came from.

So having given you a little background, this is no little wish for you when I pray happy celebration of life, do it, enjoy it, relish it. There are too many sick, crazed people who hold it in contempt. May you appreciate and enjoy the gift and opportunity that you have. Happy, happy birthday!

Love,
Ita

98. *July 18, 1980*

Dear Mom,

I wrote you yesterday, but since it depressed me to reread it, I junked it. Ugh! It was beginning to sound like most of the conversations here. Anyway here I am at Maddie's halfway House and pretending I'm in Bermuda — sleeping late, reading and doing my best to ignore the national reality while Carla frolics up and down the hills of Chalatenango. Next week maybe she'll do the same.

There was some good news this week for a family here. Their daughter survived the Arizona desert and sun. She must be in fair shape at least because she was able to speak by phone to some relatives in California and identify herself. It was her third attempt to enter the promised land!

Getting to the States, legally or illegally, to work and send back money to the family is a very widespread phenomenon here. So many people that we meet have, at least, one close relative there. Most seem to head for California. They say here that the second largest city of Salvador is Los Angeles, CA. The country is so small and agricultural that it doesn't seem to be able to absorb its own population and provide job possibilities. What I don't know is if this is true of all Central America.

My writing must be getting worse. I thought I was asking for articles from the *New York Times,* rather than *Time* magazine, but thanks for the subscription and random articles as they appear. *The News of the Week* (2) and *Commonweal* arrived. As I was reading John Cort's memoirs about the *Catholic Worker,* it made me wonder from the way he ended, if I had missed the news of Dorothy Day's death. Did I?*

Immigration is going to give us 90 more days to get all our papers in order. We lost about two months time with a run around from Chile, but now possibly we may be on the right track. Otherwise, as I told Bill about two weeks ago, we just need the county

---

* Dorothy Day, founder of the Catholic Worker movement, would die on November 29, 1980, three days before Ita.

clerk's certification of Carla's birth certificate and of the Ossining police certificates. We have a standing joke about all the trouble you and we are going through so that we can stay in a country that so many nationals are leaving!

You'll probably be getting a call from Joan Petrik. She left for some R&R this week. Since she had a heart attack two years ago, the doctors suggested a change of scene as preventive medicine. However, we're not without people passing through. Next week our Washington commuter (Peg Healy) is due. She usually brings news, jokes and trifles for fun.

This week we got a second-hand Jeep to roam the back roads of Chalatenango. Carla has baptized it *La Tonquita,* roughly "Miss Piggy." The former owner wasn't too concerned about cosmetic repairs or interior decorating touches — but it takes to the alleged roads like a pig to a puddle. It's great for the places "that you can't get to from here," — all those towns that have one bus out in the morning and one returning in the afternoon. Take care, we're certainly trying to.

Much love to all
Ita

99.

Appended to this document is a reflection on the same questions as seen by other Maryknoll Sisters in the Central American (PANISA) region.

To: the PANISA and Chile Regions
From: Carla Piette and Ita Ford
Date: July 20, 1980

THREE MONTHS EXPERIENCE IN EL SALVADOR

Three months is a short period of time but given the national and church situation of El Salvador and our own experiences in trying to find the appropriate ministry within that framework, we feel it is important to share our questions, frustrations and hopes as part of an ongoing evaluation.

A Short History

We are two Sisters from the Chile region who responded to the call of the 1979 PANISA Regional Assembly that experienced [the need for] personnel reinforcement in [the] Area of El Salvador and [a call to increase efforts to] collaborate with the Archdiocese of San Salvador. Inspired by the fourth Pastoral Letter of Mons. Romero, we looked forward to finding a way to serve and accompany the Salvadoran people during this difficult moment of their history.

We arrived April 15 as the Archdiocese was mourning the loss of its pastor, guide and prophet, Mons Romero. Theresa Alexander had already arrived from Panama to accompany Joan Petrik; Madeline Dorsey was alone in Santa Ana; so we were 5 in the country. During the first month we based ourselves with Maddie in Sta. Ana and began to investigate the pastoral possibilities in the archdiocese. Through the Vicar General we were directed to one of the archdiocesan priorities, the Vicariate of Chalatenango where there was not only several openings for pastoral workers, but also the possibility of support and collaboration with the Vicar and other pastoral teams.

At the same time that we were in this process, the repression in Chalatenango was increasing significantly, especially in several of the areas where we had been offered work. Due to the stepped up military operations to 'pacify' the area and the vigilance of the paramilitary group, ORDEN, many *campesinos* who survived the attacks fled from their homes, leaving all their belongings and food supplies behind. In some areas townspeople left for refuge in safer areas and their homes were then occupied by people from nearby villages seeking refuge etc., etc., etc. What we began to find was the phenomenon of displaced people, strangers among strangers, with great fear and suspicion of any unknown people.

At a meeting of the Religious of Chalatenango with the Vicar, we put forth our question about the feasibility at this time to begin pastoral work as we understand it from our experience in Chile, with

emphasis on forming Christian community. The group favored
another alternative, that of forming an emergency committee for the
Vicariate to respond to the needs of the present moment. To facilitate
our work, the Vicar offered us office and living space in the Parish
House of Chalatenango. This would be available once some necessary repairs and alterations were completed.

We drew up a tentative plan for the committee that, in addition
to ourselves, consists of seven volunteers on a part-time basis. The
Vicar presented the plan to Bishop Rivera y Damas and it was
approved. The main points at the beginning were: (1) to contact other
humanitarian groups and establish forms of collaboration; (2) for-
mulate projects for funding the financing of food stuffs, medicines
and transportation in case of emergency; (3) inform the parishes and
pastoral agents of Chalatenango of the committee's existence and to
encourage them to locate places of refuge in their areas as well as to
form groups to collaborate with the committee. All this has been
done. In addition, a meeting was held with the Capuchins of Honduras about the situation of the Salvadoran refugees there.

The Present Situation

Given the history and circumstances in which we arrived and
the rapid evolution of the situation, we would like to point out some
changes in the past three months.

1) We came to a local Church (the Archdiocese) that was known
for its prophetic leader, Mons. Romero, who gave witness of being the
pastor of a Church that opted for the poor in truth and justice. Under
his leadership the majority of the pastoral agents were united in this
thrust. With his death the persecution of the Church has continued,
but now a certain disunity is apparent. It seems that it is still the same
strong Church at the grass-roots that suffers daily persecution and
even death just for being aware [or] poor or young or associated or sym-
pathetic to popular organizations. On the other hand, the present leadership does not have the same prophetic gifts and charisma of Mons.
Romero. Approximately a dozen priests of the archdiocese have left the
country, some for personal safety, others for political options. Those
who remain are overworked, trying to fill the gaps; among these are

some conservatives who before responded to the proddings of Mons. Romero, but who now are falling into an ahistorical ministry. Although to a much lesser degree, there is some disunity among the Religious. As they are dependent on the priests in many pastoral situations, there is a certain climate of uncertainty of how to proceed, of waiting for a new Pentecost. The constant violations of human rights by the state and security forces produces, from our observation, a type of state of "shock" among the Salvadoran pastoral agents, as well as frustration and impotence caused by the silence of the hierarchical Church. The Archdiocese still publishes a weekly paper and has a radio which denounces the injustices and barbarities which occur, but the feeling we get is that more of a response and initiative is hoped for/longed for from the hierarchy. Given the above, there is still hope that the resurrection will come after this long passion.

2) The political situation. Formerly Mons. Romero publicly supported the project of the popular organizations. As a pastor and counselor, he upheld their right to organize, yet pointed out their faults and, when it applied, denounced their abuses. At the same time, he denounced the injustices of the government and especially of the security forces, while pointing out where truth and justice were to be found.

Since his prophetic voice has been silenced, no other voice of equal credibility has been raised to speak to the situation of a suffering divided people, the majority of whom, regardless of their loyalties, are the victims of hunger, fear and violence.

In addition, the archdiocese of San Salvador is waiting for Rome to name a new archbishop. At this time, Bishop Rivera y Damas has the responsibility of two dioceses and, as the administrator of the archdiocese, he must respond to the Nuncio who does not even reside in the country.

Some Frustrations

1) For the last three months we have had no house that we could say, "This is our home." Thanks to the hospitality of the Asuncion Sisters and the Cleveland Diocesan Team, we have a place to stay both in San Salvador and in Chalatenango. Maddie opens her door

and heart when we go to Sta. Ana and it is there that we leave our suitcases.

2) Because we arrived at a time when the Church was mourning and struggling to respond to the problem of daily persecution, we find it difficult to find someone with whom to reflect on this experience of [dis]orientation. The Vicars and capable priests all seem to have four or five full time jobs and appear just to be grateful that someone is responding to the call that "the harvest is great" without thinking that maybe the "harvesters" might need a bit of support or direction. At this point, Maddie, who is in Santa Ana alone, has quite a difficult challenge herself. Joan Petrik was here but has gone home for rest and medical care. Terry Alexander is also new here like us.

3) This situation of repression and genocide continues to grow each day in an unbelievable way. However, no war has been declared. Over 2,000 families have had to leave their homes in Chalatenango because of the persecution either by the security force or by the popular groups. All these displaced families live with terrific fear and this generates an atmosphere of a lack of trust everywhere. We are pastoral workers used to having people who we can visit, meet with, etc. Now we have no people. We cannot visit because of the times and the very real fear of placing others in danger because of belonging to the Church, which is one of the security force's biggest enemies. Our contacts are mostly with priests and sisters of this valiant Church, and some surviving catechists.

4) Given the historical moment in the region when we came here with the experimental government by area, it has taken us a while to get into this set-up, although the circumstances of the last month have immersed us into the pros and cons of this experiment. A certain spontaneous support from the Region has been present in notes and prayers. However, given the war situation, our reduced numbers and the recent illness of one member here, we have felt quite isolated and alone. Control of the mails as well as of phone calls makes it difficult to communicate what is happening, and your letters are not arriving too frequently. We feel the need of more palpable solidarity.

5) The Archdiocese gives us $100 per month. Since living a life

of pilgrims, traveling to different places each day is rather expensive (we spent $40 last month just in buses) we have asked Maddie for help which she gives us ($200 a month) that we will repay when our project money comes through. We wrote up a project in May but to date have nothing. Money for new people in this area was petitioned last year, but the petition was turned down.

6) Besides lacking our own home, a stable salary, local church and tangible regional support and inventing a job daily, neither one of us are emotional or psychological giants in this crazy situation. We realize that a lot of our energies just go into trying to keep walking down this dark road without becoming as dark as the situation.

What Do We Really Do?
1) We continue to seek out dialogue and collaboration with humanitarian groups, do translations and give in petitions for aid.
2) We drive priests to outlying country districts.
3) We drive food to contacts who will get it to people hiding from the security forces or the popular groups.
4) We transport refugees and clothes to different hiding places.
5) We try to visit Maddie in Santa Ana once a week.
6) We meet as an area twice a month.
7) We accompany Religious who are alone at present.
8) We do an infinite amount of paper work to stay in this 'nutsy' country.

Taking into account all that we have shared, we present some questions for the Region and the Congregation.

1. At this precise historical moment, is it feasible to continue to ask for more personnel for El Salvador, other than the petition made by Maddie for someone to accompany her in Santa Ana? (1 more)

2. How could the Region and/or Congregation [Maryknoll Sisters] respond better to this abnormal situation?

3. What suggestions would the Region and/or Congregation have for those who are living in this situation at present?

4. Is this system of government by area feasible in an area with so few people, in this war situation? [Reference is to Maryknoll Sisters' governance]

5. What would be a possible alternative with more direct participation of people OUTSIDE of this area without losing the mature responsibility of the people in the area?

(1 more) We would very much like to have a larger group in El Salvador, especially since we need support to live this situation. But because of this same situation — and our own experiences of trying to look for work in it — we ask, would it be just to have others go through it?

However, we do see Santa Ana as feasible for various reasons. 1) It is an established and going pastoral work — living with and accompanying the people at this time. 2) It is an urban situation and it is unlikely, except in case of declared war and attack, that the residents would leave in large numbers. 3) Maddie's ministry has credibility with the people — especially at this time. 4) There is more than Maddie can handle. 5) And, most importantly, we feel that no Sisters should be alone at this time.

Until the situation in Chalatenango has more shape to it, *we think it would be best not to ask for another Sister.*

The last reflection we want to share is what we have learned in this experience:

1) A total dependence and trust in God.

2) A deepening of our commitment and availability.

3) A coming to know the pastoral agents of the local Church and other missioners.

4) An opportunity to know this situation of repression and all its consequences.

5) An exercise in humility and faith.

6) A coming to know one's personal limitations and basic psychological needs.

7) An awareness of the ability to adapt to incredible situations.*

---

* "Sisters who were present in the PANISA region during this time offer these thoughts to balance the information given in this document.

1. Based on the particular social/political environment in that part of the world at that time, the practice in the Region for "new" Sisters assigned there was for them to visit all the houses where Maryknoll Sisters resided. Each ministry was evaluated to see if additional personnel would be of benefit. In the case of Carla and Ita, it was the

100. To Jennifer Sullivan, Ita's niece and godchild, August 16, 1980

Dear Jennifer,

The odds that this note will arrive for your birthday are poor, but know I'm with you in spirit as you celebrate 16 big ones. I hope it's a special day for you.

I want to say something to you and wish I were there to talk to you, because sometimes letters don't get across all the meaning and feeling. But I'll give it a try anyway.

First of all, I love you and care about you and how you are. I'm sure you know that, and that holds if you're an angel or a 'goof-off;' a genius or a jerk. A lot of that is up to you and what you decide to do with your life.

What I want to say — some of it isn't too jolly birthday talk, but it's real.

Yesterday, I stood looking down at a 16-year-old boy who had been killed a few hours earlier. I know a lot of kids even younger who are dead. This is a terrible time in El Salvador for youth. A lot of idealism and commitment is getting snuffed out here now.

The reasons why so many people are being killed are quite complicated, yet there are some clear simple strands. One is that many people have found a meaning to life, to sacrifice, to struggle and even to death! And whether their life spans 16 years or 60 or 90, for them their life has had a purpose. In many ways, they are fortunate people.

Brooklyn is not passing through the drama of El Salvador, but some things hold true wherever one is and at whatever age. What I am saying is I hope you come to find that which gives life a deep meaning for you. Something worth living for, maybe even worth

need of the Archdiocese to have these Sisters establish work with refugees who were fleeing the brutality of the National Guard.

2. El Salvador had been asking for additional personnel for some time. "Ministry," as it was usually understood, would have been to work in a parish doing various tasks associated with the Church. During this time of national upheaval, however, such work was impossible. The mandate of the Archdiocese, following the direction left by Archbishop Romero, was to address the urgent needs of people who were affected by the injustices of the government."Witnesses to justice" was the job description given to this ministry.

dying for, something that energizes you, enthuses you, enables you to keep moving ahead.

I can't tell you what it might be. That's for you to find, to choose, to love. I just encourage you to start looking and support you in the search.

Maybe this sounds weird and off the wall and, maybe, no one else will talk to you like this, but then, too, I'm seeing and living things that others around you aren't. I also gather that you haven't been straining yourself this year in school. Maybe you're into a drifting phase. I don't know. You or no one else has said. All I know is that I want to say to you: Don't waste the gifts and opportunities you have to make yourself and other people happy. Do yourself and a lot of others a favor and get moving again.

I hope this doesn't sound like some kind of a sermon. In fact, it's my birthday present to you. If it doesn't make sense right at this moment, keep this and read it some time from now. Maybe it will be clearer. Or ask me about it, okay?

A very happy birthday to you and much,

Much love!
Ita

101. To Sister Carolyn Lehmann, MM, August 21, 1980

Dear Carolyn,

We overnighted at Santa Ana on Monday to check and see how the others (Maddie, Maura, Terry) had passed the last strike, and also to pick up mail, and your letter was there. Thanks; it's very good to hear from you and to know that the time home is going pretty well.

Before getting into a lot of things, just let me clear the air by saying that I do trust your decision to return directly to Chile, but that I'm also disappointed that you couldn't see a stop working out at this time. To explain: in analyzing our situation and needs here, what we've found to be most helpful are short visits with friends who more or less understand the situation. With them we can dump all our frustrations and questions, then the person takes a shower and we all enjoy ourselves. It's a process that letters or phone calls can't satisfy. Basically, we choose to be here, but we need, while possible, solidarity visits to keep a bigger perspective. Also on the Chile region level, it might have been helpful if someone could have come to be able to give the "loaners" a clearer idea of what the situation is there. But maybe that will be for another time.

I don't know if you read a copy of the three-month evaluation that we sent. It pretty much reflected the situation of a month ago, and to a certain degree, still does. However, in subtle ways there's more shape to what we're doing because there's more opening up of possibilities. Sometimes, I have the sense that maybe we've passed through the stage of 'paying dues' or earning credibility. Probably those who stay around for a couple of months get accepted. So the question, "Why are we here?" is changing to, "What do you want of us here? Show us what you want us to do today." (Rosemarie Franklin would have deep depression here — long-range plans here might span an afternoon — usually it's in segments of hours!)* Again, it's not a question of should we be here or not — but what does being in this situation call for in the way of response. It's trying to order a war situation in some way so you can keep sane and functioning.

Also in the last week we have installed ourselves in the *Camino Real*,† our lodgings in the Parish House of Chalatenango. It's a zoo scene as we have extended close-hand living with about a dozen people — but it's a place to call ours, and psychologically, I think, that's a help. Although we're a block from the army *cuartel* and the *guardia*‡ and they have some noisy night exercise that takes getting used to.

We get very favorable coverage of *Pinochet* here. It's probably just as well that we're not there for the buffoon plebiscite and all the *teatro* leading up it to it.** One of the major differences I see between here and Chile is that the latter still tries to keep up the pretext of law

---

* Sister Rosemarie Franklin was in charge of Congregational Planning at the time.
† A play on the name of an expensive hotel.
‡ The National Guard headquarters.
** References to the elections (Pinochet's) in Chile and the coverage it receives in Central America.

and to point out to others that there's a legal basis for operating. There's no pretense of that here.

Carla asked me to leave her some space. So I'll continue later a general letter to the Assembly at Plum Island. Enjoy the last month. Love up your mom and Marilyn and give them my best. Take care.

                                                              Love,
                                                              Ita

102. To Sister Connie Pospisil, MM, August 21-22, 1980

Dear Connie,

Here's hoping you're back home *sin novedad,** especially if you stopped in Bolivia as planned. That scene seems nastier than usual.

How was the course with Miranda? Isn't he a firecracker? I enjoyed him very much two years ago. I also hope you had a good vacation and enjoyed being with the ladies of the World Section.

If luck and history are with us, we hope to go to Guatemala in mid-September for retreat with the Sisters there. It should be a nice opportunity to get to know the Sisters there, to say nothing of a change from here. (Isn't it weird that the oppressive situation of another country seems more remote and, therefore, will affect you less than the one you live in!)

Our own situation is getting somewhat better. We now have lodgings called *The Camino Real* (after one of the luxury hotels in San Salvador) in the Parish House in Chalatenango. There's still a lot of touches needed to make it homey, but at least we can now say we have a place. Actually we live in a *sala* [hall room] of the parish, but it now has a door and some divisions for bedrooms. Showers and "johns" are in the patio. There's a kitchen "next door." There are about dozen or so residents in the parish and the number fluctuates on weekends and people use it as a halfway house as they

---

* Without incident.

look for refuge. It is quite an experience of extended, if not integrated, community.

Also our project for funding (our salaries) was approved at the Center. So now we can begin to repay what we've been borrowing.

Maybe this is as good a time as any to ask some questions through you to the [Regional Governing Board] re: financial arrangements. There are some things that probably have to be clarified because 1) 'loaning' from one region to another seems to be a new phenomenon and I guess no one really knows exactly where affiliation with one ends and another begins and 2) PANISA has a different financial policy than Chile.

When we went to Nicaragua, we were told to write for financing for the rest of the year, which we did (taking as budget figures those from a year ago, and for an established house, which may or may not work out, but at least, we have to use some aid). We did not include in the request the $35 per month assessment for the Center because I just presumed the Chile region would take care of that. Later Peg Dillon asked me why it wasn't included. Anyway, what I would like you to consider would be the following:

Probably within a month or two it will be time to draw up another petition, assuming that we'll work out some kind of evaluation, and also keep praying to see if we should be here. My questions are:

1. Do we include the $35 assessment in the request?

2. Carla is due for a furlough in 1981: Does that money come from Chile or is it to be included in the request?

3. We haven't received any information of our sponsors and/or gifts being sent here. Again, I'll check.

We're not having money difficulties. It's just nothing seems too clear, so I'm asking just so we'll all be informed of the same thing, once some decisions are made or guidelines emerge as crazies like us get loaned.

These are some of the questions that occur to me now. Probably some more will come to mind later. By the way, we haven't received a copy of the Assembly minutes. Maybe if there's an extra around, we can see if it gets here. Mail is most unpredictable.

Maura Clarke arrived two weeks ago. She'll be with Maddie in Santa Ana at least until November, [a decision] to be reevaluated at the regional assembly. That's the longest long-range plan that we have in this country. We usually think in terms of days or weeks! Anyway, Maura is a wonderful asset. She's just one of those lovely kind of women who respond so warmly. We're into accepting all the support that's offered.

August 22

P.S. Since I wrote the last sentence yesterday afternoon, the electricity has been cut throughout the country. It's not too clear yet for how long. Some say three days, others mutter [it will be] indefinitely. It affects the city much more than the *campo* and is a great pressure on the government.

Love,

Ita

103. The following letters and documents refer to the Jeep accident on August 23, 1980, in which Carla Piette drowned.

Sept. 7, 1980

Dear Mom,

This letter sort of goes along with the tape I made for all of you last night. I'm not too much into that sort of thing, but I thought you might like it. Anyway there are a few things to add because the tape ended.

I told you on the tape I wasn't afraid and had no sense of panic on the night of the 23rd. I neglected to mention that must have been an extraordinary gifting of God for that experience. For all the physical things I had to do. I was "old Ernestina,"* as Carla called me. "There's something you have to do," so you do it, like getting out of the river and not giving up. I think I get that trait from you. For the rest of the time — bobbing down the river and huddled under the bushes — I just knew however it turned out it would be okay. Stiff, sore, probably sick, but okay.

---

* Reference is to one of comedian Flip Wilson's characters.

The other thing I was saying as the tape ended was that I know this is a very hard time for you. I know that you're concerned and worried about the situation and I don't know really how to alleviate that. I truly believe that I should be here, and I can't even tell you why. A couple of weeks ago Carla and I were praying and we both cried because it was so unclear to us why we were here, although we felt strongly we should be. Well, it's now quite clear for Carla, but I still have to keep asking to be shown. I can't tell you not to worry, that would be unnatural. It would be like someone saying to me, 'don't hurt because Carla died.' In fact, the last few days have been really hurting ones, probably because the shock of the whole thing, the event to my system is wearing off. All I can share with you is God's palpable presence has never been more real ever since we came to Salvador. He's made a lot of things clear to us. What we should be doing, etc. I trust in that and hope you can too.

Everyone will be delighted to know that the American Embassy is as bureaucratic and insensitive as any other office. I went with Carla's passport and five copies of the judge's report to be authenticated (in Salvador, a dead body not in a hospital cannot be moved until a judge comes and "recognizes" that the person is dead and usually guesses what the cause was). Anyway, first they told me that Carla's name was spelled wrong. I said that was no problem. I'd sign a notarized statement that it was the same person. Then they told me they couldn't accept the judge's statement because it didn't mention in what volume and on what page her death was noted and if anyone ever wanted to prove that she were dead, this wouldn't be good enough. I offered to sign another statement that I personally saw her buried, but they said I had to go back to Chalatenango and get official papers with lots of seals, etc. Civil servants might make the government function, but they sure do a tremendous job of disguising their humanness. I can't remember the last time I was so angry at people for being so incredibly stupid. The Latinos have much more red tape but they show some human decency and sensitiveness under the same situation.

So the authentication and certification continues, alive or dead. I think I'm at the stage where I turn all the English documents in to be legally translated. Then, I think, everything gets turned in to another office to see if it's all okay. And, then maybe, I'll get residency. I can't say it's one of my burning concerns today.

I decided to use another address in San Salvador, because it's more convenient. It's the convent where we stay in the city. The Sta. Ana address is okay too. We usually get together at least every two weeks. As Julie or someone probably told you, we've consolidated two places. Mary and Terry in Sta. Ana; Maura and I in Chalatenango. Dorothy [Kazel] and Jean [Donovan] of the Cleveland team might be doing some part-time helping out in Chalatenango as different things come up. I've also been told that a chauffer has been hired and I guess the big decision is whether a Jeep or a pick-up truck is the most suitable vehicle. Those are things I don't bother to bother about.

There are too many things on for the week and Saturday we bus to Guatemala (about five hours). I think that retreat is coming at the right time.

I'll be in touch. Take good care.

Much love to all,
Ita

104. Ita recorded this letter for her mother on a tape recorder, possibly September 6, 1980. It was transcribed by Judith Noone, MM. Further editing was done for this compilation. The sequence in this transcription and the letter previous to it in this collection follows that of the archives.

It's sort of awkward to begin a tape. I'm never very good at it, but . . . Two weeks ago, today, was the accident, Carla's death, and because someone's traveling to the States on Monday, I thought, since you've probably heard a lot of versions about different things that, maybe, it was time I said something. I'm going to sit here, have a cup of coffee, smoke a cigarette, and say what happened that day and that night as well as a few of the other things.

I guess there's quite a bit that you've heard, particularly if you went to the Mass at Maryknoll on Wednesday after Peg Hanlon and

Julie got back. I think they had a chance to talk to a lot of not only Church people of El Salvador but also some of the simple people. I had said to Peg and other people that Julie wanted just to park herself in the hospital next to me for a couple days of meetings before she left. It was a very supportive type of thing for a group to appear on the spot almost instantly. When the funeral was over I just sort of did what everybody told me to do — go to the hospital and deal with the stress, that type of thing. It's a very unreal thing, of course, it's more difficult, being the survivor.

Carla and I had talked lots of times about the possibility of our dying because of things here being very violent. I guess we talked about that — that it would be much more difficult, if it wasn't together, for the one who was left behind. So I started thinking about what I am feeling. I saw that at the very end of St. John's Gospel is this little scene of Jesus with Peter and John seems to be in the background. Jesus says to Peter, "Follow me." But Peter turns around and says, "What about him?" And Jesus says, "You're up in your fifties. I'm telling you to follow me. He's to wait around. I'll take care of that." If John was within hearing distance, I wonder what he felt like. I think now we know. I guess that's just what it boiled down to. I really did think I was going to die.

We had caused kind of a stir at Maryknoll about a month ago. We wrote a three-month evaluation sort of saying that a lot of things we hoped to accomplish couldn't be accomplished. We had a lot of questions and expressed a lot of frustration. We weren't quite sure if this was the right time for Maryknoll to send more people in here with the frustrations we were going through. And we asked for help to think about the kind of support we might need here. That evaluation and letter caused quite a stir . . . meetings, telephone calls, and all that sort of thing. But actually between the time when the letter was written and the following three or four weeks a lot of things began to take shape. I think that, whether it was the time factor, things slowly falling into place, or whether it was actually finally moving into a place of our own — even if it wasn't completely finished, but we were in there as much as we were ever in any place of for about two weeks, things were a bit more settled. We had estab-

lished some sort of credibility with some of the people we were trying to help and it was getting, not going tremendously well, but was
getting much better than it had been.

A lot of work took the form of making contacts with small Christian communities that had contact with a lot of people in the hills
who were quite hungry. They couldn't get down to the local grocery
shop because when they tried they knew often people were killed.
Part of our job was to get food to and from different places. From
such places it often would be taken to other places by mule or whatever. We also had to get medicines and make first aid kits; such
things are considered subversive and war materials. It's a schizo-
phrenic sort of thing — all primary necessities are war materials but
of course there is no war.

But anyway I guess two weeks ago Saturday, like every day we still
had various things that had to be done. Carla was going to set out
three or four places to go to as priests would collaborate with area
communities to say Mass. At the same time we would give a list of
people who were missing. It's kind of urgent that if people are missing a kind of fuss be made about it as early as possible so that not only
do people know you're aware that they're missing but maybe they'll
think twice about these and other people just completely disappear-
ing. So we worked it, i.e. Carla's going to go off to do her chauffeuring and food delivering . . . She used to say really instead of going to
the clergy and religious meetings she should go to the chauffeurs and
stevedores' meetings — slugging around 100-pound bags of food,
and finally I got up to 50 myself. We also were constantly running
these priests up and down the mountain. So that's how the day
started. I went over that morning to the third official man at the army
base, which is up the street, and he said, "Sure, sure I'll check all the
forces and everything in town." About an hour and a half later some
man came up to me and said, you know, "Are you a nun? I'm supposed to be looking for the lady with the yellow blouse on." I said,
"Yes." He said, "The commander wants to see you." When I went
back the commander was outside and said, "Can you come at 4
o'clock? I have some prisoners I want to give you." I said, "Fine." So
the day went on and the stories could kind of last a few days.

What happened was that we have finally about five families, these were families of people whose husbands or sons were killed the week before in the same town, San Antonio de los Ranchos. In fact, one of them was the mother of that boy, about 16, the one I wrote Jenifer about. Anyway they had come during the week and at one time we had them with us for awhile and, then hopefully move them to a central spot. So that I guess one was . . . another was four . . . There were about fifteen people living in our extended house, more like a tribe set up. Our ceiling is the floor of a loft and up there are just all these people in a big room where everybody spends all day. So at four o'clock I went over to the army base and we had had meetings with this Colonel, an eccentric man. We knew he doesn't want to meet me, but I was to get these prisoners and the question for him had been what to do with them. He had three choices. He could kill them. He could give them to the courts, but the courts wouldn't do anything because all the judges are threatened they'd let them loose. Or he can turn them over to the Church. He does this periodically. At least every week they have a handful of prisoners. I think that he usually had no reason to hold them at all and handing them over to the Church is a way of saving face. I'd never seen any of these people before; but it turned out that one of them was on the list that I had turned in that morning, a young man of 18 who had gotten arrested [the] Sunday before. His parents, we'd seen his father the day before and he seemed very concerned, said he wasn't exactly retarded but wasn't too swift, you know. Finally after a lot of 'to-do,' it was five to six and I had the prisoner.

So we went back to the parish and as we came in two of the ladies were there and we had some coffee. They said they were very concerned about this young man. He had at one point joined one of the organizations, they said. What they were afraid of was that once he got back to his home, he would tell the people there where they were. These women felt that their lives were in danger. We were thoroughly upset. Carla was returning now with a couple of more people. So what we decided to do was get him out of here. Hide him in the corner and distract him and then we'd take him home. So I guess it was about 6:30 or a quarter to 7 when the two came home.

They brought back a whole other group of people who we took to the house across the street where the Asuncion Sisters live and where we had been staying. I talked to Carla and she thought it was the smart thing to do. So she, I, and the two young men, one about 17–18 years old, the other one about early 20's, started off to where he lived in San Antonio.

What happens in the rainy season, usually around seven, it begins to rain. Sometimes it rains very late. Usually the trip would take about half an hour. So we started off when the rains started. We were outside Chalatenango, maybe ten minutes, and it was just one of these really freaky heavy rains. The road that we had to take, there are actually two roads, to where we were going. On one road you cross the same river five times. Ordinarily it is like forging a tiny little stream. The other road has no rivers on it, but it had a lot of landslides. They said the landslides were so bad that night, so probably the way we went was the best way to go. We didn't make very quick time and when we crossed the river the fourth time and then came to the fifth crossing it is just like you are right there. The Church is right in front of you and you're right in the town. So when we got to the fifth crossing and Carla looked at it, she said, "I'm not going through that. It looks kind of ugly and I'm not sure I can cross that." So we said to the guy, "Okay, out you go." There were trees to climb over. In the Jeep we had had a few negative points of safety, one of which is if anybody sat in the back of the Jeep, the door doesn't open from the inside. So I got out and opened the door and he got out and we started to turn the Jeep around. He came running back and said, "It looks like it's going to be hard to cross." And we said, "Here's the story — we're not staying here. We're not crossing the river. We're going back to Chalatenango. If you want to stay here, you stay." So he thought well, he really wanted to go home so he stayed.

We then proceeded down about ten feet to get across. Now I don't know, time wise, from the time we first crossed it to the second time, might have been three minutes, four or five, it couldn't have been more than five minutes and all the things that happened couldn't have been five minutes. What happened is here was — it was like a flash flood ... They say that when it starts to rain that in some of the mountain streams there just comes a point when a current comes and it's just a very uncontrollable thing. We had to cross about . . . I don't think it was more than fifteen feet of water and, usually maybe it was about, since it was rocky, three or four feet deep. We went into the water. Instead of going straight across we were just all of a sudden . . . just, the car was pointed . . . that you can turn to the right and then it was off. I said to Carla, "The land is over there." And she said, "We're being taken." And the water started to come up through the bottom and one of the fellows said, "We' re all going to drown, we're all going to die!" And I said, "No, we're not going to die, let's see what happens." So the car was kind of taken, kind of brushed up against an embankment.

Now we were three in the front and one in the back. Also the other wonderful point about this Jeep was that the Land Rover has screw windows that only open halfway. The window does not roll down like a regular one. It's a window that goes right to left so actually the window only opens half the width of the glass. It's in two pieces. So we got the door open and, of course, the water came in.

One guy got out and was holding onto something, and then the other one got out. It was going to be my turn and just as he was saying, "Come on, now it's your turn," something else happened with the current because the Jeep turned over and in the turning over it turned over so the driver's side was going down and the door closed. What happened then was the river started to come through the window. So my memory — besides being mostly of falling back on top of Carla — was this: I don't know what you call it . . . all this water with a lot of force coming through this window. So I think Carla must have pushed somewhat and one of the fellows still had a part of me so when a break came there was a tremendous amount of force coming on top of me but I tried to get out through that window. At some point the guy who had me — the current changed again — and he got thrown — and I just went bobbing down the river. The first thing I thought was it must be very far down and when do you get up to get air? I just couldn't believe it was so far down. They said later that when the Jeep went down on its side at that point it probably was two meters, six and a half feet, under water. But with the force in those currents you were kind of fighting that to get up to get some air.

For some strange reason, I had in my hand a flashlight. And it was on and for a while I was going up and then as I was being taken down another time I went down very, very deep. I just said to myself you're not going to get up, so I said, "Receive me, Lord." Finally, that's just all I said and I was a little curious about what was going to happen, but at some point I came up again. It just kind of went on — I don't know how long. It went on — these two things I can tell you: I had no panic and I really wasn't afraid. I was like all along, like a piece [of wood] that was being turned around and upside down, scratching rocks. Sometimes the stream would be very shallow and sometimes very deep and I was just going along. Then there just came a point at which I got taken towards what in the morning I found out was like a bamboo grove. There were these roots and I reached out and finally got a hold of some and I got myself out of the hold of the current. I just kind of stayed there for a while very quietly. I guess to just kind of calm down and figure out what next. I guess the thing I had most was hope. Eventually, there was lightening so I could see a tree but I'm in the middle of the *campo* [countryside], and it's very, very dark. So I looked around and there was an enormous root that was horizontal between the water and what would have been the top of the bank of the river which was about four or five feet over my head at this point. This root had, like, a fork in it, so I got one arm through the fork of the root and when I had the one arm through, I was at least anchored onto something. The other was kind of looking around for something to grab. I was in the water and the root was, maybe, a foot or two over my head. As I looked up I saw there was this tree trunk on the bank but that was about three feet up. So I thought, well, I have to get myself up onto this root that seemed very strong and then get myself on the tree trunk. Then I would be out of the water because the water was still rising. I tried a couple of times. I put my feet against the bank and tried to push myself but the bank was just mud, wet, and I slipped. I think that was the most difficult part physically. I just kind of estimate that maybe it took me an hour to get out of the river. I might be wrong. I tried to swing up. I tried to boost up and I just nearly didn't have any strength left. I had the feeling I was wasting my strength. I was moving around and somehow found as I was feeling around with my feet that there was something else that I could get a foothold on and on which I could boost myself up a little bit. It was still . . .

The land just kind of falls off, canyons. So I just had this feeling, get up and away from the river. I went plowing through this man's cornfields and knocked down several stalks and just kept pulling myself up the mountain. I got beyond the cornfield and I got into beans and beans just kind of . . . they wrap all around you — I can't even think of the word in English right now, but anyway the vines wrap around you. I went up there and I could see there was a row of trees, and I thought, maybe I could spot a house. I went quite a distance up the mountain and as I got up there and looked around all I could see was more hills and more trees. There didn't seem to be anything at all around and I said, well, pick your spot. So there were like wild bushes and things. I curled my head under a couple of bushes thinking, for some reason although I was absolutely soaking wet and it was raining, that I was going to get warm. Anyway, I found that I had no broken bones or anything like that. I knew, without a doubt, that I was going to have a good case of something in the morning, either bronchitis or pneumonia. The other thing I knew was that I had some bleeding around my left eye. I had a very superficial cut, but I didn't have any idea what it was. I took some leaves and put it on the cut. I couldn't work with my other hand because it was covered with dirt. My hands were quite dirty.

Well after I lay down, I realized I had a body that was shaking all over for over half an hour. I just went into the shivers all night, but it was just a body reaction, something like a spasm. I guess I've never been so cold in my life. For some reason, I told God off about it. There were also an awful lot of mosquitoes. I said to God that being this miserable was unbearable, "Why do you have to have mosquitoes around?" The thing was either to brush these mosquitoes off or kill them because they were attacking me. But then I'd have to take my hand off my side, which I was holding, trying to keep every piece or ounce of body together.

So the major scene for me the next morning was somebody whose arms and neck were a mess with innumerable bites. But while I had no idea what had happened to Carla or Esteban or Alfredo, I had to think that they could be alive or they could be dead. I prayed for each and then thought about a lot of people. First, I thought about a lot of people who made things very difficult for us. I said, "If this is worth anything, maybe it will touch them." Then, I thought a lot about a lot of you. I guess, at one point, I felt particularly with Rene. Then, after a while I said to myself, "Well now, you have to start thinking pleasant things, because you just can't dwell on what's happened." There didn't seem to be any way that I was going to sleep. So as long as my mind was going a thousand miles a minute, I started thinking about nice things.

Then, it must have been about midnight when I could hear loud-speakers saying, "We're looking for the nuns, we're looking for the nuns." But I didn't know if they were looking for Carla and me. I didn't know if — knew the boys were with us — that somebody knew that something had happened, but I couldn't do anything about it because I couldn't move. It was so dark. I'd gotten so far without doing any tremendous damage to myself. I thought, if I start out now, I'll probably kill myself. I didn't have the energy, no energy whatsoever. So I said I'll stay here until it's light. When it gets light I'll work my way down the mountain.

It turned out that what happened was that actually after one of the fellows had gotten onto a safe place and the other one, who was thrown [trying to help me] somehow made it to another bank — the two of them ... and didn't have to have this hastily. One of them went to a house. I guess he almost got killed because they thought he was a robber. Somehow they spread the word around quite a bit and got a truck and went back to Chalatenango where they got everybody out of bed. They came out with lots of lights including that famous lamp that you sent down with us. They got people up and they started searching and diving. Some of the people went out with ropes.

At some point they found the car completely upside down, the tires in the air and nobody in it. So that was the state of things. At six o'clock in the morning, when the announcement came again calling for everybody of goodwill to get out and start looking for Carla and me, well, I got myself up. I got tremendously sick, but I had rolled and kept purposely changing my position all night and kept moving, on my side, on my back so I wouldn't be too stiff. I knew that I was going to be terribly stiff anyway and I started making my way down the mountain. I was quite amazed how far I had gotten up the mountain. This time I found a path around the beans and the corn so I didn't have to go through them. So I got down to the riverbank. I started to call and some man came along. I said, "Did you hear what they are saying? I'm one of those people." So he crossed the river and he took me home to his house.

Afterwards, he had given me a towel to put around me to keep warm and we started to walk toward town. You know these farms in outlying areas have small country towns, it's a drop on the bucket — a little nothing — but anyway, and even that area had little subdivisions. As we were walking I met one of the men I knew who was a member of the Christian community so that he came with me. He had with him a tablecloth and so we switched the towel for the tablecloth and wrapped me with the tablecloth. Then to get to town we actually had to cross the river four times. It was still kind of going pretty fast. So we walked across and started meeting a lot of the men coming downhill with boots and machetes and different things to go along the bank. I had the idea, well, maybe Carla had broken something, broken a leg and, maybe, actually gotten a hold of something and just couldn't make herself known. So the men were all very concerned and they brought me to the Parish House.

I saw one of the seminarians wrapped up in a bedspread. He had spent the last couple of hours diving into different sloughs in the river. It was just a tremendous response on the part of the people trying to find us. Well, some ladies there brought me a set of clothes and took my clothes. They got out the first-aid kit and it's kind of funny. I looked at it, because I had made that first-aid kit just the day before. I made the first aid kit on Friday and it was delivered there on Saturday and they were using it on me on Sunday — you know this special kind of soap and stuff like that. I kept asking for coffee. I was so cold inside.

So Teresa came out again. They had come from Chalatenango about five o'clock in the morning. They went and, I guess, they made some phone calls, called the *Arzobispado* and the chancery to say that we had disappeared. They had called the Cleveland team but they weren't too specific, they just got them kind of confused. They said that something had happened but they weren't too clear. So they said [to me] now it was about 7:30 and the best thing we could think of is that we get you back to Chalatenango and have a doctor check you out and to call people and let them know that one of you has turned up and alive. So I said OK. So we went back. The first thing I did was call the Cleveland team and because they had one phone number [which was easier and they were] English speaking people, they were glad that I called them. So they got the message and said, "Yeah, yeah, they'd be right out." They got somebody and called Maddie, or somebody went up to Santa Ana, to get her to come out.

At some point the Red Cross also got involved. The colonel [I had seen] at six and for various hours the day before, came over at some point and said they were very sorry and that he was going to send out some soldiers. Some of the local people said, "Please be careful, because these soldiers were out there usually killing people." They get a little frightened. Remember that these people were doing a work of mercy and are looking yet for a body [Carla's] and let's not get confused about the subject [militia violence]. So whether the soldiers ever really got involved in the act I really don't know. But anyway that was part of the story.

About 20:30 [8:30 p.m.] or so, Jean Donovan, who's a lay missioner with the Cleveland team, but who I know even more because she happened to be in the training program at Maryknoll when I was home last year, said to me, "Where do you keep your sheets?" I said, "We keep them over there." I thought, well maybe Carla was dead and they weren't telling me. But actually what happened, she [Jean] said somebody had come in and they thought they'd make something like a hammock or something they could use if they find her. But it was shortly after that that the Red Cross people did find her, and it was Jean, and I think, the chancellor of the archdiocese and someone else who told me, very close to Chalatenango. They said the river took Carla and banged her up quite a bit. I don't know where Carla died. I think Carla must have died in the car because the car was just completely, really badly wrecked. The steering wheel wasn't so there was a lot of bumping against that and when Maddie looked up, Maddie said Carla's neck was broken and certainly other things were broken. As I said, I don't know. They brought her back to the house and wrapped her in a blanket.

Right behind her came in three men with television cameras. Well, I kicked them out very quickly. Then I probably . . . a doctor had come in the meantime or was there then, and said, "Would you believe you have an infection in your lungs?" Of course I believed it. I guess I had a fever and what else. There wasn't too much of keeping me down. I guess I was kind of hyper, but not that hyper. But all the people came in and as I said, Carla was on her bed and wrapped up with a towel and a sheet. And they kept taking the towel and looking at her face, this and that, and, you know, they had to find out how tall she was, actually the archdiocese did. Various—a couple of coffins showed up and finally to get Carla into one of the coffins they had to leave off the shoes and she just fit. Not too many people 5'8" around.

Maddie took care of Carla and that. They took her to the hospital, I think, to prepare the body there so we had some quiet then. The Bishop, you know the one who is Apostolic Administrator, Rivera y Damas, the Vicar General, and Bishop Fabian who we work with came out at 3 o'clock and we had a Mass. Then, it was after that that Carla's body came back. Then the two men, whom we worked with most closely, had a Mass and, then, the Sisters, several groups of Sisters and the people, stayed all night in the Church. That's the custom, you know, they pray and sing for reflection.

Some of the others — there were Maryknoll Sisters there too — told me to go to bed. So the only thing that I was concerned about was the readings for the funeral Mass. I wanted one from Romans 8: ". . . nothing can separate you from the love of God," and the Gospel that reads, "there's no greater love than to lay down one's life for your friends," because I think basically the job we were doing was secondary to taking that fellow home. What we actually thought was that he was not particularly trustworthy or anything like that. Thinking about that later, it was on account of his being a shmuck, and yet Jesus died among all shmucks. The people were all very concerned. We were trying to help them because they had gone through so much and especially because that's what the work's about, and I don't think that probably Carla would have wanted it any other way. I think she died doing what she was intended to do.

I think everybody was really touched by the reflections and, I think, very challenged. I think many of the Salvadorans were touched. So, the next day was the funeral. It was really quite a beautiful Mass. The people were very touched that Carla was going to be buried in Chalatenango and well, they asked me why, and I just said, "It is where she worked." You know, we had been offered the opportunity to have the wake in one of the Sisters' chapels in San Salvador or have her buried in San Salvador. I said, "No, she died right here working for these people and it's like robbing the people of — you know, she kind of belonged to them and they belong to her. This is not the time when you now march somebody off to some kind of a solemn Church thing."

Considering the time, there were a lot of things going down on the Church radio station, yet 15 priests, I knew 14 and one guy I'd never laid eyes on before, and a host of seminarians came and, of course, the Sisters. During the Mass instead of a homily there were about eight people, and, in fact, I asked one of the sisters we stay in town with, with whom Carla was quite friendly, who said just a few words. Well, she, six priests and some of the people from the communities where Carla brought the food said something. It was like pass the microphone type of thing. Afterwards we went to the cemetery that is down about two streets and then down a big long hill to the entrance to the town. All the Sisters, who were there, walked the coffin down. I thought and had this funny thing, had to sort of laugh, this would be the last time, I felt, I was trying to hold Carla back. Because sometimes, when she was very spontaneous and about to take off to something I wasn't too sure of, you'd have to put a brake on her . . . and the coffin was down hill . . . you had to put a brake on it a little bit. So I was thinking about that. It was the only thing that sort of embarrassed me. It was very (anti-)Anglo-Saxon that we were just at the point of putting the coffin in the grave and I felt like I was about to get sick. They said, "You're not going to get sick." All of a sudden I said, "I am going to get sick." So I had to move over behind two other places. They had insisted that I eat before the Mass and, I guess, later we found out in the hospital, when they took the tests that when I had to keep warm that night that all my reserve was used up. The calories and carbohydrates and minerals in my body had been used up. Actually, I didn't have digestive type of stuff left in my system, so I couldn't keep food down. But I hadn't known about it. They had to give me some special intravenous to replace the minerals necessary to just keep warm [body temperature normal]. I was at the hospital five days and, then, we had a couple of meetings.

You probably know that Maura Clarke will be coming out to Chalatenango. Maura is a tremendous woman. She has a lot of experience in Nicaragua. She has been home for the last three or four years doing Mission Education, World Awareness. She is very Irish and has a big, loving, warm heart. I think she's going to be fantastic for all these people who come in, who are traumatized, who have been fleeing or scared for their lives. I just think Maura's going to be God's greatest gift to them. I said to her, and I said to all the people, "She's not Carla. Each person is gifted and they're gifted in their own way. We can't lay trips on each other . . . that you're not this one and you're not that one. Let's all be free to be who we are."

Next week I'm going to Guatemala to join the Sisters there for a week of retreat. I think, just for a change, to see some green and probably to integrate some of this experience that is still very unreal. However, at least in the last day or two I've had some time to myself. From the 24th until this past Thursday (today's Saturday), I was never alone. I just need a little time. So I stayed with these nuns in the convent who let me alone. I mean you can do what you want. Eat with them or pray with them or sit with them or not. They are very respectful. They care very much, but they know when to back off and so that's what I've been doing for a couple of days. I was just kind of quiet, trying to put some things together. I don't know — there's mail for Carla and stuff to answer, so I'm just going to let some of the stuff go for a while and just kind of sleep and finish off my medicine.

The only other funny thing was that after the funeral we were reading some of the scripture when we were — the Maryknollers — reading about Peter. It was about Peter walking on the water and, it seems that Carla had written somebody in Chile (and the whole reflection was on this) that the Lord had called her out of the boat and she got out and she was sinking and He grabbed her hand or something like that. I realize that I said to them that during the whole thing I never said, "Help." It had never occurred to me to say, "Save me." It never occurred to me that I was drowning or to panic. It was just that something was happening. I just didn't know what it meant, but I just realized it never came across like, "Save me." I said, "Receive me, I'm coming." But any kind of being saved from drowning or panic or something, I didn't feel any of that.

I don't think I'm angry. I'm confused. I don't feel guilty. Some people talk as if there's a survivor's guilt but I don't think I have that. There is still a lot of work to do and I want to get well and get back to it. I know it's important what we are doing.

I know this is kind of a heavy experience. It might even be heavy for you to be listening to it. But, I guess, it just says that God is extremely active in our lives and is certainly the Lord of Life, the One Who's in charge. The One Who decides. I thought, you know, I've come in contact with a lot of people who sleep outside at night.

They say they slept in the *monte*. Well, now I've slept in the *monte*. These are the things that kind of bind you to people. I'm sure that what all this means will come about and be clearer later on. I think I'm pretty much together. I'm not jumping for joy or anything like that. But I miss Carla very much, but I still rant and rave at her. I don't know whatever that last letter was that she wrote that was so terrific since that was a private thing going between you and her. But whatever it is I'm really glad. As I was going through pictures, I found that one of your birthday with that crazy shirt so I'll include it with the tape. Any minute this thing is going to end. So, you know it, and I know it . . . that I love you and you love me. I know God loves us all and I don't mean that in any kind of a trite way. I think there are several extraordinary examples of that. I don't know how to tell you not to be concerned. But I hope that you can really hold on there in trust and faith.

105.

THREE MONTH EVALUATION OF THE CHALATENANGO MINISTRY

Due to the circumstances of being asked to begin a new work for the *vicaria,** months after the formulation of the area's targets and goals, the Emergency Committee does not fall directly under the area's goals. However, it does correspond to the Regional objectives, namely:

I. In accord with our Christian principles, we are committed to collaborate with those groups, organizations and movements that are actively working for justice and liberation.

II. We deepen our commitment to the cause of the urban and rural poor who are most affected by unjust structures.

Given that this was a new work to be created as the need arose, that within 2 1/2 months of beginning one of the two full-time members of the team died and another has come who needed time to get a 'feel' for the situation, an ordinary evaluation does not seem to be feasible. However, we would like to share some of the accomplishments, problems and possible solutions we are able to surface at this time.

Accomplishments

a) Insertion into the local Church, working in team effort with sisters, priests and lay leaders.

b) Organization of means for relocating people, especially women

---

* *Vicaria* — Spanish for Vicariate, an administrative region within a Catholic diocese.

and children fleeing from the terror of real or potential danger and violence, to other safe living areas or to refugee centers.

c) Setting up channels for the distribution of food and medicine to displaced people.

d) Research and presentation of a project for funding for emergency needs of the *vicaria*.

e) Establishment of contact with organized groups to collaborate and coordinate emergency aid.

Problems and Failures

a) The lack of any existing model to follow in this *Pastoral de Asistencia*, the title given to this work by the *vicaria*.

b) The need to reorganize after Carla's death, including Maura and Ita's process of learning to work together.

c) The inability to fully give of ourselves to the work because of the mourning process and adjustment to a new situation.

d) Our own limited background and knowledge due to being recent arrivals in El Salvador.

e) The problem of often feeling overstretched because of demands to respond to situations we know nothing about.

f) The nature of the work is such that it has no predictable shape or structure.

g) This emergency has no immediate end in sight, and we really do not know how to plan around a war.

h) The lack of organization within the groups with whom we collaborate.

i) The need to work within restrictive limitations due to military vigilance.

Possible Solutions

a) Broader based collaboration beyond the limits of the *vicaria* so as to tap others' abilities, skills and knowledge.

b) With time, learning to live in an ongoing emergency situation.

c) Additional personnel.

d) Faithful prayers for the happy, holy and proximate passing to the rest of the just for Ronald Reagan.

106. *To the Sisters of the Chile Region, Maryknoll, NY, September 7, 1980*

Dear, dear friends,

As I count you up, I believe that there are about 10 of you — and maybe even more if some of the furlough ladies haven't returned yet. What can I say to you who knew and loved Carla for many more years than I. If we were together we would cry and tell stories and laugh and pray. And I'm sure you all did that together with some wine to celebrate the occasion.

As I am writing to you I'm realizing that maybe there is something I'm missing — persons who knew and had had relationships with Carla for more than three or four months. Some of those were exceptional probably because in this situation there's really very little that's superficial, but it's still a different thing. To many people here, she's a heroine, a person larger than life, a mystery. In her unique way, she got a lot of things going, threw firecrackers around at meetings and sort of shook up a very *machista* Church. And, of course, her outrageousness got a few things moving, as did her own testimony of putting her body where her mouth was.

Yet, there was no dramatic difference between Carla in Chile and Carla in El Salvador. I know she was burnt out when she left Bandera and that Coelemu was a restoring and renewing time. She often said she was a product of Chile — fifteen years — and what she brought to El Salvador came from Chile.

We weren't here too long before we had to have a couple of conversations about death. It's just part of the violent situation. Not that we thought that some soldiers were going to gun us down, but there was the possibility of some drunk member (or other), the paramilitary right, or something else, whatever. There's not a high trust level operating here. We thought it would be rather nice that should it happen, that it would be together, because the one left behind would definitely be on the short end of the stick.

The Thursday before she died, we were talking about the reading of the day, "I'll take away your heart of stone and give you a heart of flesh" (Jer. 3). She said to me, "God's done that." A couple of years ago she told me that when she left Chile, she asked for a heart of stone! She never really explained the whole thing, but I presumed it was a very painful situation and the only way to handle it was to shut off all feelings. Well, I guess you can just do that for so long and then you have to start working with them or God intervenes in some way. You all know the history, the years with Teresa Corquera,* the family problems, all of it. But in that something was happening. The stone got porous, and then fleshy. She told me, "God has really done it. I now have a heart of flesh." And the heart ached for what's going on here. A lot of nights after coming home from listening to horror stories or consoling people she'd get her "toys," her magic markers, and some paper and begin to draw. She would draw birds crying and their tears forming mountain streams. She would draw wounded doves of peace. She would draw the Salvadoran countryside of cornfields going up the mountains. She also wrote a couple of songs, one, "You Are The Lord Of The Road," was sort of our theme song as we went out with a Jeep loaded down with sacks of food and medicine. As we continued talking, she said to me, "You walked a lot of that road with me." Then she said, "Now you can dismiss your servant in peace, Lord" (Lk. 3). I thought she was referring to me, so I said, "I'm not so sure I get dismissed so easily." She answered, "We'll see."

I'm not sure Carla had any special feeling that she was soon to go to the Lord. (I doubt she would have told me.) But it seems that she wrote to Kathy Gilfeather the week before with a reflection about feeling like Peter getting out of the boat and going to Jesus across the water. Although she was sinking, he was holding her. We all know that He did.

As for me, I feel like John in the last scene of his gospel. Jesus tells Peter to follow him and Peter turns around and asks about John. Jesus says — I'm talking to you, Peter. John's later. For some reason it's meant for me to keep at it. So I will. Right now, the pain is a lot. For the first week I think I must have been in some sort of shock, body-wise, and probably spirit-wise. After twelve days of not being alone for a minute, I've taken some days with some Sisters who 'are

---

* Carla's therapist in Chile.

around,' but not around. So the pain and the reality are coming out and that's good. Then next week I'll go to Guatemala to join the Sisters there for a retreat.

Maura Clarke is coming to Chalatenango. She'll be a beautiful gift for the hurting, traumatized people. I think she'll be a gift for me too.

I miss you all very much. It's one of those mysteries that God asks me to mourn alone and work it out here while all those with whom Carla was so involved are at a distance — in NY, Chile, Bangladesh, etc.

I keep counting on your love and support. (I just remembered, in another envelope some things about Carla are coming. Maybe one of you could translate them for her family. Thanks.) Take good care.

Much love.

Ita

107. *To the Maryknoll Sisters of the Chile Region, September 7, 1980. Some of the previous letter is found also in the following.*

Dear, dear friends,

Jessie has returned and possibly has filled you in on every imaginable detail, but there's something in me that urges me to add my two cents.

I just finished writing the Chileans in NY and while writing the letter I had an insight. When someone dies we all get together, cry, tell stories, laugh, reminisce, pray, have a liturgy and celebrate the fullness of life. And I know you all did that, so many of you who have known and loved Carla longer than I. What hit me was that there is no one in this country that knows Carla for longer than four months. She did already have some relationships because this is a country where there's very little superficiality. But it's just so different (for me) than if she had died in Chile. Already she's a little bit larger than life, a heroine, "an angel of charity." I guess it's useless for me to protest that my beat up old friend is an example of God's strength being manifested in our weakness; His goodness and love through our vessels of clay.

The Carla of El Salvador was a Chilean import. She claimed to be a product of Chile — 15 years worth — and what she could offer came from her life experience there. Except for Pam, Patricia, and Mary Ann you all know Carla's history, the ups and downs, the pain and the resurrections. What I want to share is something we talked about the Thursday before her death. The reading was "I will take away your hearts of stone and give you hearts of flesh" (Jer. 31,29-31). She said to me, "God has really done that for me."

A couple of years ago she told me that when she left Chile, she asked for a heart of stone! She never really explained the whole thing, but I presumed it was a very painful situation and the only way to handle it was to shut off all feelings. Well, I guess you can just do that for so long and then you have to start working with them or God intervenes in some way. You all know the history, the years with Teresa Corquera, the family problems, all of it. But in that something was happening. The stone got porous, and then fleshy. She told me, "God has really done it. I now have a heart of flesh." And the heart ached for what's going on here. A lot of nights after coming home from listening to horror stories or consoling people she'd get her 'toys,' her magic markers, and some paper and begin to draw. She would draw birds crying and their tears forming mountain streams. She would draw wounded doves of peace. She would draw the Salvadoran countryside of cornfields going up the mountains. She also wrote a couple of songs, one, "You Are The Lord Of The Road," was sort of our theme song as we set out with a Jeep loaded down with sacks of food and medicine.

As we continued talking, she said to me, "You walked a lot of that road with me." The she said, "Now you can dismiss your servant in peace, Lord." (Lk. 3) I thought she was referring to me, so I said, "I'm not so sure I get dismissed so easily." She answered, "We'll see."

That along with her letter to Kathy may or may not indicate that Carla had some kind of intuition that soon she would be with the Lord. (I'm sure I would have been the last person she would have told — given the circumstances) but we had talked about dying several times. (It seems to be a topic you can't avoid in El Salvador.) I think we both accepted the possibility as part of our being here . . .

After being here for a while, Carla couldn't help but be known in some circles. Her initiative, her firecrackers at meetings, her knocking heads with a machista Church, her putting her body where her mouth was, just being Carla, certainly did an awful lot to help earn us credibility in a difficult and disturbing ambiente.* Yet, she wasn't superwoman nor was she doing crazy things. Anything that we did that was the least bit shaky or maybe shady, we checked it out first with the vicar.

Her *Adamic*† streak of naming people and things was very strong here. And most were quite apt. I can't say I gloried in her last name for me. It was "Mrs. Coathanger" because I lost some weight.

We caused quite a stir in New York with our three-month evaluation, that wasn't our intent. It was merely to ask for some input and help in a difficult situation. Some of you instinctively must have recognized that, because there were almost weekly letters to Carla from Rebecca, and Ceci almost as often. Others of you, too, have written. It's not the receiving or not of letters. It was just some sort of void where we couldn't feel your support, even though we felt part of the Chilean region and somehow sent by you. Marge Lyons sent a letter from NY that sort of captured it. We went through a very hard time and, I think, Carla was working herself up to return in January for the meeting — and probably with a firecracker or two. (I really don't know if you're safe or not!)

After not being alone for twelve days (I was even accompanied to the hospital), I'm just taking some time alone at the *Asuncionistas*‡ to let the pain and hurt come out. It's one of those mysteries to be asked to mourn alone when everyone else with whom Carla shared life is in Chile, NY, even Bangladesh. But that seems to be the present script. Next week we'll be going to Guatemala to join the Sisters there in a retreat. I think that's a good idea. After that, Maura Clarke and I will go back to Chalatenango. Maura's great gift of kindness

---

* *Ambiente* — atmosphere.

† A reference to Adam naming the animals in Genesis.

‡ *Asuncionistas*, the Sisters of the Assumption, with whom Carla and Ita lived for a time in Chalatenango.

and love will be great for the traumatized, hurting people there. She'll be great for me, too.

I'm sending along some of the materials that have come out about Carla. A few I noted for some of her friends. The rest is for all of you to multiply or divide as you see fit.

I keep counting on your love and support, even though I, too, am a poor correspondent.

Much love to each of you.

Ita

108. To Sister Rose Guercio, MM, Treasurer of the Maryknoll Sisters, September 7, 1980

Dear Rose,

Enclosed is a copy of the project sent to HIVOS, Holland. I'm sorry if the English is a little stilted in spots. I was doing a quick re-translation tonight to get this ready for the courier tomorrow.

Just so you know, there seems to be a wrinkle about the funds. The bank account number is one the Archdiocese uses for projects funded from the outside. Money has been deposited, but no confirmation has been sent. So the committee cannot withdraw the money.

I've telegraphed a contact in Honduras, but got no answer and, unfortunately, the telephone number I had is in a book at the bottom of a river in Chalatenango. But I'm sure it will get straightened out somehow, eventually.

The project was written the beginning of June. The estimate of displaced people is ridiculously low as the months have passed. But all that is getting clearer. This was to start the ball rolling. I think it's fairly self-explanatory.

Love,

Ita

109. To Sister Catherine Verboten (Carla's aunt), September 12, 1980

Dear Sr. Catherine,

By now you have probably received word from Maryknoll, New York of Carol's* death. Since 1973 we have shared faith, friendship, and community in Chile and for just a few months in El Salvador. We were together the night of August 23 when the flash flood caught the Jeep and turned it over. One of the last things she probably did was give me a push through the window as the river was pouring in on top of us. I humbly must stand before the wisdom and love of God who chose to call Carol to himself that night, and not me. Yet, if in some ways we could choose the way we would die, Carol's was consistent with her life. She was serving the poor and 'beat up,' as she would say. Our years together are a great gift and source of strength.

In one of your recent letters, a check of $25 was enclosed. My instinct would be to apply it to our work with the displaced people in El Salvador. However, one of the Sisters said I should consult you first. It can also be returned if the donor wishes. I will wait for your response before doing anything.

I miss Carol very much, yet I also believe that we are still bound in a relationship whose depths I still must discover. I believe she is fully alive and I rejoice with her.

May she help us both to continue serving those whom the Lord puts in our lives.

Sincerely,
(Sr.) Ita Ford

110. October 9, 1980

Dear Mom,

I was about to begin once again by apologizing for not getting a letter written, but each day seems to evaporate and I flop into bed not

---

* Carol was Carla's given name, and the name by which friends and family knew her.

having done half of what I thought I would. Things keep turning up that take time and moving around — and no day is ever predictable. So, maybe there just will be fewer letters, but I'll keep trying.

The visit with Carolyn was good for both of us. Mostly we just caught up, talked about Carla, Salvador, Chile, etc. And then we moved ourselves to visit some of the Sisters in Guatemala. When I saw your present, I thought it might be better to fly back here because the land checks are much more of a hassle, and nastier. I had a little bit of back and forth with customs even so, but it turned out fine.

These last few days have been rough ones. The front part of the seminary and the chancery got bombed the other night, probably because the people who had occupied the [Organization of American States] offices asked to be taken there for protection. Also a member of the human rights commission and a priest from here were killed. That probably makes more news than all the 'beat up' who die. Who are many. Someone remarked the other day that all our conversations are about death. It's probably true, because it's all around and often so barbaric.

Maura, who is with me, is really a beautiful person. She's tremendously kind and considerate and so warm with those who wind up under our roof for a while, and with me too.

I guess this is a "I'm still breathing" note, because it's time to hit the road. I hope everyone's OK. Take care.

Love to all,
Ita

111. *To Sister Carol Hassey, MM, who was in charge of the Congregation's Health Services, October 9, 1980*

Dear Carol,

How do you like this for a 'summary discharge?' Well, we tried!

A couple of weeks ago, I saw Jane Buellesbach in Guatemala during retreat. I asked if it was possible to be in partial shock and she said, "Yes," and that I probably would be for a while. I guess it all takes time. The psyche doesn't recover as fast as the old 'bod!'

How are you? Well, I hope. Thanks for telling Jeanne the news. Take care.

Love,
Ita

112. To Sister Peg Hanlon, MM, October 17, 1980

Dear Peg,

Thanks so much for your letter. Sorry it's taken me so long to respond, but I think I'm now beginning to emerge from shock, at least somewhat.

The first thing to say is thanks so much for your visit and support and love. I really appreciate that you came. Also it seems that you all outdid yourselves on the Mass (at Maryknoll). So many people have commented and written (and we have a tape). In fact, I guess in some ways the liturgies in Chile and New York had more 'flavor' of Carla because those who prepared them knew her for a much longer time. (That was hard for me in the beginning. No one here knew Carla very long, even the Sisters, so I missed part of the process of shared remembrances.) Here in Salvador the little people took over, in a sense, and still are. The Christian community of Chalatenango must have thought we were very slow moving, so they took it upon themselves to have a marker made for the tomb. We were shown the inscription about two minutes before the lady was getting on the bus. It was quite elaborate and she wasn't in too much of a mood for compromise. I got one or two changes made, but essentially I lost. And it's not that important! I guess it will be ready before November 2.

The other thing I wanted to respond to was about the Jeep. After a lot of back and forth, [Father] Fabian has decided to replace "La Tonquita" (which is still parked in Chalatenango — so I have my reality therapy daily) with a new diesel Jeep. The cost is $8400. He has funding for $4800. Just this week we got official confirmation about our project for emergency aid for food, etc. Fabian told me he was going to borrow from that fund so we could get the Jeep as soon as possible — because we're now using a borrowed gas one. Then he hopes to slowly replace the money as he can. He hasn't directly asked me to help find money, but given the tone of your letter, I would say that if there could be some help, I'm sure it would be more than appreciated. Most of the help coming has strings, such as food, medical, refugee center, etc. I really don't know if there are quantities coming in to be used as seen fit. So in response to your offer I'd say we need help and would be grateful for what you could do.

Carolyn Lehmann and I had a good get-together in Guatemala for almost a week. If things work out, Julie might be dropping in next week. Some of that depends on the climate here, but we're hoping it will work out.

Much love,
Ita

113. To the Maryknoll Sisters from David Helvag

David Helvag, a journalist in El Salvador, interviewed Ita Ford in October 1980 (see #114). He later wrote this account.

On February 10th 1982 six members of the Salvadoran National Guard were indicted for the December, 1980 murder of four U.S. church women, three nuns and a Catholic lay worker active in refugee relief work.

Two of those killed, Ita Ford and Maura Clarke, had spent several years working with the poor people of El Salvador. In the late fall of 1980, I briefly met with, and was greatly impressed by Sister Ita Ford. A photographer and I had just returned to Chalatenango city after spending several nights under fire with the National Guard contingent in the small border town of Arcatao. We decided to visit the church refugee center we'd heard about before continuing on to San Salvador. It was there we met her. She was a thoughtful and attractive woman, small, light boned and watchful, casually dressed in blue jeans and cotton.

We sat around a low table on a couple of plastic school chairs drinking tea and fruit punch, passing the afternoon in conversation, some of which I recorded.

"From my own limited experience I think the majority of the rural people in some way have sympathy for, if they're not actively collaborating with, the popular organizations, the revolutionaries," she told us.

"In the militarized towns this is not true, of course, but the majority feel they're being terribly repressed by the security forces. A death squad will just drive into town and stake it out, just lean against the wall and there's nothing the people can do. People have identified their cars, seen these men walking in and out of the National Police stations. Who do you go to to put in a complaint? There's nowhere to go to complain about murder."

The Catholic church and various human rights organizations estimate that some 35,000 people have died in El Salvador since the U.S. backed 'reform coup' of October 1979, the majority of the dead being civilians killed at the hands of the security forces and right-wing death squads. I asked Ita how she felt about U.S. aid to the Salvadoran Junta.

"As a U.S. citizen I'm highly disappointed and mostly outraged by the type of support we're giving to this junta," she said. "I think the U.S. is upholding a myth that there's a center ground and a third way. This government doesn't represent anybody at this point. It's fearful to think of the U.S. now training Salvadoran troops and sending in equipment. It's reprehensible."

"Sometime the United States will have to realize it does not own Central America or any other part of the world, that people have a right to shape their own destiny, to choose the type of government they want and make their own choices and we don't lose anything. We don't lose Cuba, we don't lose Nicaragua, because they were never ours to lose."

Several weeks earlier Ita had been in a Land Rover that had overturned in a river while on a mission trying to save the life of a 19 year-old government informer. They were trying to get him out of a guerilla-controlled area where he would have been killed. Another nun she was with at the time died in the accident.

"Afterwards we got him away and I tried to say, 'Look. Look at this life that was lost for yours. Life's too precious. You can't just buy and sell it like you've been doing. You have to think what life means.'"

She showed us the smashed remains of the Land Rover that had been pulled out of the river and towed back to the refugee center. "When I got out of the water after the accident and had to walk for hours through the forest to get to a town, it was so cold. All I could think of was, 'Why her God? Why did you call her and not me?'" She tried to smile. "I don't know. Maybe I've been chosen for another purpose."

One month later she and three other church women would be dead at the hands of the Salvadoran security forces.

114. An interview with Ita Ford by David Helvag

This interview, described above, was transcribed by Judith Noone, MM. It has been edited for this compilation.

Ita Ford, a Maryknoll Sister, had been working in El Salvador during the last year. On December 4, 1980, her body was found with those of two other nuns and one missionary lay woman. A few days before her murder *Pacifica* reporter David Helvag talked to her in El Salvador.

Helvag: As a Sister, a North American who has been working here in Salvador for several months, maybe you could tell me about some of the work you are involved in.
Ford: One of the works we are involved in is with the people who are displaced or refugees. Those who are fleeing [do so] for various reasons. Some are fleeing [from] a climate of terror, some are fleeing because members of their family have been threatened and they, themselves, have been threatened. Others are fleeing because they're afraid of the popular group organizations. [The result is] a variety of uprootedness, in which the people have left their small plots of land and their homes and they come to another town or they come to the city. What you have then is a whole phenomena of [people moving] to one place, [while] other people, then, who are also up-rooted, move

into their homes and their land. Since this pattern has been going on, for at least this year, there has been in this area 50% less sowing of the basic grains. So we are looking forward to not a famine, but a scarcity of food by the end of this year and the beginning of next . . .

So what has happened is that there now exist 7 refugee centers in San Salvador, the largest one being 800 people. At this point, it is on the property of the Archdiocesan Seminary. Some people have been there since January. It's a very difficult situation because most of these people are rural people, particularly women and children, who are used to a very basic busy day of washing and cooking, and there they are — it's a type of a jail and I would say morale is low. The difficulty with those centers is also that there is no government guarantee of security.

H.: Like official Red Cross or Green Cross guarantees?
F.: No. In international law, as has been explained to me by the International Red Cross, only when a state of war has been declared can protection of that type be guaranteed. [As a result] the army can always go into a refugee center and take somebody out.

H.: It really has involved no war at this stage?
F.: Well, it depends on who you talk to. In my estimation it's a civil war. But how many people need to die — what sort of conditions are necessary to say it is a civil war? It seems the government is not going to say that this is a civil war. The popular organizations, at this point, have not yet made steps to claim territory or to say we are a government in exile, in opposition . . . and so the thing erupts.

H.: They talk about several thousands of refugees having crossed over to Honduras including a thousand just in the department of Chalatenango. What you were talking about is different forces affecting and generating refugees — what do you think is the main force that is creating the refugees in this country?
F.: The main force, I think, creating the refugees in this country is actually the conflict between the security forces and the popular organization forces . . . .

H.: *What do you know about the massacre on the Rio Sumpul? What was that as far as you know?**

F.: As far as I know, [this was] a military operation, one of the first of this type to go up through the canyon, up near the border [between El Salvador and Honduras] into a place that the people call *tomba,* which is where people had resettled up in that area. It was an operation that included air cover and helicopters from which they were shooting down at the people. In one place, bodies were found shot as they were taking cover underneath the trees. It was sort of a two-day thing with the people going through the mountains and getting to the border, which is the river there. And as they crossed over the adults went first and the soldiers said if you don't come back we'll kill the children, and eyewitness reports said the children were thrown into the river, at least one or two were thrown up into the air and shot at. I don't know if this is apocryphal or not but somebody said that one of the Honduran soldiers started screaming, "Cut it out," and one of the Salvadorans said, "Mind your own business. This is our problem." . . .

H.: *[Among the refugees] who come to the church, who come to the city, are they the people caught in the middle, or what do they say in terms of the testimony you receive?*

F.: I guess you could say they are the people caught in the middle, but I feel there are few people caught in the middle. I feel, from my own limited experience, that the majority of the rural people in some way have sympathy, if they are not actively collaborating with the popular organizations.

H.: *Which are the revolutionaries?*

F.: Right. In the militarized towns, no they're not. But I would say that the majority of the people that I have come in contact with, the feeling I get is that they want a change. I mean, they are the ones who do not want what exists now in the way of government and secu-

---

* On May 13–14, 1980, the Salvadoran army massacred several hundred refugees, who were trying to cross the Rio Sumpul and escape into Honduras.

rity forces. In fact, maybe these people don't even understand government. What they understand is that they are being terribly repressed by the security forces and that they just kind of live in fear. A truck or car comes along and it's the death squad and everybody just kind of trembles and that night somebody is killed. Where I've been is that the death squad will come in and a few men will just lean up against the wall and stake out a town and stand for a while and go around, and the people just feel that there is no defense. As far as we can at all investigate — and people have seen with their eyes — I can find the cars and [I've seen] the [same] men walking out of national police stations and seeing them — who do you go to, to put in a complaint? There is no place to go complaining against the death squad, and that seems to be much more active, I think, in places like Santa Ana. It is very, very bad there. It is becoming more of a phenomenon in this area now. It wasn't before. It [has been] within the last few weeks. It's really picked up.

H.: Here in Chalatenango?
F.: Yes, in the different centers of population.

H.: Now, what's your impression of the role, socially, politically of the local church here, throughout Central America, particularly Salvador? The right has actually attacked the Catholic Church for their being leftists, or Catholic liberation theology for putting the Church in collaboration with the Left. How do you see all that?
F.: The Colonel of the local regiment said to me the other day that the Church is indirectly subversive because it's on the side of the weak. There's been sort of a conversion process going on in the Church, a realization that before the Church was very aligned and alive with the government structures, with the *status quo* and, therefore, was an arm of oppression. I think that probably beginning with the Second Vatican Council, and particularly with the Medellín meeting of the Bishops' Conference (CELAM) in Colombia in 1968 and, more recently, in Puebla, Mexico, the Church has taken a preferential option for the poor. The government finds this difficult to understand. I mean, they don't understand, exactly, the whole evolution, and it's very contradictory.

H.: *Recently there has been a noticeable expansion in the presence of evangelicals — particularly U.S.-based evangelical groups in Central America. Do you think this is in some sense a politically approved reaction to what's happening?*

F.: I can only say that from my experience in other Latin American countries where once the military government took over there was official support and funding of the evangelical groups. Seemingly [this is] because they are very non-political in the sense that they do not make any association between the spiritual and real life and don't lead the people to reflect on what's going on in their life. In that way they are very non-threatening and it's a very nice control type of situation.

It seems to be in Salvador, the amount of money that's going into even just a campaign in the way of posters and TV time, radio time, having found new [life] in Jesus Christ, it's obvious that that type of money is not generated inside the country.

H.: *As a U.S. citizen, as a human being, what do you think of the role of the U. S. government in its support of the military Christian Democratic junta that rules here?*

F.: As a U.S. citizen I'm highly disappointed and mostly outraged at the type of support. I think the U.S. is upholding a myth that there is a center ground and another way. It's just a creation of the whole State Department rather than . . . .

H.: *That this [government] is centrist in fighting both extreme right and left?*

F.: That's not the truth. This government doesn't represent anybody at this point. It's fearful when you think the U.S. is now going to train Salvadoran troops in Panama. The different equipment they are sending in — you know, it's reprehensible and I think sometime the United States has to realize that it does not own Central America or any other part of the world. That people have the right to shape their own destinies and choose the type of government they want and make their own choices. We don't lose anything. We don't lose Cuba. We don't lose Nicaragua. They were never ours to lose.

115. Mimeographed letter, October 27, 1980

Dear Sisters and Friends,

This is a belated attempt to express my appreciation for your letters, wishes, prayers and caring that you have sent my way since the accident and Carla's death. It is humbling and comforting to be the recipient of so much love and concern from many parts of the globe. I guess it is one more manifestation of our ties and concern for each other.

Some of you knew Carla well, others slightly or not at all. Yet, her death has made us all ground ourselves again in the Lord of life and deepen our commitment to the coming of His Kingdom, especially among the poor and oppressed. Carla's commitment, fleshed out in her own inimitable, creative way, is ours too — also to be lived to the full with our own gifts and possibilities. Her death has meaning because her life was full of meaning. May the same be true for us.

The work in Chalatenango goes on. Maura Clarke has joined me and together we are continuing to collaborate with the local church communities in the emergency situation. Since El Salvador is in a state of undeclared civil war, we count on your solidarity and prayers that we remain faithful servants to those suffering and those struggling for a society of brotherhood, justice and peace.

Much love to you,

Ita

116. This is a postscript added to Jean Reardon Bauman at the bottom of the previous letter.

Dear Jean,

I resorted to a mimeographed letter because I got paralyzed as the mountain of mail kept increasing. Carla keeps generating lots of mail and she's not around to respond — in this way.

What can I say? Being a survivor isn't romantic or glorious; it's a bitch that you have to work through. Carla's death and my not dying when I thought I would is a lot to absorb and it takes time. I don't understand it. I don't like it. I have to humbly stand before the Lord and ask Him to make sense of it since He's in charge.

Meanwhile, we keep plugging along here because life is threatened by other evils worse than death, i.e. hatred, manipulation, vengeance, selfishness, etc. That's what we have to keep struggling against so that life-producing possibilities have a chance to flower.

Love to you and John,
Ita

117. *An additional postscript sent to Maryknoll Sisters Jessie Poynton and Laura Magallanes, October 27, 1980*

Jessie and Laura,

Please excuse the form letter. I had to do something like this to get going so I could face the mountain of mail.

First of all, I want to thank you again, Jessie, for coming to Salvador. I know I was out of it, I guess — some degree of shock, but I really appreciate your coming. I'm sorry the last day was 'nutsy.' I can't even remember what happened, but I do know what I was feeling. I hadn't been alone for a minute from the time I was helped across the river and back to the *pueblo*. All I remember is that I had to get to the *Asuncion*, be by myself for awhile. That wasn't particularly gracious, but I couldn't do anything else. As Carla used to say, "A drunken driver should get off the road."

Also I'd like to tell you how much I appreciated the newsletter and your own reflections on Carla. It was well done.

The enclosed cards, a custom here, didn't turn out as I had hoped. First they lost my picture and had to use the plate from the paper. Then they changed the paper I asked for. So now with the glossy swirl, the face is even less clear. However, it's something. I'm sending Connie about 100 for Barbara and other people who you think of.

Julie Miller and Pat Murray were here the past weekend; that's one solidarity visit for the month. Since the regional assembly starts with Thanksgiving dinner, our next morale builder will be across the border. Periodic visits really make a difference!

Several letters from Chile have asked why I don't return. I guess where I am right now is that, in order to absorb what happened, that is, not only Carla's death but also my own being saved that night, I have to do it here. Leaving at this time (or right after the accident) could reinforce some of the unreality it still seems. At some later point, we'll have to evaluate. I'm not sure that I could do a decent job right now. As Carolyn would say, "[Everything] is hitting the fan [at once]," but in selected places and not yet in a general concentration. It's messy and hard, but there's still space in which to move. I don't see a short-range solution.

It appears that these poor people still have a lot of suffering ahead of them. Keep asking with us that our small efforts in some way reduce the suffering and contribute toward a just tomorrow.

Once I conquer the two mountains of accumulated mail, I'll try and be more regular about writing. In some ways I feel like the surviving relative and, maybe in a sense, I'm the one here who not only was Carla's friend, but also who knew her for more than just a short while. So besides friendship, it falls to me by default!

I look forward to your letters and their realness. Take care.

Much love to you both,

Ita

118. *November 13, 1980*

Dear Mom,

I'm not sure what silverfish are, but stick it to them. The other night a rat fell down from the cement beam overhead and was scurrying up the partition of Maura's bedroom when one of the Sisters in Chalatenango knocked it senseless and then did it in. I'm glad it dropped while the lights were on. It could have been heart attack producing in the dark. I also think I handle military roadblocks better than falling rats!

Peg was here last weekend and passes on your donation and insistence about new shoes. She is also looking forward to returning to Central America in February. If it works out, maybe she'll be working here. It's her first choice anyway. I'm sure she'll be giving a blow by blow of her visit around Thanksgiving time when she gets back. She livened up Chalatenango for twenty-four hours and the people asked her to return.

These days I'm buying grains, sacks of corn and beans, lots of them. When I'm not doing that I'm also looking for masons and contractors to check out the house structure to make sure the house doesn't cave in.

On the whole we're pretty busy, although we don't always know what we're doing. Being busy is fine for me now, especially on some days when I just don't feel like myself. I guess it's the blahs that come after someone close to you dies, but I notice that there are times when I want to keep others at a distance. I don't want them making claims on me. I presume it will pass with some time and in the meantime I think I'm running Maura ragged.

Two weeks from now we'll be at the regional assembly in Julie's country [Nicaragua]. If it works out, we'll probably try to go a day or two earlier to flop. Maybe I'll curl up with one of the books Billy sent through Peg. I love the subtitle of Barbara Tuchman's book on the fourteenth century, *The Calamitous Century*. That's how some of our days seem.

I'm off to buy plane tickets and drop this in the Post Office. Take care.

Much Love to all,
Ita

119. *November 18, 1980*

Dear Mom,

A year ago we celebrated your birthday early. Maybe this year you'll be celebrating with a new grandchild. Wouldn't that be nice.

This morning I've been aping one of your chores, shopping for the ladies in Nicaragua. They sent word for things one can still find here and that aren't available there. I consider it fitting and just to be doing it for them, since you do it so often for me.

The week ahead should be a good shot of R & R. It will be good to be with a larger group — we'll be almost twenty-five, I think. With only four in Salvador, it's hard to get a sense of group and think through problems or projects that call for a corporate response. I'm beginning to appreciate how Mary Ann Junas might feel in Bangladesh and I think this is not the best arrangement and, then, I think of the four of them in a non-Christian environment, working out their support system. Here we're very interested in the local church and even have three other Sisters under our roof at night. Then there's the Cleveland team who help us out quite a bit, since they have a fleet of cars at their disposal and are quite ready to show up in a microbus, pick up truck or Jeep as the need presents itself. Their biggest asset is being blonde, which makes roadblock passing easier. Carla kept threatening to bleach her hair when she saw how the others get through.

Since life is fairly hectic, I don't think there's much point in getting more subscriptions to *The Way* or others. There just isn't time and usually at night we fall into bed exhausted. Also, the present situation is such that we're never alone. So there's no sort of normality to say, "Okay I have an hour every day to do whatever." I keep saying to myself when the war is over, I'll do such and such, maybe. It boggles the mind to think that what's happening now could be the norm for a given time to come. So a lot of human things are on hold now and when we can, we'll pick up these threads of our lives.

I thought I'd get to a tape before, but maybe next week — that's a hope, not a promise.

Warmest wishes for a happy birthday!

Much love,
Ita

120. *To Maryknoll Sister John Bernard, also known as Gertrude Vaccaro,*
November 13, 1980

Dear JB,

Thanks for your letter that only arrived today (waiting en route
or held up somewhere). As best I can, I'll fill you in, although I don't
have Peg Hanlon's letters at hand.

About a week after Peg returned to Maryknoll after her visit
here, she wrote me, asking about follow-up on what we were going
to do about replacing the Jeep. She had had some conversations with
the Cleveland team while she was here and they had several ideas.

I didn't answer Peg right away because I was waiting to see what
the Vicar would decide to do. In that interim Jean Donovan visited
Maryknoll and spoke with Peg and wrote up a request for Jeep main-
tenance for $2000.

About a month ago, the Archdiocese decided to give us monies
allocated by *Misereor** for transportation. The amount allocated, however, does not cover the full cost of the Jeep. So, since I was unaware
of Jean Donovan's request, I wrote to Peg, saying that although we
had not been asked to look for funding, if Maryknoll wanted to help,
possibly they could help with all or part of what the *Misereor* funds
did not cover. I don't have a copy of that letter here — San Salvador
— but I believe it was $3600.

I wrote to Peg in the same spirit that I found in her letter, that is
if Maryknoll could help our work in some way, she'd try and get
some help. Since this is a poor Church with many claims on it right
now because of the refugees and other needs, I said anything Maryknoll could do would be very appreciated.

So because of the timing of the letters, you possibly may have
two requests on your desk. I leave it to your judgment which to
process. I'm sure I can express the gratitude of the Vicar, Fabian
Amaya, and others in the Archdiocese, for whatever help you can
obtain.

Maura and I are doing fairly well. For myself, I just appreciate so

---

* *Misereor*, a funding agency of the German Catholic Bishops.

much the person she is and the support she extends at this time. There probably isn't a worse time to come into a situation, yet she's so gracious and kind — seems to roll with it. For myself, I have downs and some ups, which I guess I should expect for a while. Yet, the momentum of the work carries me on. These days I feel like a Chicago merchant specializing in grain futures, or maybe Joseph in Egypt storing grain against the coming shortage. There's nothing more absurd than two Brooklynites judging the quality of red beans and corn!

Please give our thanks to the Center Sisters for their great caring and solidarity — and many to you.

Much love,
Ita

121. To Sister Carolyn Lehmann, MM, November 14, 1980

Dear Carolyn,

The Western Zone [of the Maryknoll Sisters in Central America] did it again. Thanks so much for all you ladies, Brendan and others did to organize the day. The response here to the letter and all that it carries in solidarity has been touching. We're trying to circulate it as best and as far as we can.

In the last few weeks we've had visits from Julie and Pat and last weekend from Peg Healy. The agendas were very similar to the Guatemala visit, picking up spirits and just talking out some things. It's as though we get monthly gamma globulin shots for the *animo!**

Today I'm into the *tramites* to get us out of the country for the Assembly. It's a three-day process, at least. It's like getting temporary parole from prison. The control is fantastic. And of course, no one thinks of scheduling meetings in non-conflictive areas, like the Virgin Islands.

I'm also trying to get some input from different church sources regarding their opinion of why or why not we should be here now.

---

* *Animo* — energy.

I'm sure that will come up at the Assembly, but it's also for us. A priority was named, but I don't feel it was promoted in any way. So, if we can clarify and, then, articulate to others maybe the Spirit will zap a few others to think about joining us. It's almost impossible for four of us to feel and act like a functioning body here.

Of course, I shouldn't talk about feeling or acting like a 'functioning body.' Many days I don't know myself. I have a tendency to keep people at a distance, to not want claims placed on me that I feel I can't handle, to be very 'functional' — ugh! I presume it's all part of the process of mourning, but it's 'blahsville.' I'm not so bad keeping at the work, but personal things, especially writing letters really costs me to do. I'm sort of ashamed that I haven't written to the people of Bandera, or Eduardo or Ariana's family, but just can't seem to do it yet.

I heard from Marie yesterday. Please thank her for her letter, the money stuff I'll figure out with Rose Anna at the Assembly.

Lots of love to all the ladies — Peg, Ina, Inez and [illegible], our gang. What to my wondering eyes should appear about two weeks ago in the *arzobispado* was the pastor of Villa Francia. I interrupted a meeting to say hello. You just never know who's going to turn up on your doorstep, but there wasn't much time to talk. Also he's been out of Chile just a little less than myself, which was a surprise. Anyway, friend, take care.

Much love,
Ita

122. *November 22, 1980*

AN EVALUATION OF THE MINISTRY OFFERED TO THE PANISA REGIONAL ASSEMBLY IN MANAGUA, NICARAGUA

Four months ago Carla and I wrote a report on our first three months' experience in El Salvador. That paper, written during a very difficult period, tried to communicate our frustrations as well as our hopes and questions, and caused more reaction than we anticipated. It was meant to be input for an on-going evaluation; the questions we raised were meant for dialogue and exchange with others in the region, as well as those outside. Since that report was written, Maura arrived to accompany Maddie, Carla died. Terry withdrew from the Tamnique work to join Maddie in Lamatepec and Maura joined Ita in Chalatenango.

In addition to Maryknoll history, there have been on-going political, social and ecclesial changes in El Salvador since the last regional assembly. As this assembly has the right and responsibility to reevaluate the priorities named last year, I would like to offer some points not just for reaffirming El Salvador as a priority, but also to ask that the priority be actively promoted on the regional and other Latin American regional levels.

A letter from the PANISA Region to the RGB's [Regional Governing Boards] of South America, dated Nov. 29, 1979 states:

> *The purpose of this letter is to call your attention to perhaps the most significant decision of our assembly, which was the naming of El Salvador and Nicaragua as priority areas for the placing of personnel in the next few years. This decision was backed by the Mexico-Guatemala region and a letter was sent to the CGB as a request from the World Section that priority status on a Congregational level be considered for these two countries for the naming of personnel during this period. At the same time the assembly voted that letters be sent to the RGBs of other Latin American regions, making known this request and the special need for personnel in these areas.*
>
> *As you no doubt are aware, recent developments in these two countries have placed them in unique historical positions that are having and will continue to have, great importance for all third-world countries struggling in the process of liberation. For this reason we are particularly concerned with having an effective Maryknoll presence there, not only by increasing our numbers, but also for what this means as a support and a renewing of the strengths of our Sisters there . . .*

The two conditions for assignment to El Salvador were: 1) that ministry must be exercised in the Archdiocese of San Salvador due to the guidance of Mons. Romero and 2) that only experienced Latin American missioners be considered at this time. It would also be important for anyone coming "to have certain clarity of ideas of the political options at stake, with an openness and willingness to accompany the people as they pass through different stages for them to assume active roles in shaping their destinies."

Since that letter was written a year ago, only one of the four sisters who were in El Salvador at that time is still here. Four others have come, one of whom has died. In other words, the number of personnel is exactly the same as when the request was made for more.

The bases on which the priority was set last year have altered, yet the changes need not affect the decision. The Archdiocese of San Salvador was considered a priority because of the prophetic leadership of Mons. Romero and the experience of the Church there. Following his assassination there was a period of confusion and a sense of scatteredness. However, in the last few months a stronger pastoral direction is evident and there is a greater cohesion and sense of purpose among pastoral agents who are creating a pastoral for the actual moment. San Salvador is the only diocese that is responding as Church to the overwhelming numbers of displaced persons throughout the country. To date, nine refugee centers are in operation and a tenth will open on December 1. The Office of Social Communication's weekly newspaper and radio (when it is functioning) have been heroic in transmitting the national reality. Though lacking a charismatic leader, the Archdiocese, as Church to the national situation, because of this response is encountering a notable increase in hostility and in incidents that indicate a pre-meditated persecution. (From January through October, 1980 there have been twenty-eight assassinations of church personnel, three woundings, twenty-one arrests, four profanations of the Eucharist, forty-one machine-gunnings of church properties.) In its choice to opt for the poor and support the right of the *pueblo* to search for its own alternatives, the Archdiocese continues to be a local church that we should support.

While the Lamatepec work was not included in last year's priorities, the history of this year makes us ask, that given the overall suffering of the Santa Ana area, should we not continue to accompany and support the people where we already have a base of service and credibility? When the war is over, an evaluation of the diocese's leadership, unity and overall pastoral direction would indicate if we should continue there. (In El Salvador, the process has accelerated to the point that almost all informed people agree that the country is in a state of undeclared civil war.)

The Present Moment

In July we said, "Until the situation in Chalatenango has more shape to it, we think it would be better not to ask for another sister." Since then the emergency committee has taken on a shape and purpose in the context of the Archdiocesan *Pastoral de Asistencia*. As will be mentioned later, the Vicar could see up to four more sisters in this work. (Our experience of trying to begin a new work in this situation was most difficult, I wouldn't suggest that anyone coming new to El Salvador be asked to do that. Rather the present needs and job possibilities flow from collaborating with already existing works that are adapting to the war reality.)

Lamatepec is presenting a separate request to the Assembly for personnel. What can the Maryknoll Sisters contribute to El Salvador at this point, at this special moment? Within the past few weeks Maura and I have consulted with people at different levels in the local Church, asking their opinions on the advantages and disadvantages of Maryknoll Sisters in El Salvador now and what would they think of more coming? What follows is a summary of their responses.

In El Salvador there is an overabundance of work due to the evolving war situation. Maryknoll Sisters, due to their charism, formation, flexibility of lifestyle (as contrasted with a more structured, conventual style) and experiences in similar situations are seen as very appropriate and needed collaborators in this historical moment. There just aren't that many Religious available or capable of emergency and refugee work at this time.

Another important task is confirming or strengthening the faith of the Christians who are committed to the liberation of their *pueblo* as well as of those who are suffering reprisals for collaborating with the militants. Religious have the possibility of getting closer to and gaining credibility with the people, especially with those who are suffering.

Being foreigners can be a two-edged sword, but the advantages seen at this time are: a demonstration of international solidarity, a testimony of service by some North Americans, a freedom of movement denied to Salvadoran church personnel, a reputation for honesty (in the handling of project funds, etc.) responsibility and practicality.

The disadvantages presented are: a possible anti-gringo backlash and our present number of four sisters seems too few to act or coordinate as a body within a war situation or to sustain more losses due to sickness or death.

Regarding Sisters who might come, the following suggestions were made. Although ideal people do not exist, the person should have good nerves and no major emotional problems, be flexible and able to learn in the situation as it develops, want to work in a team effort, have some practical skills (such as driving or some organizational ability, etc.), have a realistic attitude about the situation and its risks, have a certain political clarity as how to situate themselves in the situation. Orientation would be provided/possible from the local church people with whom one would be collaborating.

Possible Jobs

Nursing: in refugee centers and in mobile teams serving areas of refuge where people have fled.

Refugee Centers: organization, handicrafts, alphabetization, work with women, children, religious presence, etc.

Emergency Committee: organization of food and medicine distribution, relocation of refugees, etc. on-going contact with Christian communities.

Personal Request

Before this gets too long, I would like to add a personal preoccupation. From past experiences I have a nagging hunch that as Maryknoll Sisters, we name priorities but aren't quite sure how to promote them, except by assignments from the Center. Is there some method we could develop to challenge or call each other from where we are, to encourage each other to respond to other needs that are seen as more pressing or important? What I'm really asking is:

How do we promote the priority of El Salvador — that there be an effective Maryknoll presence — when no one will be assigned here and, given the situation, people will try to discourage or dissuade Sisters from coming?

This is very important for the morale of those of us who are here and I'd really appreciate your thinking about it.

123. Ita's last letter to her mother, from Nicaragua, December 1, 1980

Dear Mom,

I guess we're into celebrating life — birth, birthdays, and my own grudging acknowledgement that I'm still alive for some reason. So here's to three generations of Fords thankful for the gift of life!

I should have known better than to plan on the time for a tape at an Assembly. We generate work for all the margins of the day — sigh.

Central America is so different than Chile! But they're a good group of supportive ladies.

Much love,
Ita

124. Translation by Ita for prayer service, December 1, 1980

For a prayer service at the conclusion of the Maryknoll Sisters' regional meeting in Managua, Sr. Maria Rickleman asked Ita to translate this text by Archbishop Oscar Romero, "The Poverty of the Beatitudes." The next day Ita and Maura Clarke flew back to San Salvador.

"The Poverty of the Beatitudes" by Archbishop Oscar Romero

In my thought today, I would like you to hear this idea . . . that poverty is a force of liberation because in addition to being a denouncement of sin and a force of Christian spirituality, it is also a commitment. These words of scripture are a call. Christians, this word is for me first of all. I must give an example of being a Christian. And it is for all of you, my brother priests, and for you religious, and for all baptized people who call themselves Christian.

Listen to what the Medellín conference says.

> *Poverty is a commitment which assumes, voluntarily and through love — the condition of the needy of the world in order to give testimony to the evil this represents. It also is a spiritual freedom towards goods — following Christ's example who made his own all the consequence of man's sinful condition and who "being rich, became poor" to save us.*

The commitment to be a Christian is this: to follow Christ in his incarnation. If Christ is the majestic God who became humble unto death on a cross and who lives with the poor, so should be our Christian faith. The Christian who doesn't wish to live the commitment of solidarity with the poor isn't worthy to call himself a Christian.

Christ invites us not to fear persecution. Believe me brothers, he who is committed to the poor must suffer the same fate as the poor. And in El Salvador we know what the fate of the poor signifies, to disappear, to be tortured, to be captive, to be found dead . . .

He who would want the privileges of this world and not the persecutions of this commitment — hear the tremendous antitheses of today's Gospel.

Happy you, when people hate you and exclude you, insult you and consider you an outcast for the sake of the Son of Man. Rejoice and be glad because your reward will be great in heaven.

AFTERWORD
by Melinda Roper, MM

Twenty-five years is a long time in a human life, and yet in the story of the universe it is but a moment. Each person's experience of time is unique, while at the same time shared with all creation. From within this uniqueness we make choices, we form relationships, and we make commitments. From within these relationships and commitments we choose to remember. Those of us who have chosen to read this book about Ita Ford have chosen to remember. For Ita's family and friends, your memory goes beyond what is written here. For those of us who knew Ita briefly or not at all, we join Ita's family and friends in becoming part of a collective memory that was revived dramatically in the 1970s and 1980s through the suffering of the people of El Salvador.

Ita is an integral part of this suffering and memory. The collective memory to which I refer is rooted in human experience from its beginnings and becomes acutely conscious in the person of Jesus of Nazareth. The night before he died, Jesus shared a meal with his friends and tried to help them understand the magnanimity and totality of his love. When Jesus said, "Do this in memory of me," I believe he meant for us to live the way he did, in total commitment to the good of others.

In the midst of betrayal, denial, misunderstanding, ridicule, sleepiness, and fickleness, the totality of commitment and love becomes integrated in the goodness, beauty, wisdom, and justice of

---

Sister Melinda Roper was President of the Maryknoll Sisters at the time of Ita Ford's death in 1980. She works today in Panama.

249

the universe. As we become part of this collective memory we begin to understand the totality of Ita's commitment as well as the commitment of so many sisters and brothers in ages past.

In our living memory today, I look back in appreciation to the valiant people of El Salvador for their gift of hope, fortitude, and struggle from deep within the spiral of violence and injustice in which they were immersed. I look back with a grateful heart for the courage and living faith of my Sister in Maryknoll, Ita Ford. I was and am inspired by her openness to search for and stand before the truth. I admire her choice to be with the poor of El Salvador during a time when there were no clear answers to her heart-rending questions, and no solutions to the daily problems of survival. Ita's gift of herself to family, friends, community, and the people continues to invite and challenge me to become part of the living tradition in which the totality of her commitment continues to reveal the mystery of new life in suffering and even death.

During the last twenty-five years there have been many El Salvadors. We don't need any more — or have we not yet learned and realized its lessons? During the last twenty-five years many good and just persons have lived and died. Some have freely given their lives and have been assassinated. We don't need any more assassinations — or have we not yet learned and realized their meaning?

In our living memory today, I look toward the future in faith, choosing to believe that our lives are not in vain, that Ita's life, reflections, struggles, love, and death have become part of the energy of the universe, part of the living memory of Jesus today.

For those not yet born twenty-five years ago, we who know the story invite you to become part of a wonder- and mystery-filled future. Your goodness and the totality of your commitment are a blessing for us as well as for the next twenty-five years and beyond.

May we live into the future with the blessing of all who have gone before us.

Santa Fe, Darién, República de Panamá